Harpur's
HEAVEN
and
HELL

Harpur's
HEAVEN
and
HELL

TOM HARPUR

TORONTO
Oxford University Press
1983

FOR SUSAN
She knows why

ACKNOWLEDGEMENTS I would like to thank my editors at Oxford University Press Canada, Richard Teleky and Sally Livingston, for their assistance, as well as Phyllis Wilson for her patient typing and retyping of the manuscript. All photographs are used by permission of *The Toronto Star*: 3, 4, 7, and 8 are by Dick Loek, and 1, 2, and 5 are by Bob Olsen.

TOM HARPUR

Canadian Cataloguing in Publication Data

Harpur, Tom.
  Harpur's heaven and hell

Bibliography: p.
ISBN 0-19-540425-4 (bound). — ISBN 0-19-540428-9 (pbk.)

1. Christianity — Addresses, essays, lectures.
2. Christian life — 1960-   — Addresses, essays,
lectures. I. Title.

BV4515.2.H37 1983   248   C83-098970-6

1 2 3 4 — 6 5 4 3
Printed in Canada by
John Deyell Company Limited

Contents

Whither shall I go from thy Spirit? Or whither shall I flee from thy presence? If I ascend up into heaven, thou art there; if I make my bed in hell, behold, thou art there. If I take the wings of the morning, and dwell in the uttermost parts of the sea, even there shall thy hand lead me, and thy right hand shall hold me. If I say, Surely the darkness shall cover me; even the night shall be light about me.

FROM PSALM 139

Introduction

This is a controversial book both by nature and by design. It could not be otherwise, for it is in part an attempt to answer the question most often put to me after twelve years as religion editor of the largest newspaper in the country. That is: 'As a former Anglican priest and professor of theology, with more than a decade's experience reporting on and discussing religious issues in the mass media, what do you yourself believe?' While the answer will probably shock some people, I hope that it will encourage others—that vast company today who, in spite of their goodwill towards the churches, have lost heart, and no longer know what to believe.

As a way of approaching that central issue, however, I want to answer as briefly as possible a second question that crops up almost daily in my interviews and correspondence: 'How is it that a person with your particular academic background would leave the security of the university to become a journalist and commentator on religious affairs?'

The year was 1967. An ordained Anglican priest lecturing on the New Testament and teaching Greek at Wycliffe College in Toronto, I preached every Sunday at an active downtown evangelical parish. Around me the world of religion was in a state of turmoil and ferment unknown since the Reformation of the sixteenth century. It was the heady period following the Second Vatican Council (1962-5) called by Pope John XXIII to 'open a window' in the Roman Catholic Church. The key word at Vatican II was *aggiornamento*—updating Catholicism to modern realities. Priests and nuns had already begun leaving their orders in droves. Trendy clergy were experimenting with new life-styles and modes of worship that sometimes bordered on the bizarre: I know one cleric who invited a local motorcycle club to bring their 'hogs'—bikes—into the chancel area for 'a blessing of the motorcycles', but succeeded only in scaring his congregation and getting grease on an expensive new carpet. The air was still echoing with the debate over the 1963 best-seller *Honest to God* by John Robinson, then Anglican Bishop of Woolich, and the extraordinary phenomenon of the 'God-is-dead' controversy. The dust of this tumult had barely settled when, in Canada, Pierre Berton's shocker *The Comfortable Pew* (1965) gave the faithful and the media alike another jolt. Conflict over the war in Vietnam was beginning to divide church people and everybody else, north and south of the border.

I had had a successful parish career—a year as curate at the posh Anglican Church of St John's in York Mills, Toronto, and then seven years building up my own suburban parish, including a new rectory and a large sanctuary, at St Margaret's-in-the-Pines in West Hill. I had even had the luxury of a year's post-graduate work back at Oxford, studying under some of the great theological minds of our time. Moving to the seminary in 1964, I had thought I would be at the centre of things, shaping the minds that in turn would shape the new, more relevant church of the future. But things didn't quite work out that way. I found to my surprise that the majority of theological students were ultra-conservative, so afraid of new ideas that they were unwilling to be influenced, let alone shaped, by anybody. (Recent conversations with theological professors suggest that would-be ordinands today are, with notable exceptions, much the same—perhaps not surprisingly, given the conservative mood that seems to have fallen over most denominations and religions with regard to basic beliefs.) The academic life itself, rather than sparkling with wit and discussion about the great theological and practical issues being raised out-of-doors, so to speak, seemed almost incestuous, bent on a holding operation—anything to avoid the radical change that was to my mind essential. I felt bored and frustrated.

But my life was about to change. Reading Berton's chapter on the church and mass media—in which he claimed the church was acting as though the telephone had just been invented in an age when a media revolution was about to drastically alter our whole culture—confirmed what had gradually been building in my own thoughts. There was an urgent need for Christians to become involved in media and begin talking to people outside the church, instead of always talking to ourselves.

In the spring of 1967 I met with the only media person I knew, the co-owner of radio station CFGM in Richmond Hill, just outside Metropolitan Toronto. I proposed an hour-long talk-show on religion, with me as host, to commence that fall. He called back the next day to say he thought we should begin the following week! I felt rather the way Peter must have when Jesus told him to get out of the boat and walk to him on the water: a radio show seemed much safer to talk about than to do. 'By the way,' the owner said, 'I've already got a name for the program: *Harpur's Heaven and Hell.*'

The title did little to ease my fears. Friends and colleagues, mostly clergy, urged me to back off. It was bad enough for a theology professor to broadcast on a country-and-western music station—a name like *Harpur's Heaven and Hell* was downright un-Anglican. I almost took their advice when I heard the show's first promo, after which the disc jockey jauntily announced the next record: 'I won't go huntin' with you Luke, but I'll go chasin' women.' However, after a faltering start, the show became a success and eventually evolved into a five-nights-a-week format. Sometimes we had guests, including a stripper who had found God, and Beatle John Lennon, who made a lengthy appearance by phone from his famous Bed-In For Peace in a Montreal hotel. Most often, though, there was no one but me, facing a microphone and a line of telephone buttons, and talking to anyone who cared to call about whatever was on his or her mind.

The show lasted for five years. As the owner had predicted, the title was effective: once people heard it they never forgot. There was plenty of controversy; some listeners were so offended they tried to pressure my bishop to have me unfrocked (to use that quaint term). I even received bomb threats—notes left under the windshield-wipers on my car—because of my stand against the war in Vietnam. Eventually I was to 'unfrock' myself, voluntarily laying down the exercise of my ordained ministry in 1979, partly because of a conflict of interest in doing my job as a journalist (would I counsel people as a preacher or interview them as a reporter?) and partly because of my diocese's new strictures on what one could or could not preach as a loyal subject of the bishops. But that is another story. The point is that because of *Harpur's Heaven and Hell*, I was soon asked to write opinion pieces for *The Toronto Star* and other papers, and to appear regularly on various radio and television shows to discuss religious trends and events. Before long I realized that what

I was doing free-lance, as a hobby, was really much more stimulating and fulfilling than my teaching career. And so in 1971, after a talk with the bishop, I left Wycliffe College to become the religion editor of the *Star*.

Now, after a dozen years of travel—to Italy (including over ten trips to the Vatican), India, Japan, the Middle East, Africa, Central America, Scandinavia, France, the British Isles (many times), the High Arctic, and most of the principal cities in North America—I have covered two papal elections and three papal tours, interviewed every notable religious figure of our time, from Billy Graham to Mother Teresa to the Dean of Canterbury Cathedral, and examined every kind of cult as well as all the major religions. And as a result I can say that my views on religion and faith have been profoundly changed.

After seeing the grace and glory of God at work in saintly men and women of other faiths, I could no longer believe in only one right and true faith. I could no longer hold that one denomination's view of Christianity was the unique reflection of what Paul calls 'the mind of Christ', when I'd seen at first hand the havoc each denomination, in its own way, is capable of wreaking in people's lives. (It is significant that in South Africa, where there are more orthodox believers in the dominant Protestant church, more people who give to missions, more people who attend prayer- and Bible-study meetings, and more who take the Bible to be the inspired, inerrant word of God, than in most other countries of comparable size, the worst forms of racism and injustice reign supreme, fully supported by selected biblical texts. In the United States the battle for racial integration and equality found its bitterest opposition in the 'born-again' Christians of the so-called Bible Belt. And in Guatemala, where born-again Christianity has been growing faster than anywhere else in the world, the rate of official terror and massacres—especially of the Indians—under the 'born-again' former dictator Efrain Rios Montt was second only to that of El Salvador.) I could not look with equanimity on religion's claim to bring peace and unity when I had witnessed the tragic controversies and divisions it is capable of producing. (I will never forget walking the streets of strife-ravaged Belfast in the fall of 1979, investigating the effects of years of sectarian violence and hatred upon the children.) I could not simply accept Christianity's claims to relieve guilt when I knew the inside story—how much unnecessary guilt can be incurred by its often cruelly rigid dogmas. (I cannot restate Dietrich Bonhoeffer's words emphatically enough: the church must stop trying to act as a kind of 'spiritual pharmacist'—working to produce acute guilt, and then in effect saying: 'We just happen to have the remedy for your guilt here in our pocket.') I began to grow both sad and angry at the number of people in most major faiths who want to compel everyone to jump through the same verbal hoops, follow the same ritual formulae, that they do, and who refuse to grant standing as a real member of their faith to anyone who will not. I have found that people who claim that they (or those who believe, talk, and act as they do) are the only true Christians—or Muslims, or Jews—hold little attraction for me as human beings. The rigid mind-set is the same no matter what the faith.

So to return to the question with which I began: what do I believe? Religion is at once the most powerful force for good or evil, and the most controversial aspect of human affairs today. There are many positive things to be said about it; but there is also a lot to criticize. What follows is not for the religiously squeamish, nor is it for those who are so content with their religious outlook that they will not question it. But the people I have met in the course of my own inner search have convinced me there is much in the following pages that will strike home to a wide audience. This book is not intended for scholars, but for all those concerned and thoughtful people who are not willing to settle for easy answers to the deeper issues we all face.

I believe in God, the one divine Creator-Spirit, who is above all things and yet in and through and under all creation—transcendent or wholly 'other', and yet at the same time immanent, in-dwelling in the whole of the cosmos and in each member of humanity. I believe this in spite of the problem of evil—the horrors of nature 'red in tooth and claw', the abomination of Auschwitz, the terrible accidents, the cancer wards, the sufferings of innocent children. I have struggled for many years with this agonizing problem—reconciling a loving God with undeserved and inexplicable pain—and yet I believe.

I believe because a deep-rooted awareness within me tells me God exists. ('Deep calleth unto deep,' the Psalmist says; when the philosopher Immanuel Kant tried to sum it up, he said the two things that compelled him to believe in God were the starry heavens above, and his own sense of the moral law within.) I believe, because the opposite conviction—that all of the cosmos, from the miracle of a baby's birth to Mozart, to the harmony and play of the distant galaxies, is all the product of a chance collision of atoms and the lottery of nothingness—requires more faith, or credulity, than I can muster. I believe because I see God at work in my own life and in the lives of others. I believe because of the constant testimony of ordinary folk down the ages as well as the great spiritual geniuses of our species. I believe, in short, because I cannot do otherwise.

I believe in Jesus as a unique revealer of this God. To be a Christian, for me, means to be committed to his vision of God, to try, by God's Spirit, to follow him as his disciple or learner. As the earliest Christians said, it is to will to be a follower of his way. He himself was not God, nor did he claim to be—for him, as a pious Jew, that would have been the greatest blasphemy of all (see Mark 10:18). But he was a man completely open to God's will, and filled with his Spirit as no other man has been. Luke's Gospel particularly states that Jesus was led and empowered by the Spirit of God—not by his own, as it were, innate 'divinity'. Jesus calls us not to worship him, but to obey him, following in his way as disciples. Thus he lays no dogmatic burden on us. Rather he calls us, in a radical challenge, to share in and help to actualize the kingdom of God on earth. Sadly, the church has always found it much easier to argue about Jesus' divinity or other doctrines than to do what he plainly said we should do: above all, to love one another and to establish justice among all the inhabitants of our planet. I believe that Jesus is alive today in a spiritual way, not because he somehow rose from the dead by his own power, but because God raised him up (as the Bible makes very clear) as a sign of the new humanity towards which we are all moving. The imagery that has him ascending into heaven and sitting at the right hand of God is clearly archaic, based on simplistic notions of a two- or three-tiered universe and some extremely anthropomorphic ideas about God: there is no 'throne' and no 'sitting' in a specially favoured place as in an ancient royal palace.

I believe in the forgiveness of sins, not because an angry God has somehow been crudely appeased by the sacrifice of his only son (what an extraordinary theology for twentieth-century

man!) but because that is how God deals with human sin. He forgives it. Long before Christ (which means 'the anointed one')
died on the cross, he told his disciples to ask God for forgiveness
of sins, as in the Lord's Prayer, and on numerous occasions
made it plain that one has only to ask, in sincerity, to receive.
The cross speaks deeply to me of God's love for each and every
person who has ever lived—of any faith, or of none. Here the
Spirit-filled one suffers in his innocence and yet prays, 'Father,
forgive them . . .'. The message is clear: Jesus is saying that the
kind of love he has come to see and to know in the 'Father' can
take rejection and mockery: you can spit in the face of God, and
he still forgives. This is indeed amazing grace. It does not mean
that offences against oneself, one's neighbour, or God are without consequences that must be met, suffered through, and
finally overcome. There is a 'hell' right here and now, and all of
us have experienced it to some degree. The familiar sermoniz-
ing to the effect that Jesus somehow 'paid the price' or took our
punishment—for all the sins of all people from the beginning of
mankind—not only boggles the mind, but seems to me to be fun-
damentally immoral. We suffer the results of our mistakes ourselves, as anyone who has made wrong choices knows full well.
But the knowledge of forgiveness relieves the gnawing, corrod-
ing pain of guilt, and sets us free.

I believe in prayer, something fundamental to all religions,
but I am also convinced that more nonsense is talked about it
than about almost any other spiritual matter. In its simplest
sense, prayer is the soul's communication with God, an inner,
often completely unverbalized conversation with the ground or
core of all being. Prayer, above all, is not magic—the polite coercion of an unwilling God into doing our will. Nor is it the
attempt, by wheedling, pleading, and cajoling, to get God to
change his mind, as though he were some capricious tyrant in
need of obsequious courtiers. Prayer makes changes in us, not in
God. It's a little like tuning the radio or TV dial in order to open
the right channel to the in-filling of his Spirit. Nor is prayer for
others an attempt to alter God's actions. Rather, it unleashes an
unseen but very real energy towards others. The power of the
mind, tuned to God and directed to the good of others, is a
dynamic that may be as yet little understood, but it is undeniably
active in our world.

I believe in a life to come, beyond the grave—as I explain more fully later in this book. God will ultimately raise up all of us, as he did Jesus, to share with him in a glory as yet to be revealed. No one who remains willing will ever be excluded. What will 'heaven' be like? Perhaps we will be allowed to share with God in the design and creation of new worlds, new galaxies, new races of people who will not know war any more. Whatever the new life will be, it will certainly not consist of sitting around in celestial robes playing music for the angel choirs. The writers of the Bible did the best they could to describe 'heaven', but it must be admitted that their imagery falls flat on the modern ear. One can't help sympathizing with the agnostic who claims that such a paradise would be an utter bore. The God who made this universe as marvellous as it is must have something infinitely better in store for us than human minds can ever conjure up.

The vast majority of adults in our Western society are, and have been for some time, experiencing an aching spiritual void. Millions of people of goodwill towards religion, millions who even still consider themselves church-related (at least for censuses and other official purposes) as well as millions who continue to attend services if only at Christmas and Easter or for 'rites of passage', such as baptisms, weddings, and funerals, nevertheless find that their traditional faith does little or nothing for them. They dimly suspect there was once water in the well and there may be still; but somehow they never get any of it. The problem is not simply that church services are often dull and irrelevant, or the majority of sermons bland, boring, and not infrequently insulting to the intelligence of the congregation. At a very deep level the whole religious 'package' strikes many people as incomprehensible. It communicates not life, but a haunting confusion. Wrapped in dogmas and rituals that defy common sense, and seem completely unrelated to twentieth-century realities, the central message of God's love and of his kingdom is clothed in unnecessary mystery and robbed of its true bite. Frankly, I often find myself longing, in the midst of all the business of Sunday morning worship, that everybody—minister, choir, readers, acolytes—would cease all the activity and 'God-talk', and be still for five minutes. Then perhaps one could get on with one's own meditations, or simply sit in silence to reflect on the week behind and the week ahead *sub specie aeternitatis*, that is, in the light of eternal values. It would do more for my spirit—

and that of many others, I suspect—than twenty minutes of eloquence from the pulpit.

Holy Communion, also known as the Eucharist, the Lord's Supper, or the mass, is a case in point. The simple actions and brief statements attributed to Jesus in the Gospels, as he broke bread and passed a cup of wine on the eve of the crucifixion, have been turned into a solemn spectacle that buries the essence of the thing in an avalanche of words. The Anglican Prayer of Consecration, said over the bread and wine, is one of the worst offenders. The lengthy prayer repeatedly reminds God of almost every possible detail of Christian doctrine—as if somehow he had forgotten. It is high time the real drama and truth were allowed to break through: that as people share in the same loaf and the same wine, they are made to know again that there is a deep mystical bond between each of us and God, and between each of us and the whole of humanity.

More importantly, it is one of the greatest scandals facing modern Christianity that the Lord's Supper is treated as though it were the private preserve of each particular denomination or sect. The simple meal, meant as a sign and a source of human unity, has become the point on which Christians are most divided. The more orthodox a group is, the more anxious it apparently is to forget the law of love and bar outsiders from approaching its altars. How can people with such an outlook hope to be believed when they talk about 'healing' for the world?

The truth is that the churches have taken Jesus' relatively simple message and so overlaid it with mystifications, traditions, dogmas, rituals, and rules that it has become almost wholly unrecognizable—even falsified. I remember well coming on foot into Bethlehem in December 1976 after spending five days and nights hiking from Nazareth, in the north of Israel, down the Jordan Valley and through the stark yet hauntingly beautiful wilderness. Visiting the Church of the Nativity and seeing what is alleged to be the site of the manger was a profound shock. The marble manger, bedecked with pious bric-à-brac, symbolized forcefully what is wrong at the heart of the faith. It has been layered over with a façade, a fancy husk, while the living kernel goes largely unnoticed. The words of Jesus to the scribes and Pharisees of his day are as relevant to the church today as they were two thousand years ago: 'Woe unto you, scribes and Pharisees, hypocrites! for ye shut up the kingdom of heaven against men: for ye neither go in yourselves, neither suffer ye them that are entering to go in!' (Matt. 23:13.)

The fact that something is seriously wrong has been documented by many sociologists, most notably in Canada by Professor Reginald Bibby of the University of Lethbridge. Bibby has conducted the first major comprehensive national surveys on religious trends and attitudes in this country—two in the past eight years. He has found that while there is a massive search for answers to questions about meaning and purpose in life, the trend away from organized religion—which has traditionally provided these answers—is going on apace and 'seems likely to continue in the years ahead'. Such studies confirm that while nearly ninety per cent of Canadians, according to census figures, claim to be either Protestant or Roman Catholic, 'the vast majority engage in a religion without content.' The 1981 census figures show that the number of persons in Canada claiming no religious affiliation increased in the decade since the last census by ninety per cent, to reach one and four-fifths million, or over seven per cent of the population. However, these statistics do not reveal the full extent of the decline, since most people still tell the census-takers that they are Anglican, Roman Catholic, United, or whatever, depending on their background and the religious ties of the past. Thus the 1981 census shows an Anglican membership of two and two-fifths million, when that church itself only claims about one and a half million *members and adherents*, with an active membership that has now slipped under the one-million mark. The most recent Gallup Poll research in the United States, done for the American Catholic Press Association, shows that there has been a drastically sharp drop in church attendance among Catholics in the past five years. In 1978, seventy-four per cent of the Catholics polled said they had been to mass in the previous seven-day period. Today this figure stands at fifty-two per cent. The overall figure, for all denominations, regarding weekly church attendance now stands at forty-one per cent, according to this same poll.

Bibby goes so far as to say that Canada can no longer be considered a Christian country in any meaningful way, since only about forty per cent claim any active Christian commitment—and a good portion of these are highly non-traditional in their beliefs. Some comparisons may help to underline the crisis. Near the end of World War II, two in three Canadians attended religious services weekly. That figure has now dropped to one in three. Only one school-age child in three is currently exposed to religious instruction in a church, whereas two in three of their parents once were. What is more, surveys of children and young people even in the Catholic Separate School system, where religious instruction plays an important role, reveal that knowledge of key church teachings is alarmingly vague. Obviously, if the faith is not being communicated to the young, the number who share it is destined to go on decreasing.

This brings us to an important junction. Dietrich Bonhoeffer, who was put to death by the Nazis at Flossenburg just before the allied troops arrived in 1945, has become, through his *Letters and Papers from Prison* (1972) and other works, the most seminal Protestant theologian of our era. From prison he wrote: 'The most crucial question for the church in a post-Christian age is, who is Jesus Christ, for us, today?' The question of what theologians call Christology, that is, how to understand the person of Jesus and explain him or communicate about him to modern men and women, is of fundamental importance to the churches if they are to have a future. They have yet to begin to recognize the supreme urgency of this issue—one which has played a significant role in the current decline in church membership and, in spite of the frothy seeming-success of the TV evangelists, has foiled most attempts to communicate the gospel effectively to the masses.

A basic problem lies in the fact that the ancient creeds and their intricate formulae about Jesus having two natures, 'very God and very man', are largely incomprehensible today. The Gospels, it should be noted, always insist on his humanity—and if he were not fully human, of what possible help could he be to our common race? It is worth quoting a passage from the Epistle to the Hebrews (author unknown): 'Who in the days of his flesh, when he had offered up prayers and supplications with strong crying and tears *unto him that was able to save him from death*, and was heard in that he feared; though he was a son, yet he learned obedience by the things which he suffered; and being made perfect, he became the author of eternal salvation unto all them that obey him. . . .' (Heb. 5:7.) Obviously the author does not subscribe to the view that Jesus was divinely perfect from birth—he 'learned obedience' and was 'made perfect'. Nor are we to believe that in his prayers Jesus was praying to himself. God is the one 'able to save him from death'. However, in the opening verses of the letter, the writer makes it plain he believes Jesus was pre-existent with God and that he was God's agent in creation: 'By him also he made the worlds.' We have to ask, then, what kind of 'real humanity' is he talking about? Surely this, like the similar ideas expressed in the prologue to John's Gospel, is a case of mythologizing after the event of the Resurrection. Jesus' disciples knew he was human, but to emphasize the power of his vision they came to use terms that suggest more.

Pressing the matter of his full humanity a little further, it has to be said that a man cannot be human, 'in all things made like us', if he has only one parent. To be human means, among other things, to descend from genetic material, with a specific human ancestry, supplied by an earthly father and mother. For the genetic contribution of the male to be mysteriously created out of nothing and then added to the female ovum may be a miracle, but it is not the conception of a human being. The doctrine of the virgin birth demands that Jesus have no normal genetic traits of any forebears whatever on the male side. Significantly, only Matthew and Luke, in the obviously later legendary material on the birth of Jesus (on these passages, see Revd Frank W. Beare's *The Gospel According to Matthew*, 1982) specifically mention the virgin birth. John and Paul apparently knew nothing about it. Stories of heroic figures said to have been born of virgins were, of course, well known in the classical and Hellenistic periods. Justin Martyr (who lived from about AD 100 to 165), the early Christian apologist, even defends belief in the virgin birth on the grounds that the records of pagan religions were full of such marvels.

After the incident in which the boy Jesus talked with the scholars in the temple, Luke says he returned home with his parents and 'increased in wisdom and stature and in favour with God and man.' This sounds more like the normal development of a highly spiritual, sensitive youth than it does a description of God in human form. What is most revealing is the attitude of Jesus' mother and family to him during his early ministry. If Mary and Joseph knew his birth was miraculous and indeed really heard all that the angels are said to have told them in the accounts of the Annunciation, why did they reprimand their son for spending time in religious discussion with the temple authorities at the age of twelve? Jesus' reply to the scolding, and Luke's comment on it, are worth noting: 'He said to them, "How is it that ye sought me? wist [knew] ye not that I must be about my Father's business?" ' (Luke 2:49.) Luke adds: 'And they understood not the saying which he spoke unto them.' More significantly, one would presume that his close relations would know something, if only rumours, of his unique birth and destiny. Yet they come during the period of his early popularity with the crowds (Mark 3:21) and try to take him home forcibly, 'For they said, he is beside himself', that is, insane. When his family, including his mother, arrive to call him home, Jesus replies that his real family consists of all who do the will of God, in effect disowning his relatives (3:31-5). It is interesting that Matthew and Luke (who, according to the scholars, had Mark's Gospel, the earliest, in front of them when they wrote theirs) both leave out the incident in which Jesus is referred to as 'beside himself'. This is far from the only place where either or both feel free to alter Mark for reasons of taste or their own theological slant.

Though Jesus is given many titles in the New Testament, he never refers to himself as God, nor is he called God directly. His own term seems to have been the enigmatic 'Son of Man'. Debate over the meaning of symbolic epithets such as 'Son of God', 'Messiah', and 'Christ' has filled whole libraries. While scholarly and detailed, the discussion is at the same time inconclusive, if not outright contradictory. What is absolutely clear, however, is that none of these epithets, when applied to Jesus, means Jesus = God. The equation was only elaborated later, in church councils of the fourth and fifth centuries.

In the current, and in my view heretical, Jesuolatry that is rampant in the so-called 'electronic church', as well as in thousands of pulpits and 'pop' religion books, Jesus is spoken of as though he went about proclaiming, 'I am God'. Plainly he did nothing of the sort. What seems to have happened is that after the Resurrection a tortuous and lengthy process of theological development began, in which the messenger became, mistakenly, the message. God's unique agent came to be viewed as another God, in spite of herculean efforts to preserve the doctrine of monotheism, leading eventually to the full-fledged doctrine of the Trinity. The entire process (over which much blood has been shed down the ages) illustrates again the statement made earlier: it is easier to worship Jesus than to do what he said. Jesus himself made the point abundantly clear in several parables and sayings such as this: 'Not everyone that saith unto me, Lord, Lord, will enter the kingdom of heaven, but he that doeth the will of my Father who is in heaven.' (Matt. 7:21.)

Trying to reread the New Testament afresh, putting aside all one has learned in Sunday school or church, can be exhilarating. What did Jesus come to do? He came, the Gospels say, to preach the good news of the kingdom of God: the good news that, contrary to all appearances, evil is not on the throne; there is a loving centre to the cosmos. Intelligent, continually creating, and ultimately in charge, God reigns over the whole cosmos, the chaos and the hurt as well as the glory, according to Jesus. This kingdom of right relations in the presence of God is available here, now—even within us—if we will but let go, relax and enter into it, or let it in, as little children. The recognition that God indeed reigns and wills that every person on the face of the earth should join in making his kingdom a reality here, 'as it is in heaven', liberates us from mankind's single greatest enemy: fear. Fear is at the root of all human misery and hell; fear is the underlying cause of war and, in our day, the growing threat of nuclear holocaust. Fear, as the Bible rightly says, 'has torment'.

Jesus, it should be noticed, actually said very little about sin, apart from attacking all forms of rigid, self-righteous religiosity. His attitude was that once we have faced and rejected our sin, it can be—and is—forgiven. But he said a great deal about fear and its single antidote: faith. Not faith in a set of religious propositions, nor in dogmas about himself or the Trinity, nor in church traditions made by men; but faith in the sense of a child-like (not childish) trust in a living, gracious God whom he called, in imagery, 'Father'. 'Fear not' is Jesus' most characteristic saying, and at times he grieved, asking: 'How is it that ye have no faith?' His view of human destiny is a joyous, liberating vision, not a heavy burden of guilt and condemnation. As he says in John's Gospel: 'I am come that you might have life more abundantly.' (10:10.) His uniqueness, as I have already said, lies in the degree to which he was open to and filled with God's Spirit or presence. He was, in this sense, God's son, but not in any 'supernatural' way: the same possibility is open to all of us. Indeed, it is in John's Gospel, the latest of the four, and the one with the most highly developed view of Jesus' person, that he quotes from Psalm 82:6, as evidence that God himself has called all his people 'gods' and 'children of the Most High'. In John 1:12 we are told that all who receive him 'to them gave he power to become the sons of God.' According to Jesus, all are destined to become 'sons' of God, and his promise was that those who followed him would exceed him in their accomplishments or 'works'. It is highly significant that Jesus' parable of judgement (Matt. 25) includes nothing about a person's credal beliefs, sexual orientation, or political ideology in its criteria for God's acceptance or rejection on the last day. The question simply is whether or not one has done the will of the Father and 'lived the kingdom' by feeding the hungry, clothing the naked, and visiting the sick and imprisoned. All the rest, to Jesus, was window-dressing.

Today's new vision of Jesus as the liberator—the champion of the poor and the oppressed, who identifies with the refugee, the outsider, the social leper—does not represent some kind of 'leftist' takeover of the Bible. It comes from taking a fresh look at Jesus' humanity and his passion for justice and healing. The 1983 New Year's statement of the Canadian Roman Catholic Bishops regarding the economy, which has caused such wide repercussions and debate, is not some kind of 'Marxist Manifesto', as various critics would have us believe, but a direct attempt to apply his teaching to the crucial issues of our time. The whole new emphasis on social action and social justice in all the major churches, here and abroad, is based on what Jesus taught as a successor to the Old Testament prophets. It is the result of attempting to read the Gospels with fresh eyes, unclouded by the churchy presuppositions of the past. It is born of the realization that Jesus did not come to 'pour holy water over the status quo' but, as he says in Luke 4:17, quoting from Isaiah: 'The Spirit of the Lord is upon me because he hath anointed me to preach the good news to the poor; he hath sent me to heal the broken-hearted; to preach deliverance to the captives and the recovering of sight to the blind; to set at liberty them that are bruised. . . .' Wherever in the world these actions are carried out, the kingdom of God is present and at work.

In Canada and elsewhere there are now many inter-church and inter-faith coalitions concerned with social action on native rights, racism, the social responsibilities of big corporations, peace research, the problem of nuclear arms, immigration, refugees, and human rights. But this is not social action for its own sake, worthy though that may be. It is social action undertaken at the moving of God's Spirit and modelled on the life and example of Jesus himself. It is the wave of the future and one of the brightest signs of hope I see in the current religious scene, which otherwise gives much cause for distress. The churches and synagogues are showing evidence of their will to become the conscience both of the nations and of humanity. What they must do now is exert an equal effort to meet the inner cry for meaning and purpose at the level of the individual's spiritual searchings. Mere repetition of old dogmas is not enough.

I personally dislike labels of any kind, but for those who insist on them, the term 'Christian humanist' probably best describes the position to which I have come. As I state later in this book, humanism (or concern for all things belonging to and enhancing our humanity) is a noble concept. The real enemy today is anti-humanism: all the forces that reduce people to mere things in the system or 'game'. In a world where torture and barbarism of every type are on the increase, all who care deeply about human values and rights must join together to fight for them, no matter how different the bases for their particular brand of humanism may be. I don't see how it is possible to call oneself a Christian, orthodox or not, without being a humanist, that is, one who is vitally interested in the preservation and further evolution of what it means to be human. There could be no higher basis for humanism than the idea that God became man in Jesus, as traditional Christians have held for centuries. Or, as St Irenaeus put it in the second century AD: 'The glory of God is man fully alive!'

What is most distressing to me, as I look back on my experience as a reporter, is the sharpness with which religion continues to divide people into different camps, even to the point of violence and bloodshed. You can see it in Ireland or in Iran, but there is plenty of *odium religiosum* (religious hatred) much closer to home. I have a special file for the most extreme forms of hate mail I receive—all from people professing to be deeply religious—and much of it is filled with latent violence. Broadcaster Gordon Sinclair and others who have dared to question or criticize religious institutions and their doings tell me they have found the same thing. Tragically, each sect, cult, and denomination seems convinced that it alone has 'The Truth' in its entirety. All others are heretics. In spite of much talk and some movement towards ecumenical understanding, the major Christian churches remain as divided today as they were twenty-five years ago.

The Anglican and Roman Catholic scholars on a Joint International Commission seeking a compromise to heal the more-than-four-hundred-year-old split between their two churches have concluded that there are no irreconcilable differences. But despite the historic embrace of Pope John Paul II and Most Revd Robert Runcie, Archbishop of Canterbury, in Canterbury Cathedral in 1982, no real progress has been made. Under the very conservative leadership of John Paul, Rome once more seems to have reverted to the attitude that 'we can have reunion any time you wish to submit and return to Mother Church.'

In similar fashion, twice in England and once in Canada, the Anglican Church has spent years negotiating to bring various Protestant churches to the altar, only to turn them down abruptly before any union could be consummated. The Anglicans find it much easier to talk about Christ's prayer, 'That they may all be one', than to comply with it. As one said, somewhat archly, in defending his wish to stay Anglican: 'There may be other ways to God, but no gentleman would take them!'

All too many Christians, especially in the more fanatical churches and sects, still believe all other denominations and faiths to be schismatic or heretical and their followers bound for hell. This opinion is often reciprocal and so, as Kurt Vonnegut says, it goes—on and on. Unless world religious leaders come to realize the full seriousness of this situation and decide no longer to allow their various dogmas to blind them to the profoundly practical ideals they all profess in common, religion will continue to contribute as much to humanity's deepest problems as it does to their healing, if not more.

What is urgently needed right now is a world summit conference of the leaders of all the major faiths, not to consider some kind of homogeneous union into a single world faith (bound to be a fearsome, unworkable mish-mash), but to ponder together the great truths they share. The brotherhood of all humans under the sovereignty of a divine being (or beings), whose will is justice and love of neighbour, could unite these faiths into an extraordinarily powerful, virtually universal force for peace and the common good.

The fate of the world itself hangs in the balance. Enlightened religion—religion true to its basic, central message, not caught up in external packaging—could become the dynamic that tips the scales towards survival and helps God's kingdom draw nearer. If every one of the world's one billion Christians could agree and resolve, even just for one twenty-four-hour period, to jointly perform the will of the God they all profess, the planet would never be the same. If they were to join with the nearly one billion Muslims in the same commitment, and then with the Jews, then the Buddhists . . . !

On absolute certainty in religion

The single greatest foe of true religion and of the individual's own spiritual life is the seductive belief that somewhere, somehow it is possible to possess, with absolute certainty, 'The Truth'. This statement applies to all religions, cults, and sects, to all gurus, saviours, or alleged 'enlightened ones'. The tragedy of Jonestown is not the only modern example of where this belief can lead. It is behind the slaughter of the Baha'is in the Ayatollah Khomeni's Iran today. In the case of Christianity, no error has caused more bloodshed, cruelty, intolerance, division, and just plain misery than the view that 'we alone have God's revealed and infallible word and fiat'. The same can be said of Islam, Judaism, Hinduism, and all the rest.

Protestant Christians are divided into a myriad of camps because most of them have mistakenly elevated the Bible into an infallible 'paper pope'. Taking a view of the New Testament that would have astounded its authors—whose only Bible was what we call the Old Testament—they have to an alarming degree become Bible-worshippers. The Bible has become an idol, assuming a place reserved for God alone; in their mistaken zeal, they have broken his first commandment. Yet the New Testament authors themselves adapted or changed the Old Testament passages they quoted, and at times Matthew and Luke quite cavalierly altered the materials they found in Mark. There is no suggestion that they believed every line of Mark's work to be sacrosanct or infallible.

The battle over what seems to me a preposterous notion—that the Bible is totally free from error (known as the 'inerrancy of Scripture' debate)—is raging in several major Protestant denominations at this very moment. Even in the liberally minded

United Church of Canada, the nation's largest Protestant body, a growing fundamentalist wing is rallying around this theme. Anyone familiar with the Greek of the New Testament, however, knows there are hundreds of thousands of variant readings in the different manuscript traditions—variations due to scribal errors in the process of recopying older versions. Admittedly, the vast majority of these are of minor importance, but there are some key areas of uncertainty. Take, at random, the incident of the centurion at the cross. Did he say: 'Surely this man was *the* Son of God'? Or: 'Surely this man was *a* son of god'? In the one case, it's an orthodox Christian confession; in the other, simply an admiring admission that Jesus died like a hero whose father and/or mother was a pagan deity. Scholars are aware that the original ending to Mark's Gospel has been lost. From the ninth verse on, the final chapter is the product of a later attempt at a fitting conclusion. The manuscripts, in fact, contain two variant endings, one very short, the other considerably longer.

The very earliest manuscripts we know had virtually no punctuation, since space was at a premium and the scribes simply crowded as many letters as possible into each line. Yet there are places where the later addition of punctuation makes a vital difference. For example, the only time Paul expressly says that Jesus is God is in one highly debatable passage in Romans 9:5. If a comma is added to the original Greek text, it reads: '. . . Christ came, who is over all, God blessed forever, Amen.' If, as seems more likely, a period is intended after the word 'came', it then reads: '. . . Christ came. May God, who is over all, be blessed forever, Amen.' This kind of sudden, ejaculatory prayer of praise to God is common in the literature of the time and indeed is used again by Paul in this same letter (Rom. 11:36).

Serious differences appear when the four Gospels are compared. The two accounts of the birth of Jesus in Matthew and Luke abound in contradictions, as do the four accounts of the Resurrection. Even the two genealogies of Jesus given by Matthew and Luke bristle with so many inconsistencies that they are impossible to reconcile. Matthew (1:2 ff.), for his own theological reasons, begins with Abraham and works towards Joseph—who, he then tells us, was not Jesus' real father anyway. Luke (3:23 ff.) goes the other way and begins with Joseph, the 'supposed' father, and traces the ancestry back to Adam, 'the son of God'. Try to find out who Jesus' grandfather or great-great grandfather was from the two texts, and you can begin to see some of the problems. As for the birth narratives, in Luke's account (2:5 ff.) Mary and Joseph live in Nazareth and go up to Bethlehem where the child is born in a stable, whereas in Matthew (2:1 ff.) it seems that Bethlehem is their home; here the Magi enter the 'house' to find the child, and the holy family only goes to Nazareth after the flight into Egypt to escape Herod's wrath.

It is even more difficult to make the four accounts of the Resurrection agree. For me, the contradictions are actually advantageous. The differences, together with the emphasis on the disciples' initial reluctance to believe that anything notable had happened, all have about them the ring of reality: certainly there was no collusion among the evangelists to tell a flawless story. To ignore these differences or try to force them into harmony is to practise intellectual suicide.

Two additional examples will suffice to illustrate the point. If you compare the Gospel accounts of the cleansing of the temple, you will find that the first three place the story just before Jesus' arrest and execution—at the end of his ministry. But the fourth Gospel, so radically different in so many obvious ways, puts it boldly at the very outset of his public preaching (John 2:13 ff.). It is up to us to decide which chronology is the right one. Finally, take the well-known story of Jesus' healing of the wild demoniac whose evil spirits were cast out into a herd of swine, which then rushed down a cliff and destroyed themselves. Mark, whose version was the original, says there was one demoniac (5:2-13), but Matthew (8:28-32) improves on this account, claiming there were two. (Scholars have often commented on Matthew's penchant for doubling, which they say is based on the Old Testament ruling that two witnesses were required to prove a case.)

This discussion is not intended to detract in any way from the power, beauty, and essential importance of the biblical record. The point is simply that the infallibility notion doesn't stand up under honest critical examination. In fact, those who make the most noise about the Bible's truth, 'from cover to cover', have never undertaken the discipline of comparing the texts themselves—for all their Bible study. Even though we are commanded to love God with all our mind as well as our heart and soul, they still regard any attempt to apply reason to the Holy Scripture as a betrayal of God, if not a 'satanic' plot.

Worst of all, some even insist that the King James Version alone contains the pure, undefiled Word. Certainly no new translation—of the seeming scores that have recently appeared—can touch the King James for sheer elegance and beauty of language. But it is undeniable that the great scholars who produced it were working from very late manuscripts; that is, inferior Greek texts. Since then dozens of much earlier manuscripts have been discovered in Egypt and elsewhere, giving modern translators a far more accurate version to work with. The Revised Standard Version and the New English Bible may not sound as glorious as the King James, but they are much closer to what was really said and done.

For me, the realization that the biblical records are very human documents, bearing the mark of their time and of the people who wrote them, has been a liberating experience. The fact that God's Spirit did not treat the authors as mere automatons (as in alleged automatic writing) shows once again that he does not force anyone, but works in and through human beings as they are. The authors of the Bible were inspired, yes. But they were also people of their day, with all the limitations and weaknesses that humans are prone to. Today, for example, we realize that instead of providing a single, uniform 'theology of Jesus', the New Testament offers us several theologies. Each evangelist is seen as a theologian in his own right, in his own milieu, handling the source materials and presenting the gospel from his own distinctive point of view. Certainly these men were not historians in any modern sense of the word, nor were they interested in Jesus' biography. We are never told what he looked like, how he spent the years between his experience at the temple and his baptism by John the Baptist, or his precise age at the time of his death. The evangelists' concern was first and foremost to create faith and to nourish the churches of their day. The Gospels are a form of evangelism and catechetics, not scientifically researched documents for the archives of history.

The Bible speaks to us as perhaps no other book has done, not because the inspiration of the writers was different from that in or behind any other great work of art—God is one and the same—but because they were dealing with the most sublime of themes: God's revelation of himself to the world. The sacred texts of other world religions are seen in a similar light by their followers.

The Bible continues to speak to me personally as no other

inspired book has done. Knowing that it is part poetry, part high myth, and part consciously religious 'propaganda' (in the best sense of the word—preaching rather than mere history) only enriches its appeal and deepens my appreciation. Portions of it are difficult to understand. But as Mark Twain once said: 'It's not the parts of the Bible I don't understand that bother me, it's the parts I do!' In other words, it is a ringing challenge 'to do justly, to love mercy, and to walk humbly with thy God.' (Mic. 6:8.)

Significantly, those who claim to take the Bible as literal fact often contradict their own position and apply their doctrine with an uneven hand. They are fundamentalist only selectively. For example, while they insist on reading the Genesis stories of creation and the fall of man at face value, treating them as science and natural history, they take a less literal view of the passages that command the stoning of fornicators and adulterers. Most of the Old Testament rules and regulations are simply ignored, as are Paul's words on the subject of women covering their heads in church.

When Jesus says, 'I am the door', fundamentalists know he is speaking in poetic imagery. In fact, they uniformly reject the literal interpretation that Roman Catholics give to Jesus' statement in reference to the bread at the Last Supper: 'This is my body.' According to them, what Christ means is: 'This represents my body'. Yet when they come to the almost psychedelic Book of Revelation, they return to a literalism that leads to ludicrous absurdities. Wading in boldly where angels fear to tread, they deduce from this document, written for a precise situation in the Roman Empire in the late first or early second century, a complete blueprint for the late decades of the twentieth century. Since each would-be expert in 'Bible prophecy' interprets the book, and related works such as Daniel, according to different principles and biases, there are nearly as many blueprints as there are preachers expounding them. Attempts to predict the future in this manner are exercises in futility, whatever the commercial success of efforts such as Hal Lindsey's and C.C. Carlson's book *The Late Great Planet Earth* (1976). In the past, calculations as to the date of the return of the Messiah and the final Apocalypse have led to tragic results; even now there are communities of deluded people who have quit their jobs and sold their houses in immediate expectation of the 'Rapture' to heaven.

Today, incidentally, such speculations have relieved many Christians who should have known better from any sense of responsibility concerning the most pressing problems of our time—global hunger, poverty, environmental destruction, war. Looking forward to their own miraculous escape from the wrath to come, they are content to let the world itself go to hell. After all, they say, it's all predestined: it's 'in the book'.

On papal infallibility

Until Vatican II, Roman Catholics were virtually committed to a fundamentalist view of Scripture, although independent study of the Bible was not encouraged for rank-and-file members. Now Catholic scholars have almost as much freedom as other critical scholars. Catholic Charismatics or Neo-Pentecostals still maintain a literalist approach (in some cases to their detriment, as in their emphasis on demons, the so-called 'second baptism', etc.), but the church itself maintains the official position that historical-critical treatment of the Bible is acceptable.

The Pope and the teaching Magisterium of his office, however, remain the final arbiters of truth. Such scholars as Hans Kung and Edward Schillebeeckx, along with several Latin-American liberation theologians, have been severely reprimanded (Kung was even stripped of his status as an official Catholic theologian) when they have followed to their logical conclusion the leads suggested by this new approach to the texts. Kung's book *On Being a Christian* (1977) is the most readable and most complete development of this modern mode of interpretation.

The papal claims to infallibility—the dogma that the Pope is incapable of error when speaking officially (*ex cathedra*) on matters of faith and morals—represent an attempt to impute absolute religious certainty to a man rather than to a book, but they are no less idolatrous than the fundamentalists' claims. Furthermore, their basis in Scripture and church tradition is of the flimsiest sort. As an official dogma, infallibility went from being very much a minority opinion at the beginning of the nineteenth century to become an essential teaching that was solemnly defined at the First Vatican Council in 1870.

The Swiss Catholic historian A. Bernard Hasler, author of *How the Pope Became Infallible* (1981), was for five years a member of the Vatican Secretariat for the Unity of Christians. In July

1980, he wrote an open letter to Pope John Paul II. Declaring that 'the truth is at stake', he asked for answers to two questions: How can the dogma of infallibility be justified in the light of the Bible and of church tradition? And how can the ruling of Vatican I be considered valid, when it flew in the face of the best information available and was made through the use of pressure? Soon after writing the letter, Hasler died—without receiving an answer.

Theologians know full well what history has demonstrated time and again: that popes have erred and continue to do so. Not infrequently through the centuries, a ruling pontiff has wholly contradicted his predecessors. Still—and tragically, for the current cause of church reunion—the present Pope holds steadfastly to the dogma in question. Thus Hasler, in his open letter, wrote: 'You continually protest that you want to work for the unity of all Christians. But all this remains lip service as long as you are not prepared to tackle the main issues raised by the First Vatican Council. . . . On the subject of ecumenicity you have repeatedly said how necessary and vital dialogue is. But anyone who listens carefully soon recognizes that you don't mean *real* dialogue. For you preclude any alteration of your own position.'

The attempt to move the notion of infallibility from one man to the church itself (as Kung tried to do in his own book on this issue), maintaining that the church as a whole would be free from error, seems to me of little use either. There are verses in the New Testament promising that the Spirit will guide Christians into 'all truth', but historically the church as a whole has made too many horrific mistakes for anyone to believe that it possesses any in-built guarantees of total freedom from error. Remember Galileo, Copernicus, all those who died in the Crusades—the list of witnesses stretches back a long way.

The more trendy temptation today, especially among young people, is to attribute infallibility to a particular mystic, sage, or guru. But this tendency, like the attitude of fundamentalist Muslims to the Koran, of Jehovah's Witnesses to the *Watchtower* publications, or of the Mormons to the writings of Joseph Smith, stems from a single basic illusion: that absolute objective certainty is possible about eternal things. Moreover, there would be no room whatever for faith or trust if it were. That kind of certainty doesn't require faith; it demands, even coerces, total acceptance and obedience. The truth cannot be stated boldly enough: God is not a Fascist, and his followers are required to use their own minds, consciences, and wills. It may seem less secure, but it is an exciting and liberating experiment in human responsibility.

In closing, I would like to say a few words about how this book came into being and how the selections from my work were made. When Oxford University Press approached me with the idea, just after my return from Hiroshima at Easter, 1982, readers had been urging me for some time to provide two things: first, a clearer statement of my own beliefs and personal positions on controversial topics, and second, a collection of some major articles and series—such as the trip to Israel ('The Tale of Two Mountains') and 'The Christmas Story'—in a more permanent form. When the series on death and dying appeared in the fall of 1982, the number of these requests increased sharply. After looking through the hundreds of articles I have written in the past twelve years, we decided to concentrate on three distinct kinds of pieces: some with a personal or 'here I stand' note; some critical, stressing the need for renewal; and some of an openly inspirational or 'spiritual' nature. Among them are the articles that met with the most response (both pro and con); those that illuminate some of the crises facing religion today; and a few that are simply favourites of my own, such as the visit with Mother Teresa in Calcutta. If regular readers detect any differences between the pieces in this volume and the originals, they are not mistaken: I have taken advantage of this opportunity not only to rework, expand, and develop certain themes, but to speak much more frankly than I could as a journalist covering the entire spectrum of religion. What ties all of these pieces together is the fact that they have been written 'from faith unto faith'. That is to say, even when I am most outspoken and critical of current religious trends, I write as one who is himself in the midst of a spiritual pilgrimage, who though often despairing of all churches and religions, still feels love and even hope for them. An 'uncomfortable Christian', yes—but a Christian all the same.

The uncomfortable
Christian

The problem of evil

The first funeral I took as a rector of a small historic church in Scarborough, many years ago, was that of a teenaged girl struck by lightning on her way to school. Her companion, walking only a foot or so away, was stunned by the blast but relatively unhurt. At the parents' home, and later at the service itself, I struggled to find words of comfort. None of the ready clichés so prevalent in today's electronic religion seemed honest, logical, or simply persuasive through sheer emotional appeal. I found it impossible to say: 'This tragedy is in some way, beyond our knowing, part of God's great plan; you don't see it now but one day you will.' Or: 'God has taken your daughter to a much better place; he needed her; she will be young forever, spared the pain of living in this troubled world. . . .' A host of spiritual placebos came to mind in all their seductive array. But in the face of so much shock and sorrow, I could not force myself to utter them; even before I had framed them for speech, they sounded hollow.

These parents, like all people confronted with one of life's sudden, often horrible accidents, fatalities, dread diseases, needed more than anything to grieve—to feel anger at the situation, to shed bitter tears, to ask hard questions even of the God in whom they believed. Above all, they needed to be assured that this tragedy was not their fault; that it was not because they had fought the previous day, or failed to attend church regularly, or forsaken family prayers. They needed to be reassured that they were right to feel stricken, enraged, desolate; and that others in the faith community shared their awful sense of loss and bewilderment. But they needed much more as well. They needed assurance that although God does not 'send' cruel tragedies, his presence and strength do come to those who mourn. His help, and the caring love of friends and family, can bring meaning out of the most senseless events. And those who eventually conquer in this way remain his most cogent witnesses to the power of life and love.

The problem being faced here is the oldest of all religious questions, the ultimate one: 'How can a just and good and loving God permit evil, pain and suffering—especially that of the innocent?' Or, to use the title of a recent book by Rabbi Harold S. Kushner, *When Bad Things Happen to Good People* (1982), what are religious people to say? Kushner's book is invaluable at a time when many are suggesting a view of God that makes him (or her) seem like a capricious monster whose cruelty, if true, would make him more the object of hatred than of devotion.

Take, for example, a recent speech given to a group of Canadian businessmen attending a Full Gospel Businessmen's breakfast. Prayer is as important as it was centuries ago, said Norman Williams, a man who survived the 1977 mid-air collision of two jets in the Canary Islands in which five hundred and ninety-three people were killed. Williams credits his survival to his widowed mother's prayers with him before he undertook the journey. 'My Bible-believing mama asked me to pray with her for a safe return, and I did,' he said. 'That's what made the difference.' Does he think for one moment that none of the five hundred and ninety-three or their families were praying for safety? Does he presume that somehow the others—some of whom, he said, were cursing as their plane burst into flames— were of less concern to God than he? Was Pastor Dietrich Bonhoeffer not praying when his Nazi captors led him out and hanged him in Flossenburg, just two days before the allies liberated the town? Did no one in Auschwitz, or Buchenwald, or Dachau pray before being sent to the crematorium?

The plain fact of the matter is that bad things happen just as regularly to 'good' people as to anyone else. Cancer, accidents, bereavements strike without any moral aim whatever. It may be true, as C.S. Lewis put it in his not-very-good book *The Problem of Pain* (1943), that 'pain plants the flag of truth in the fortress of a rebel soul'. But to suggest that God sends the pain for this purpose is only a little less than blasphemy.

Kushner, rabbi of Temple Israel in Natich, Mass., is eminently qualified to tackle the thorny problem of what is technically called theodicy: how to reconcile God's goodness and power with the obvious injustices in human experience. His book is dedicated to his son Aaron, who died in his early teens of the strange disease known as progeria (premature aging). At two, Aaron was a bright, happy child who could identify a dozen different varieties of dinosaur and would patiently explain to any adults willing to listen that dinosaurs are now extinct. Before long the child lost his hair and began to look like a little old man. The Kushners lived the next decade knowing they were on borrowed time. Having comforted others in their hours of grief, the rabbi came to know what it means to need comforting yourself. The more he read, however, and the more friends tried to offer condolences, the more he realized there was something very wrong with most religious thinking on this crucial point. Most of the books, he found, were much more concerned with defending God's honour and proving that experienced evil is really necessary to make this world good, than with curing the bewilderment and anguish of a parent with a visibly dying child. Thus even before Aaron died, he pledged he would write his own book.

One of the first problems Kushner deals with is the feeling—universally recognized by clergy trying to minister to those caught by tragedy—that God is somehow punishing people by making them ill or taking their loved ones. He blames conventional religion for this horrendous theology, which only succeeds in adding guilt to an already overburdened soul. 'Why did this have to happen to me?' or 'What did I do to deserve this?' are the first questions most people ask as their world begins to collapse. Behind the questions is the unexamined assumption that everything that happens is sent by God or designed for a purpose, however inscrutable. In Kushner's view this is a fundamental error, leading in the end to a God who is less moral than we are ourselves—torturing us for a spiritual 'good' that every fibre of our being cries out is evil to the core. There are, he argues, some things over which God has no control. There are such things as luck, chance, or fate; there are corners of chaos in this world still waiting to be made part of the ordered universe. There is no reason why some parents have retarded children and others do not, why some people are killed in a crash and others are not, apart from the 'natural' laws of genetic codes, gravity, and so on.

Whatever meaning there is in such events is not there of its own accord, nor is it instilled by God; the meaning is one we impose on or draw out of it. There was no special meaning in

Aaron's death, except that which his parents, by the grace of God, were able to extract from it. Aaron's death makes sense and has point only because his family were enabled to draw from it the inspiration to be of realistic help to others who are hit by similarly inexplicable assaults of chance. Kushner goes on to point out that there are other areas over which God has no control, because in creating the universe according to 'laws', he gave up the power to intervene like the *deus ex machina* of Greek tragedy. A bullet once fired cannot be diverted. A person whose life is filled with prayer cannot survive jumping from a cliff, any more than the worst criminal can. The laws that make this an ordered universe in which we can delight are not to be suddenly changed in order to suit personal whims or ensure individual safety. In giving people true freedom, God also made possible the choice of evil. The pain inflicted by the torturer or the death-camp overseer can't be blamed on God. That Hitler was a maniac was not God's will.

Kushner writes: 'I don't believe God causes mental retardation in children, or chooses who should suffer from muscular dystrophy. The God I believe in does not send us the problem; He gives us the strength to cope with the problem.' And, we could continue, to bring good out of the very jaws of any evil. We can turn to God for help in the face of tragedy, says the rabbi, precisely because we know he is as outraged at it as we are. The question to ask is not, 'Why did this happen to me? What did I do?' That kind of question is really pointless, unanswerable. A better one would be: 'Now that this has happened to me, what am I going to do about it?'

Some TV evangelists today cruelly tell people caught by tragedy to 'pray for a miracle'. 'Hold your retarded child against the TV screen', I heard one say. What nonsense!—as if God were some coy potentate who could be cajoled, flattered, or bribed into acting on behalf of some and not of others. The real miracle is the incredible ability of human beings to take the most grievous strokes of fate and, by the grace of God and the caring of a community of friends, turn them to the service of us all.

I personally agree with everything Kushner has said. However, the good rabbi has not completely solved the problem of evil. He has not answered why, if God is as outraged as we are at such evils as mental retardation or cancer in children, he did not make the world better. If he is at the same time all-loving and all-powerful, how can these things be? Perhaps we have to go beyond Kushner's view to wonder whether God, who is so deeply involved in our evolution, is not in some sense evolving himself. Does he also have a 'shadow-side'? This daring, and to some unacceptable, approach to what Paul once called 'the mystery of evil' is much more radical than the traditional mythical imagery of Satan, the serpent, the forbidden fruit, and an Eden forever lost. As a character in Graham Greene's novel *The Honorary Consul* (1974) puts it, there is a 'night-side of God which causes him great pain—a night-side that will eventually wither away or be overcome.' The idea should not be lightly dismissed. After all, the notion of fallen angels or a personal devil solves little, if anything. Only a sadistic God could be all-powerful and yet allow some monstrous devil to torment the creatures we are told he loves.

Although for a more technical approach one should read the works of the creators of what has come to be known as 'Process Theology', Greene's novel presents some powerful popular arguments for the thesis of an evolving God. The leading character is Father Leon Rivas, a revolutionary ex-priest who argues that he can see no other way to believe in God than to hold that he too is part of the cosmic evolutionary process. He says that all his life he has tried to understand why God allows innocent suffering 'and why I cannot stop loving him'. Rivas accuses the church of taking a pat, easy way out of the problem of evil by blaming it on Satan, and affirms: 'I believe in the evil of God, but I believe in his goodness too. He made us in his image . . . and so our evil is his evil too. How could I love God if he were not like me? Divided like me. Tempted like me.' On such a view, God is involved in a struggle against himself, a struggle in which we share. Every evil act of ours strengthens his night-side, and every good one helps his day-side. Eventually God will be able to 'tear off his mask forever', and the time of causing destruction and creating monsters like Hitler will be over. Rivas is certain that because of Jesus, in whom God's intentions were for once completely fulfilled, a final victory is assured. In other words, we can live in the faith and hope that evolution will one day end with all of us sharing in the goodness summed up in Christ. The priest says: 'It is a terrible process all the same, and the God I believe in suffers as we suffer. . . .'

I believe that this 'process' view of God is one way to explain the otherwise horrendous deeds attributed to him in what we call the Old Testament: for example, the slaughter of the Amalekites (I Sam. 15:1-8). In any case, it certainly merits hard thought on the part of those who profess belief in God's love in the face of life's tragedies. I am not so naïve as to think it will be widely accepted by the traditionally minded. To some it will no doubt seem heretical. Still, we can hope that it will help to spark a new and creative approach to a critical problem for those who find that the stock answers are no longer enough.

Depression and faith

Many of those who come to a minister's study—or who write for help to a religion editor—are suffering from the commonest and bleakest of human ills: depression. Some can be helped by religion. They need a sense of purpose, of being accepted, of realizing they can be forgiven for some nagging guilt, of finding strength through fellowship, of release from self-centredness by discovering a higher sense of service to others. But for millions of others, religion itself has become an obstacle, and sometimes even the very cause of their feelings of utter darkness and self-loathing. Psychiatrists and saints, as well as ordinary pastors, have long been aware that depression often poses an especially thorny hurdle for those who are the most religiously inclined. Indeed, studies have shown that clergy themselves tend to suffer from this malady more than members of any other profession, except psychiatry.

Before looking more deeply at the reason, it has to be said that depression in some form attacks every thoughtful person, to a greater or lesser degree, at frequent intervals in the course of a normal life. It can masquerade in a myriad of different forms, ranging from a mild 'case of the blues' to a pit of the blackest despair and hopelessness. Central to depression is the feeling that it is never going to end—a little like the favourite Anglican chant: 'As it was in the beginning, is now, and ever shall be, Amen.' At the same time there is a sense of aloneness, a feeling that others couldn't possibly understand, which is only deepened by well-meaning friends who urge one to 'stop moping' or 'keep a stiff upper lip'. Often even ordinary decisions become impossible, ordinary pleasures are sucked dry of all joy, familiar duties become unbearably tedious, and the future seems barren of any new possibilities. Self-hate runs rampant; physical symptoms from backaches to migraines (psychiatrists speak of the depressed person's 'organ recital') begin to appear; a general fatigue or lassitude pervades everything. Nothing has any point any more.

Often, too there is an undercurrent of rage, even in those people who seem most placid and incapable of emotion when depressed. Because they have never learned to deal with anger, they may lash out in unexpected tirades, or some other form of overkill. Some people can't eat or sleep. Others want to sleep and eat all the time, as a means of escape. Some take comfort in alcohol or drugs; others look for sexual gratification. In short, depression is a hydra-headed monster with causes as numerous and as varied as its manifestations. Often it can be triggered by such a tiny matter as the tone of voice used by a boss, parent, spouse, child, or friend. It may not be much, but feeding on a wealth of unresolved deeper conflicts, a minor incident can lead to a downward spiral and full heaviness of spirits.

Religious people have the greatest difficulty with depression if they make the too-familiar error of supposing that, because they believe God has accepted and forgiven them, because they have been 'born again' or 'enlightened', or because they hold church office, they should be above this kind of experience. A severe inner conflict is set in motion when depressed persons see their condition as evidence of 'lack of faith' and thus either refuse to admit they are depressed, or begin to berate themselves for their 'sins', real or imagined. Anger is another matter in which church and synagogue have been of little help. Much depression is caused by deeply repressed rage—against one's work, one's parents, one's spouse, whatever. But religion has taught us that it is not 'nice' to be angry at anyone, least of all those closest to us, and so our anger gets pushed down, only to surface in another form: usually anger with oneself.

The spiritual directors in medieval monasteries, who knew a great deal more about the workings of the inner man than is usually credited to pre-Freudians, used to have a saying: 'Where there is torpor [lassitude and depressed spirits] always look for the rancour [anger].' The solution does not lie in flying into a rage at will. But a careful reading of the Bible shows that the men and women of God were very honest in accepting and expressing the fact that they felt anger from time to time. Jesus himself was angry on several occasions. He expressed anger at Peter—'Get thee behind me, Satan' (Mark 8:33)—and at the ravages of illness upon humanity. He could speak very tartly to his parents and relatives when the occasion warranted it, too. The Psalms make it very clear that the biblical writers had no fear of expressing their anger even against God—something that most people in grief feel is wrong, and yet may be their deepest need.

Perhaps not everyone needs a punching bag in the basement to take out his or her anger on, but I well remember a very wise professor of pastoral theology recommending this method to a class of future parish priests: 'There's one for you, Mrs Jones, and for you, head-warden Smith!' he said. 'That's a better way to deal with your frustrations after the annual meeting than taking it out on yourself or, more usually, the wife and kids.' But anger is not the only culprit.

Too many religious people, especially ministers, become lost in the great gulf they perceive between the perfection their religion demands and the way they themselves are. Christians who accept a 'perfect Jesus', whose way of life they are supposed to imitate, can do great things. They can also break down under the strain. They accept neither his humanity, nor their own, nor anyone else's, and so make impossible demands on all around. They profess to be living a life of 'faith' when in reality they are living a life of 'works' and paying for it. They ignore the fact that every major character in the Bible had his or her times of frustration, doubt, fear, failure, and depression. Instead of seeing that all personal growth follows an inevitable cycle of decision-death-resurrection, many religious people want to bypass Good Friday in a leap towards Easter. Quoting the psalmist, Jesus on the cross cried out in depression and anguished isolation of spirit: 'My God, my God, why has thou forsaken me?' Two of the Gospel writers omit these words, perhaps because even in those days, they felt embarrassed at Christ's apparent admission of feeling 'God-forsaken'—the very essence of the depressed state.

It is hard to know which do the most harm in the area of depression: the slick TV evangelists with their simplistic promise that Christ makes it possible to be 'up' all the time, or the writers of 'pop' self-help psychology books, who smoothly tell us how to wrestle every negative feeling to the ground. Both foster magic and illusion. We want to 'buy' their message because we have such a deeply rooted longing for absolute happiness, absolute security, absolute control over every aspect of life. In our human longing to return to that womb of comfort rather than accept the tough, ambiguous, growth-producing struggles of which real life is composed, we are readily seduced. But the ultimate failure of these false prophets can bring the most severe depression of all. Having been led to believe that other people can be on a constant 'high', we find we can't: therefore we must be somehow deficient in either will-power or true belief.

In his excellent book *What to Do When You're Depressed* (1975), George A. Benson, a Christian psychoanalyst, notes that people who suffer constant depression need professional help. However, he sees occasional bouts of depression as part of the true maturing of men and women of faith: 'For growth is a resisted natural process that is always foreshadowed by despair before it moves us on to the joy of change and the peace of God.' Benson does not mean that people should not seek to avoid unnecessary depression; those special 'blues' that often surround vacations, graduation, anniversaries, or Christmas, for example, can be avoided by keeping our expectations realistic. Often we need to look honestly for the source of our anger.

When depression comes, most of us do not need to be told to 'pray harder', or to 'expect great things from God', or to recite world-beater slogans. We need to understand the reasons for our blighted feelings and take the action that seems appropriate—such as eliminating or at least facing any sources of anger—while realizing that the mood will pass. Indeed, properly understood and accepted, depression may well be a major stepping-stone in our becoming fuller, more compassionate, more joyful human beings.

The Pope

The present Pope, John Paul II, is a complex man, tough, shrewd, and intellectually gifted. As the spiritual head of roughly seven hundred million Catholics (there are about one billion Christians in the world), he is without question the single most influential and respected religious figure of our time. It is significant that in the eyes of the media he can literally do no wrong.

The critical stance normally taken towards public figures and events has been virtually abandoned in the case of John Paul II. Partly this is because of the widespread delight in covering a religious figure who is not only highly photogenic, but keenly attuned to theatrics, those of television in particular. Partly the problem stems from the serious lack of qualified writers and commentators in the field of religion. It's easier to describe the grand gesture than it is to analyse what is being said and what its implications are. Examples of this failure of objectivity have abounded on the various papal tours, where the vast majority of reporters have sounded more like public-relations experts for the Vatican than seasoned newspeople. To see the full extent of this phenomenon you have only to look closely at the one-and-two-fifths-billion-dollar Vatican Bank scandal revealed in 1982, which involved several deaths, including that of Roberto Calvi, head of the Banco Ambrosiano and widely known as 'God's banker', because of his Vatican connections. This bizarre case, only one of a series of scandals connecting the Vatican and known criminals with Mafia affiliations, drew scarcely a murmur of negative comment about the Pope's role in the affair. Would the head of any other organization or business ever escape severe criticism if it were found that his main financial officials kept getting entangled with outright crooks? Archbishop Paul Marcinkus, a close friend of the Pope, who used to golf with both Calvi and the notorious Michele Sindona (now in a New York prison for massive fraud), even had to leave his lodgings at the posh Villa Stritch and move into the Vatican with his chief accountant and head PR man to avoid being summonsed by Italian treasury agents in the summer of 1982. Marcinkus heads the Vatican Bank. Few trained journalists, either religious or general, have dared to try and tell the whole truth about Pope John Paul II, so great has been the fascination with his 'charisma'. Yet it is essential that this be done, not only out of love for the Catholic Church and its people, but also because the media have an obligation to tell all sides of any story, no matter how unpopular or even dangerous it may be.

I was in St Peter's Square the night Cardinal Karol Wojtyla was elected, and I attended his investiture in St Peter's Square in all its splendour. Since then I have seen him at very close quarters day after day on several of his tours, even travelling with him on his jumbo-jet flight from Dublin to Boston in October 1979. I have read all of his major speeches, statements, and encyclicals, and written scores of stories about him. Consequently I am aware of his many strengths, his bold stand for human rights, his charismatic flare for mass communication, his love of the dramatic, crowd-pleasing gesture. He obviously has great courage, and even greater self-discipline. But I would be lying if I did not state flatly that in my opinion his papacy has been a disaster in many crucial ways. Furthermore, unless John Paul radically alters his style and outlook, the future of his church looks very bleak indeed.

The churches and the world have been led to hope that he would be the man of the hour, a modern man, one who would hold fast to essentials yet move flexibly in compassion and humility to lift people's burdens, and serve not just his own flock but the whole of humanity. Instead we find him rigid, unbending, steadfastly determined to turn back the clock to the Middle Ages. A greater contrast with the beloved John XXIII, whose name he adopted for half of his own, would be hard to find. His ultra-conservative views on everything from the role of women to the role of the papacy itself are creating a colossal crisis both for his own church and for the whole of Christendom. He simply is not carrying the majority of Catholics with him—no matter how loudly they cheer as he goes by—on such issues as birth control, obligatory celibacy for priests, the virtual excommunication of divorced persons who remarry without an annulment, the ban on women priests, and the refusal to enter into communion with Anglicans or others, except on his terms alone.

This Pope travels a lot but seems to learn little or nothing from it, since he comes only to talk (some sixty addresses in six days on the American tour), never to listen. Everywhere he is treated like a conquering hero, like the general in a Roman triumph, but nowhere is there any dialogue. As many of his own theologians have put it, his idea of dialogue is: 'I talk, you listen; then you submit.' Those theologians who don't submit are harshly dealt with, as in the case of Hans Kung. No other person in the world is allowed to make so many speeches on so many vital issues, with such extraordinary media coverage, without ever having to face a press conference or other forum where opposing questions or views are presented. This is one reason why his visits to many of the earth's trouble-spots have produced so much hoopla but so little permanent change or healing. The Irish tour was a classic example. It did nothing to heal the violence or end the sectarian strife, partly because he refused to speak with the Protestant church leaders who came to Dublin to meet him for that express purpose. Their brief (on ways in which changes by Ireland's Catholic hierarchy could help to overcome Protestant fears of union with the south) was taken over by a papal aide, and they had to be content with a short exchange of pleasantries with the pontiff instead of saying what was really on their minds. Small wonder the ultra-fanatical Revd Ian Paisley was able to gloat over the outcome, sneering that the moderate group had gone to Dublin simply to kiss the Pope's ring!

It is not just a case of ignoring outsiders, or his own liberal theologians such as Hans Kung and Edward Schillebeeckx, or the one hundred and sixty German liberals and moderates who not long ago sent him an open letter asking him to change the church's stand on contraception. This Pope doesn't even listen to his fellow-bishops. Early in his reign, enthusiasts said that because of his own experience as a bishop and cardinal in Poland, John Paul would restore the World Synod of Bishops to what the fathers of Vatican II intended it to be: an occasion for all the bishops, through their representatives, as successors of the Apostles to make decisions in a collegial manner under the Pope's governing hand. This dream was crudely destroyed at

John Paul's first attendance as Pope at a World Synod in October 1980. The topic was the family and related issues, and I eagerly joined about one hundred and fifty other reporters for fifteen days of the month-long event. More than two hundred bishops from every part of the globe discussed all the controversial issues, from birth control to divorce. Many argued courageously and passionately for changes in church policies. Yet the Pope's speech on the final day ignored all of their more progressive suggestions and rigidly reaffirmed the status quo. Apart from the experience of meeting each other, the bishops might just as well have stayed at home. As Hans Kung commented to me later in an interview, the whole thing reminded him of a 'totalitarian party congress'. Writing in *The Catholic Register* (15 November 1980) just after his return from the synod, Cardinal G. Emmett Carter, Archbishop of Toronto, expressed great disappointment that the synod had become 'a major debating society' instead of a truly collegial body able to make decisions for the church of God. The cardinal, who seems far from being a radical (or indeed even a progressive, these days) deplored the fact that the major 'propositions' agreed upon by the bishops after four weeks of deliberation have never yet seen the light of day. Even though the bishops explicitly recommended that their findings be published, the 'propositions' are to this day in the sole possession of John Paul. As Carter wrote, this is indeed 'a clear formula for confusion and frustration'. 'What did the synod say?' he asked. 'What was its thrust on the major issues that interested the world? No one really knows.'

The Pope's intransigence at the synod, in the face of earnest pleas from his bishops for some consideration of pastoral changes, is matched by his rigidity elsewhere. He persists in his outmoded opinions, which not he, but the shrinking company of his priests, have to explain as best they can. The point is that Catholics are increasingly ignoring John Paul's authority while continuing to applaud his pop-star image. What he says is far more traditional than what his predecessor, Paul VI, said; the difference is that he has a captivating smile, where Paul was vinegary at best.

One sign of the coming crisis is the fact that about fifty per cent of all Catholic missions and parishes in the world are now without a resident priest, and the situation is getting worse daily as the aging remnant retires or dies. The Pope unfortunately still sees the world through the 'tunnel' of his Polish experience, and it distorts reality for him. For example, a year or so ago Poland ordained more priests than did the whole of Latin America. In Poland, where one can grow up without ever meeting anyone who is not Roman Catholic, where roughly ninety per cent of the population is faithful to the church, one can easily get the illusion that there is no need to compromise or change to meet either other Christians or the world in general. And when there is a common enemy, such as the Communist regime in Poland, a church that is in fact the only organized opposition cannot afford the luxury of dissent, or of appearing to change its mind. However, this kind of experience is no advantage in attempting to run such a universal organization as the Roman Catholic Church.

John Paul, as has been noted, is a man of many talents. But he is too much a one-man show—and too much the product of his unique background—to be the kind of pope the churches and the world now need so badly. Like the Lutherans, the United Church, the Anglicans and many others, I would be happy to acknowledge the Pope as primate and head of any reunited Christian Church, but only if his were a leadership modelled on that of Jesus, who declared: 'I am come as a servant among you'. As long as John Paul affirms his claims to infallibility and to universal jurisdiction over all who would consider themselves part of the 'true church' of Christ, he is acting and thinking like some ecclesiastical monarch of a bygone age, and the scandal of Christian disunity will continue.

Papal infallibility

The doctrine of papal infallibility—that the pope is infallible when speaking officially (*ex cathedra*) on matters of faith and morals—is the major stumbling block to Christian unity today. Pope Paul VI himself once admitted this in a moment of anguished candour; Anglican, Orthodox, and Protestant church people have been deeply aware of it for some time. Now a book by a Roman Catholic theologian reveals just how shaky the foundation for the infallibility doctrine really is.

How the Pope Became Infallible (1981), by Revd August Bernard Hasler, is the English version of a book that first appeared in German in 1979. Hasler, who served for five years in the Vatican Secretariat for Christian Unity, met an untimely death in July 1980. Plenty of Roman Catholic theologians since Vatican II (1962-5) have questioned the infallibility dogma and a significant number of North American and European Catholics no longer believe in it. But Rome has never repudiated it (in fact, John Paul II has strongly reaffirmed it), and in 1979 Revd Hans Kung, the renowned West German theologian, was stripped of his right to teach as, or even call himself, a Roman Catholic theologian because he had dared to subject the doctrine to a devastating critique in his book *Infallible? An Enquiry* (1970). What Hasler has done—which gives his book unique status among those critical of infallibility—is to describe in minute detail the actual proceedings at Vatican I (1870), where infallibility was first defined and promulgated as a key dogma of the church. While working at the Vatican, Hasler was given access to the archives and was thus able to study the diaries, letters, and official documents of that fateful council.

The picture that emerges is one of scandal, intrigue, and power politics on a massive scale. Pope Pius IX, who officiated at Vatican I, is revealed as a man obsessed with ramming through the decree no matter what bishops or arguments stood in his way. Hasler painstakingly documents what had long been suspected by Catholics and others alike: that Vatican I was neither free to make its own decisions, nor ecumenical in the sense of truly representing the mind of the church at that time. Since freedom and ecumenicity are the essential marks of a valid council, Hasler concludes that the dogma of infallibility was passed uncanonically, or in contradiction to church law.

In his introduction Hasler makes several points often missed by those unfamiliar with the issue. First of all, he notes that Jesus himself, although he had a unique sense of authority, never once claimed to be infallible. Nor did his Apostles. We know that Peter—claimed as the first Pope—was once openly corrected on doctrine by Paul (Gal. 2:11). The truth, as Hasler shows, is that the church knew nothing of infallibility for over one thousand years of its history. When the claim did appear in the thirteenth century, the circumstances surrounding it were interesting, to say the least. Peter Olivi (1248-98) was a Franciscan priest, and he first attributed infallibility to the pope 'from something less than the purest of motives'. A fight was raging over whether poverty in the form of communal renunciation of property by the Franciscans was a possible path to salvation. Pope Nicholas II (1277-80) ruled in favour of the Franciscan view, and Olivi wanted to make this decision irreversible by arguing that the pope can never err on faith and morals. Forty years later, however, Pope John XXII (1316-34) came to a different decision on the poverty controversy. He was angry when told his predecessor's decree was infallible, since it limited his own power to decide for himself. Thus in the papal bull *Qui Quorundam* (1324) he condemned the doctrine of papal infallibility as 'the work of the devil'! Later, when pope rose against pope (at one time there were three rival popes all excommunicating each other) the papacy went through such a time of scandal that papal credibility, not infallibility, became the prime concern. People tended to look to church councils for absolute truth rather than to the pope. (In 1414-18 the Council of Constance, convened by the Emperor of Germany, deposed the three contending popes and settled that row by electing a new one in their place.)

It was the Protestant Reformation, especially the movement begun by the monk Martin Luther in 1517, that made the popes think once again with some longing about the notion of infallibility. As Hasler says, 'the more Protestants contested the authority of church and pope, the more Catholics stressed it.' Still there was no formal move to call infallibility a dogma. Even at the Council of Trent (1545-63), held to stem the Protestant tide, the notion of papal primacy foundered on the reef of stubborn resistance by the French bishops and others. Hasler's research shows that as late as the beginning of the nineteenth century, papal infallibility was generally rejected by the church except in parts of Italy and Spain. But the chaos and widespread disenchantment with rationalism that followed in the wake of the French Revolution gave rise to a general quest for stable forms of authority. French intellectuals began to look nostalgically towards Rome, and several, most notably Count Joseph de Maistre (1753-1821), wrote cogently in favour of an infallible pope. There was a similar trend in Germany.

Pius IX (1864-78) thus seized on a movement which was by then gathering momentum on every side. He saw the church as besieged by the forces of secularization, liberalism, rationalism, and a range of other '-isms', against which papal infallibility was an obvious means of defence. He set a world-wide practice of only appointing bishops who were committed to his policies. To prevent opposition, he forbade formation of national bishops' conferences. Thus the bishops had little contact with each other, and were forced to deal directly with Rome. Theology and catechisms were brought into line with the teaching of infallibility and any manuals or other books taking a different line were either put on the Index of Forbidden Books or officially burned. Praise, blame, and outright condemnation were the tools used to bring recalcitrant clergy into line. But even as the supporters of Roman centralism and infallibility began ascribing titles to Pius IX (including 'King', 'Pope-King', 'Most Exalted Regent', 'Supreme Ruler of the World', even 'King of Kings'), the forces of opposition were gathering. Bishops and professors from all over, especially Germany and France, voiced mounting concern. In particular they were appalled at extremists who had gone so far as to address hymns hitherto intended for God himself to Pius IX. Hasler reports that one enthusiast called Pius 'the vice-God of humanity'. The assistant bishop of Geneva spoke of the threefold incarnation of the Son of God: in the Virgin's womb, in the Eucharist, 'and in the old man of the Vatican'. St John Bosco talked about the pope as 'God on earth . . . Jesus has put the pope on the same level as God.' Thus, on the eve of the council, the whole Catholic world was bitterly divided on the question of papal infallibility.

The fascination of Hasler's research is that it shows, blow-by-blow, the way in which the council fathers (bishops) were manipulated, intimidated, and coerced into final agreement with the definition pushed through by the ailing pontiff. (Piux IX was known to have epilepsy, and was also thought by some to be less than completely sane.) In 1864, six years before the council, Pius had polled the cardinals in one Roman department and found only one out of fifteen in favour of his plan to make infallibility a dogma. Of thirty-two bishops consulted—mostly Roman centralists—only seven were in favour of the definition. Diaries show that even the most ardent supporters of infallibility at the council itself were desperately afraid the controversy would provoke a massive schism. But the Pope, together with about fifty bishops who were hard-core enthusiasts, eventually won the day over the roughly one hundred and thirty opponents of the dogma and the five hundred prelates who came to Rome undecided. Pius IX used the pulpit, the press, and the confessional, as well as a variety of religious associations, to exert pressure on dissidents. When it came time for the actual vote, a large number of the bishops threw their ballots into the Tiber or simply went home! The documents show they were furious at having had neither freedom of debate nor freedom of conscience.

Hasler, whose life and ministry were devoted to the cause of Christian unity, concludes that the problematic dogma of infallibility has feet of very soft clay, and should be abandoned. His case seems unassailable. But what would the papacy be like without this doctrine? In a special preface to this book, Hans Kung points to Pope John XXIII, the most revered pope of modern times, the man who called Vatican II and who more than any church leader of this century was able to command love and allegiance even from those outside the churches altogether. Pope John, he reminds us, saw the papacy as a 'primacy of service'. John made no bones about his own humanity, limitations, and fallibility: 'He lacked the aura of infallibility.' And yet 'none of the popes of this century had as great an influence on the course of human history and of Christianity itself as this pope who put no stock in infallibility.' Certainly this kind of Roman primacy, one that seeks its pre-eminence by making itself the servant of all humanity in a truly human, truly Christian way, would be acceptable to most major Christian bodies today. Pope John Paul II speaks much, and sincerely, about the cause of Christian unity. He could achieve it virtually overnight by the stroke of his pen. It could, in fact, be the last 'infallible' pronouncement: 'I and my successors are not infallible any longer.'

Doubts and belief

There are now more agnostics than believers in Canada, if various opinion polls[1] have any semblance of accuracy. This raises an interesting problem for the faithful. Since the agnostics' position is only defined *vis-à-vis* religious faith, the two groups have much more in common than either is willing to admit.

Before saying why or how, it is essential to clarify certain terms. An atheist says there is no God. This is, of course, just as dogmatic and just as much a statement of faith—since it cannot be proved—as the first article of the Apostles' Creed. An agnostic (from the Greek word meaning 'not to know') says: 'I don't know whether there is a God or not. It's an open question.' As one famous Greek philosopher put it, when asked whether he believed in God: 'I just don't know. The subject is too complicated and life is too short for me to try and find out.' But since life must be lived on one premise or the other, for all practical purposes agnostics must act—until their minds are made up—as if there were no God. In other words, agnostics too live according to a kind of faith or belief, even if from a religionist's point of view it seems to be a negative one. In that sense, an agnostic is like a polite atheist.

It is worth observing that while there are many true agnostics, people who really do keep an open mind, who are truly open to all the evidence and feel a genuine thirst to know the truth, most of those who take the name do so simply because it has an intellectual ring to it. The majority have never subjected any faith, Christian or otherwise, to the kind of research and study they would give to even a passing hobby. Their agnosticism is a fake, an excuse for not thinking of religion at all. But the real point I want to argue here is that if agnosticism is tinged with faith— and I think it takes vastly more faith to hold that the universe came into being as a pure stroke of chance than it does to assume a creator—true belief must always be shot through with a healthy dose of not-knowing. Put plainly, religious faith by its very nature must always hold within itself a certain agnostic element. There is doubt, and therefore risk, at the heart of any truly religious commitment. The kind of certainty, the rigid conviction that 'we alone have the true truth', so prominent in various religious quarters today is more the product of insecurity and an unwillingness to bear life's ambiguities than it is of actual spiritual insight.

There are those who speak with great authority about matters such as the furniture of heaven and the temperature of hell, and the precise timing of the end of the world. They claim to have an infallible road-map for life, an answer to any and every question. But the truth, based on the evidence of the Bible itself, is that they really can't know. Their religion, and their tolerance of those with differing views, would be greatly enhanced if they admitted it. The Apostle Paul (who generally gets pretty bad press) sets a good example in this regard. Paul is convinced about many things, but he is the first to admit he is an agnostic in the sense that he is very far from knowing the full reality he calls God. In the famous hymn to love in his first letter to the Christians at Corinth (1 Cor. 13), he quite expressly says that the Christian believer is like a man looking at images reflected in a mirror. As the King James Version puts it: 'For now we see through a glass darkly; but then face to face: now I know in part; but then shall I know even as also I am known.' Earlier in the same passage he makes no bones about the partial nature of all Christian prophecy and knowledge.

But there is a higher authority than Paul. No one can take with full seriousness Jesus' humanity or the Gospel narratives without realizing that he wrestled with doubts himself. Certainly the Passion story makes no sense without the element of doubt. The cry from the cross—'Why have you forsaken me?'—shows Jesus himself entering into the agony of not knowing; yet he is willing to stake his life on the outcome. Similarly, when speaking of the last days he reveals his agnosticism when he states: 'Of that day or hour knoweth no man, not even the Son, but the Father only.' (Mark 13:32.)

In the face of television evangelists (some of whom are out-and-out religious hucksters) who promise instant certainties; in the light of other gurus or sects that deal in the same; and given the human propensity in troubled times to seek absolute refuge in completely closed positions, the true agnostic comes as a helpful reminder. Honest doubt, honestly faced, can lead to deeper understanding and a more courageous acceptance both of life and of the spiritual realities that shine in and through it. It is significant that the Epistle to the Hebrews cites Abraham as one of the supreme examples of faith in the Old Testament. The proof consists of the simple statement that God called him, 'And he went out, not knowing whither he went.' (Heb. 11:8.) He had no blueprint of divine guidance in his hand. He simply decided to take the risk of obeying what he saw as a command of God, and left it to later experience to confirm or deny the validity of his decision. If this spirit of humility combined with faith were ascendant in all the major faiths today—as well as in the multitudinous sects and cults—religion would cease to be one of the world's serious problems and become a much more central part of the solution.

NOTE

[1]For example, the report of Revd Dennis Oliver—'The New Canadian Religious Pluralism'—to the Canadian Society of Church History (1 June 1979), and the two reports of sociologist Reginald Bibby of the University of Lethbridge.

Authoritative religions

One of the most sinister phrases to come out of any cult or sect surfaced in the press recently. A quote from some confidential cult training literature, it read: 'People want to be controlled.' For most of us, the initial reaction to such a statement is to deny it heartily, even hotly. The unfortunate thing is that it is to a large degree true. The only decision some people ever make about their lives is that they will never make any decisions for themselves at all. The responsibility, the ambiguity, the genuine pain of making tough choices is simply too much to handle. It seems so much easier and safer to leave the problem to some-body else.

The growing power of the state and its creeping intrusion into more and more aspects of life in the 'free' or democratic world is thus no accident. In a deep sense it is willed in an abdication of choice to others—a flight wombwards. The same kind of flight is taking place at an alarming rate in the realm of religion. It is a matter of record that the fastest-growing religious sects at the moment are the most thoroughly authoritarian (1981 census). Given the general confusion the world is in, and the constant barrage of distracting, conflicting messages we receive, many individuals are increasingly willing to capitulate to the move-ment or leader with the greatest claim to certainty. This is so whether the infallible ultimate authority is some charismatic per-sonality (for example, a television evangelist); some 'special reve-lation'; a holy book such as the Bible, the Torah, the Koran, or the Bhagavad-Gita; or simply the daily horoscope or local fortune-teller. The mass suicide and killing of nine hundred and twelve men, women, and children at Jonestown was the result of this 'seduction of absolute certainty' at its most extreme.

The problem is not just one of cults or sects, although they provide the most obvious example. No organized religious group, from the Roman Catholics to the Jehovah's Witnesses or the Mormons, is totally exempt from the temptation to keep its followers as children unable or unwilling to think and decide for themselves. The greater the authority that speaks or is quoted, the greater (usually) is the apparent success, at least in terms of numbers. Surprisingly, the clergy—who are entrusted to care for the spiritual lives of their flocks—seldom, if ever, comment on this seductive, exploitative 'shadow-side' of the religious enterprise. And yet the goal of any true spirituality is for the persons involved to reach complete maturity. In the Sermon on the Mount Jesus told his disciples to become fully developed, or completely what they were meant to be. Unfortunately, the King James Version translates this idea as: 'Be ye therefore perfect.' (Matt. 5:48.) Paul, in his letter to the Christians at Ephesus, said the aim of all Christian life and devotion is to arrive at a mature humanity measured by the full picture of the true humanity revealed in Jesus Christ (Ephes. 4:13). But Christ obviously knew the terrible agony of wrestling with choices. He had no blueprint of certainty beside him in Gethsemane, no guru, no astrological chart to assure him that the way of non-resistance and of self-sacrifice on a cross was 'the right way', guaranteed to prove victorious in the end. Although the Gospels say very little about the inner workings of Jesus' mind, and there is no material for a psychological or emotional 'study', at this critical juncture it is perfectly clear that he plumbed the depths of the uncertainties and risks and sufferings surrounding any important, life-changing choice.

Nevertheless, countless 'authorities'—pastors, TV evangelists, yogis, or whatever—together with hosts of the faithful, talk about 'divine guidance' and living the spiritual life as though everything were neatly cut and dried. They speak of stark blacks and whites, when for many of life's most crucial decisions there is only the grey of unknowing. All too often the choice is not between good and bad, but between the lesser of two evils. There are indeed 'right' decisions to be made; but often only further living can show them to be so. At the time, there are no foolproof verses of Scripture, no pronouncements from above, no safe authorities to vest them with rightness and thus ease the burden of shouldering the responsibility oneself. Taking the widest possible perspective, it is true to say we are living in one of the most religious ages of all time. The will to believe is at an all-time high, no matter what church-attendance statistics reveal. It is also true that much of what poses as true religion has a tendency, which must be constantly subjected to examination and critique, to keep people passive, dependent, and hence inauthentic in their spiritual lives.

The theme of the Judaeo-Christian tradition is that God has called people to be 'sons'—free, independent adults, fully responsible for their lives. As the martyred German theologian Dietrich Bonhoeffer so often stressed, man has 'come of age' and, as a mature son, is accountable to God for what happens on earth. The test of the 'truth' of any religion would seem to be whether it helps free people to become mature, 'grown-up' children, or whether it fetters them forever as toddling infants. When Karl Marx described religion as the opiate of the people he was speaking of bad religion. Unfortunately there is still a good deal of it around.

Fundamentalists and humanism

Full credit must be given the so-called right-wing, conservative
Christians whose resurgence in the past decade has been one of
the major religion stories of our time. They have conviction and
energy to burn, a strategy, an unequivocal message, and a will-
ingness to use all modern means of communication to put it
across. They are like 'an army, terrible with banners', and
already on the march. But it can only be said, with sorrow, that
the fundamentalists and their cohorts are making a colossal mistake. They have targetted the wrong enemy.

Careful observation of their strategy indicates that they
regard humanism and humanists in general as the chief force
behind and agents of all that they mean by the 'Antichrist'.
Somehow the Moral-Majority preachers such as Jerry Falwell
have managed to load the terms 'humanism' and 'humanist' with
all the freight historically reserved for the most blatant enemies
of God, goodness, motherhood, and the rest. If they had read as
much about Socrates as they have about the Antichrist, they
might have avoided this disastrous error. Socrates cared deeply
(according to Plato) about how words were used and defined; so
should anyone who professes to care about truth. The Oxford
English Dictionary defines humanism as the 'quality of being
human; devotion to human interests'. A secondary meaning is
'Any system of thought . . . concerned with merely human interests . . . or with those of the human race in general . . . the religion of humanity.' It defines a humanist as a 'student of human
affairs or of human nature'. In the light of these definitions, it is
not too bold to state that God himself (or herself) is a humanist.

The central doctrine of orthodox Christianity is the incarnation—God made man, the Word become flesh. What it means is that God took human life and all that pertains to it so seriously that he revealed himself in a thoroughly human life. Jesus too was a humanist: as John's Gospel tells us, 'He knew what was in man.' He told his followers that to do good to any human being was to do it to him (Matt. 25), and set the example himself by freeing people from fears, guilts, and oppression—no questions asked. If Christianity, in common with other great world religions, has any 'good news' to proclaim to modern man, it is precisely this: that God loves human beings whatever their condition, attitudes, or needs.

What conservative church people should be careful to say (if say it they must) is that they are opposed to secular humanism: i.e. a humanism dogmatic in its claim that man is alone in the universe or cosmos, and that this *saeculum* (the Latin origin of 'secular') or world-age is all there is. For the secular humanist, man alone is (in the words of the ancient Greek philosopher Protagoras) 'the measure of all things'. Such a view is clearly not Christian humanism, with its claim that true humanity is only discovered through eternal, 'spiritual' yardsticks or measures, only truly understood as being shot through with the divine. Still, these two kinds of humanism have much in common in their concern for a truly human existence. Evangelicals should remember Jesus' much-neglected words: 'He who is not against us is for us.' (Mark 9:39.)

The time has come when all men and women of goodwill who care about restoring the human face to their brothers and sisters—as well as themselves—must band together in a common struggle. The deadliest, most pervasive enemy of the kingdom of God and true Christian humanism today is not secular humanism but what, for want of a better word, we might call anti-humanism. The people to be attacked and condemned are not those who, though unbelievers, care deeply about their neighbours both at home and around the world (often more deeply than some religious types do). Rather, they are all those individuals, groups, states, 'principalities and powers' that work to dehumanize us all. It is anti-humanism that is at work wherever the poor are oppressed, wherever torture or other violence is perpetrated in the name of law and order or 'the state'. It is anti-humanism that is at the root of exploitative pornography, and makes women into objects. It is anti-humanism that relegates native people, here and elsewhere, to an inferior, marginal status in society. It is anti-humanism, today more than ever, that is at the core of the war mentality.

Nevertheless, the TV evangelists and their fellows for the most part uncritically support the current escalation of the nuclear-arms race, ignoring the fact that they are helping to prepare for the greatest desecration of the face of God in man ever contemplated in human history. If they could perceive the real enemy and realize how urgently the planet's future depends on co-operating (without loss of principle) with all others who truly care about humanity—all humanists of whatever ilk, as well as those of other faiths—Christian fundamentalists could help to change the present uncertain balance of good and evil in our world. Instead of waiting (almost eagerly, it seems) for the final Armageddon, they could be hastening the building of the kingdom of God on earth. And that is something for which Christ himself taught all of us to pray.

Searching for Christmas and Easter

Religious truth and the Christmas story

There are few human cries older than the time-worn plea, 'Tell me a story'. Thus to speak of the Christmas story is to speak a universal language. Christmas reminds us that all major religious truths are expressed in stories: the creation of the world, the fall in the garden of Eden, the exodus from Egypt, the Nativity, the suffering and Resurrection of Christ. In fact, the reason the early church remembered Jesus' sayings is that most of them are in the form of parables: the prodigal son, the good Samaritan, the sower and the seed, and many more. What was eventually written down in the Gospels had been faithfully passed on by word of mouth many times before. (When you realize that these stories originated in an 'oral society', where people were simply trained to listen and remember—albeit free from the distractions of noise pollution, Muzak, and all other kinds of electronic chewing gum—your respect for the fidelity of the transmission process is bound to increase.)

But the stories by which these and other religious truths are communicated were not written as history in the modern sense of the word. Although they are often rooted in events, they deal with issues that go beyond, and may in fact utterly transform, history itself. In religious terms, myths (which many of these stories are) are not synonymous with unreality or fairy tales—quite the reverse. A myth tells by means of a story a truth that can't be told any other way.

The Gospels are about a very particular Jew who lived in a very particular geographic location at a definite point in time. But they are primarily the work of evangelists or preachers with a message to be believed. The stories or myths of the Nativity, the first Christmas, occupy a unique place in the New Testament record. Mark's Gospel, believed by most modern scholars to be the earliest, does not include any of them. This work begins quite simply with the emergence of John the Baptist, Jesus' baptism in the Jordan River, and the beginning of his ministry. Nor does Mark repeat many of the parables. His focus is clearly on Jesus' actions, his healings and exorcisms, and, pre-eminently, his Passion and Resurrection. It is a 'Passion narrative with an introduction' as one scholar once put it. Paul, whose work was the earliest written down and whose letters play so large a part in Christian theology, says nothing of the virgin birth, the wise men and the star, or the shepherds. The crucified and risen Christ is the true centre of his thought and preaching. The Gospel of John (the Gospel that 'feels' so different from the first three, to anyone who has taken the time to read them all from beginning to end) does not have the Nativity stories either. What it does have is a statement that amazed readers in the first century: i.e. that the eternal word of God 'became flesh and dwelt among us'. The idea of God appearing disguised as a human being or dressed up in human form, without becoming a real human body, would have been no shock whatever to the intellectuals of Greece and Rome who had read all the ancient myths. It was not the Christian claims about Christ's divinity that offended them so much as the idea that God had become fully involved in the stuff of humanity. The humanity of Christ in the Christian 'myth' was their real problem, a situation that is almost totally reversed today.

For the details of the Christmas story itself we must turn to Matthew and Luke. Both must be read for the full picture, because their accounts differ—not in their main thrust, but in what they include or omit. Each has his own theological viewpoint and a particular life situation of the early church in mind. To some extent, they draw on different sources in the overall tradition. Thus, for example, Matthew alone tells us of the coming of the wise men and the Christmas star, while Luke alone recounts the experience of the shepherds. Even the genealogies or family trees of Jesus in these Gospels (Matt. 1:2-16 and Luke 3:23-38) abound in variations. Nevertheless, what all the writings and stories of the New Testament ultimately say about the meaning of the life that began at Bethlehem, they say with total unanimity: God has entered human history in a unique way; he has spoken a word of total, unconditional love to all men; abundant life is possible in this world and the next. The story or myth is relatively simple—the challenge, as Christmas reminds us, is living it out.

The Christmas story

Flavius Lentulus cursed the cold. Leaning his spear and heavy shield against a scrub olive, he fumbled with stiff fingers to find the leather flask inside his tunic. He took a deep pull and tucked it away again. Drawing his great cloak tightly around him, he looked out over the valley below. Would the dawn never come?

He cursed again. A curse on the rawness of the night, on the wretched, quarrelsome people of this backside of the empire, on his commanding officer who had condemned him to a month of night-duty for being drunk in the market-place. The *Pax Romana*, the Roman Peace, was made of iron; but it was just.

The pale moonlight caught the veteran's plumed helmet and cast a baleful glow over the ragged scar that ran from chin to right ear—a souvenir of the Parthian skirmish years earlier. Lentulus grinned sourly to himself. That was a fight! Better by far than helping that murderous old goat, King Herod, rule his scurvy flock. A curse on him too!

From the rocky outcropping on which he stood he could watch the slumbering town of Nazareth, cupped in a hollow on the hilltop just behind him. Not a light to be seen. At his feet the range dropped to the plain, giving him a strategic view of the merchant route that wound all the way from Damascus in the north to the exotic bazaars of Egypt, far to the south. He nodded, feeling weariness about to engulf him, and now cursed himself for the liquor. If he were to be caught sleeping his captain would have him flogged. He was tough enough, but he had seen men stronger than himself die after a taste of the lead-studded cat.

Lentulus thought of home, of the farm in the hills just south of Rome, of the endless days at school before he was conscripted—anything to keep awake. What was it he had overheard those two simpletons arguing about in the town yesterday? Or was it two days ago? Something about a Messiah, an anointed one who would come to deliver them from the yoke of Rome.

He stamped his feet and noticed that the bare hills east of the Sea of Galilee were now blushing with pinks and edged with a faint, silvery gold. In less than an hour his watch would end, thank Jupiter or whatever deity Rome favoured these days. Probably it was the emperor himself; Augustus was a name once used of gods alone. But the thought of school and the talk of those two old men had awakened a strange memory. What was the poem Virgil had written—about the birth of a child who would bring in the Golden Age? He could remember being forced to learn it as a penance for skipping classes to watch a general lead his troops along the Via Appia, towards Rome.

Shaking his head, he began to recite the Fourth Eclogue of the great master himself. How did it go? Something about 'a new human generation descends from the high heavens . . .' Sadly, he found most of it was lost beyond recall. But suddenly the last few lines came together and he muttered, half aloud: 'Come forth, oh baby boy, and recognize your mother with a smile, whom ten months have brought to the weariness of labour. Come forth, baby boy, on whom parents have not yet smiled; whom no god has honoured at his table, and no goddess in her bed.'*

Unknown to Flavius Lentulus, in a small clay-brick house less than a mile from his lonely post, another silent watcher gave thanks for the dawn. As the first cocks crowed a young woman, barely in her teens, named Mary (or Miriam) pulled on her coarse homespun cloak and climbed up to the flat rooftop.

As she looked southwards, out over the vast plain of Esdrae-lon where her people had fought so many battles, her mind was overwhelmed with the events of the past few hours. She could almost hear her heart pound as joy and expectation contended with fear, doubt, and amazement for the mastery of her soul.

It had all happened so suddenly. Whatever could she tell her

*It should be noted that this poem, written by Virgil in 40 BC, explicitly mentions a virgin and a heaven-descended child. Some scholars believe it may have been influenced by the prophecies of Isaiah (chapters 7 to 11). In any case, it attests to the widespread longing for a world saviour just prior to the birth of Christ.

parents? Or Joseph, her betrothed? Had it been a dream? A
nightmare? A shiver ran through Mary's slight form as she
relived it.

She had been restless all night. Usually she was so tired from
household chores—helping with the cooking and cleaning,
fetching water from the spring at the lip of the hill where the
Roman sentries always stood, and spinning to augment her
father's meagre wage—that she slept like someone drugged.
Except last night. At two in the morning, unable to stand the
tossing and turning any longer, she had lit a tiny lamp and tried
to finish some mending. But it had been no use. Her fingers
were leaden and her mind too full of extraordinary thoughts.

Why, if what the rabbis said was true, did God permit the
strutting Romans to crush his people underfoot? She remembered the scarred and drunken face of a brute who had accosted
her at the entrance to the bazaar just the day before. How could
a righteous God suffer such blasphemous louts to live, let alone
allow them to oppress what had once been King David's flock
and realm? Her Joseph, she proudly recalled, was a direct
descendant of that royal house.

For a moment her sympathies flowed out to the Zealots, those
young men everyone whispered about but feared to speak of
openly. They came mainly from the hill country around
Nazareth, she knew. And that was where they hid, out in the
wild places; bands of desperate men, armed to the teeth and
determined to make the Romans bleed. Their ultimate aim was
to overthrow both the puppet Herod and his Roman overlords.
But for now it was guerrilla war—ambushing a patrol here or a
sentry there, setting off an avalanche from some steep precipice
to disrupt the traffic of empire along the accursed imperial
roads. Sometimes they were caught. Mary shuddered at the
memory of those broken corpses, spread-eagled on the cross-
shaped gibbets the Romans used. When she was barely eleven,
she had seen a dozen of them silhouetted against the sky to the
west of Nazareth. She had had nightmares for weeks.

All at once, in the midst of her troubled thoughts, an
unearthly stillness, so deep it was almost palpable, had flooded
her chamber, and a silver iridescence, soft yet all-compelling,
flowed in at the narrow window until it filled the room. As she
sprang back in terror, flinging one arm over her face to shield
her eyes from the light that was, in an instant, more blazing than

the desert sun at noon, Mary heard a voice of overpowering strength and at the same time gentleness, reassuring as the sound of wind in the pines atop Mount Hermon. 'Do not be afraid,' the voice said. 'I am the angel Gabriel, Mary, and I have come from God as his messenger to you.'

She had not dared to look. But a strange calm had echoed in the words as if they themselves possessed a healing balm. Astonished, she sank on the edge of her straw pallet. 'The Lord is with you, and you have found special favour in the sight of God. Listen! You will conceive and give birth to a son, and you are to call him Jesus. He will be mighty,' said the angel. 'And he shall be called the Son of the Highest. God will give him the throne of his father, David; and he will be King over the house of Jacob forever. His kingdom will never come to an end.'

Weak and close to fainting, Mary had stammered out: 'But how can any of this be, when I have never been intimate with a man?'

The strong voice resounded in tones she was sure the whole world would hear, and yet she knew the words were meant for her ears alone: 'The Holy Spirit of God will come upon you, and the power of the Most High will overshadow you with his protection. Thus the child you bear will be called holy—the Son of God!'

Then the dazzling messenger had revealed another marvel: Mary's cousin Elizabeth, in spite of her years, had also conceived a son, and was six months pregnant. 'Nothing said by God can ever be looked upon as impossible,' said Gabriel.

Barely knowing what she was doing, Mary heard herself say quietly: 'Behold the handmaiden of the Lord. May it all happen to me as you have said.'

Seconds later, the light had faded from the room. The energy that had made the very air seem taut with power was gone. Normal night sounds, the barking of a dog, the distant bleat of sheep, came in at the window again. All that lingered was a faint yet haunting scent, like rarest incense. On the rooftop Mary felt the light wind, rising with the sun, cool her flushed cheeks.

Suddenly a neighbour's donkey brayed, eager to be let out to greet the morning. Thus shaken from her reverie, she descended to the kitchen and, with an overflowing heart, began to light the charcoal fire. There was the day's bread to be made—and many grave decisions.

Off in the distant east, across the burning sands and trackless wilderness on the other side of the Jordan River Valley, a foreign caravan was once more under way. The servants, half-blinded by the swirling dust stirred by their masters' camels, and footsore after months of travel, fought with each other as they struggled to keep up the pace. Most of them rued the day they had left their homes to join in this mad quest. But hunched above on their swaying beasts, their eyes straining at the shimmering horizon, the Magi, or wise men, rode on. Men possessed, they followed their vision westwards, towards the land of the Jews.

One of the donkeys at the mouth of the cave stamped and let out a low whinny. In a flash, Joseph Ben David slid out from under the sheepskin wrap and seized his cudgel. Stepping warily over his sleeping companions, he flattened himself against the damp wall and edged towards the opening. His heart skipped a beat as he made out the dark figure etched against the starlit sky. Wait! There were two of them, fumbling with the rope tethers, intent on stealing the beasts.

Joseph took a deep breath and lunged. He caught one kneeling thief behind the ear and sent him sprawling. Then, with a crack like a snapping bone, he hit down on the arm of his knife-wielding companion. The two were on their feet and running before he had a chance to raise his stave again. Leaping and weaving like mountain goats down the bouldered hillside, they vanished in the inky blackness of a dried-up river bed, clattering stones the only evidence of their flight.

Inside the cave, Joseph's aged uncle struggled to find the short, broad-bladed Roman sword he had hidden in his meagre baggage. Several young men, relatives of Joseph, were in various stages of waking.

'Sssh . . .' he whispered hoarsely, pointing towards the women and children who slept at the end of the cave, beyond a smouldering fire.

'There were only two, and I gave them such a fright they'll still be running when the sun comes up.'

Thus reassured, the men—except for his uncle Mordecai, who finally found his sword and took up a position near the animals—were soon asleep once more. They had walked more than sixty miles so far, and they were bone-weary.

But Joseph was too excited to rest. He looked anxiously to the corner where Mary, now in her last month, lay sleeping, her pale hand, palm uppermost, flung across her forehead as it to ward off a blow. Dear God, she was beautiful!

He sat hunched under the sheepskin, chin on his knees, gazing into the fire and beyond it into the astonishing events of the past few months. First there had been the joy and celebration of his betrothal. He had often seen Mary from his stall in the bazaar, where he worked making furniture, plough-frames, and yokes for oxen. Watching her as she bargained with Simon the vegetable dealer or Ben Hadad the linen merchant, he had been struck by the amazing aura of stillness and wisdom that graced her lovely features.

When she had come on that unforgettable day to ask him about a yoke for carrying water, he had scarcely been able to speak. But the encounter proved beyond a doubt what he had known for over a month: he was hopelessly in love. He grinned ruefully as he recalled how he must have looked at that first meeting: dust in his red beard, wood-shavings clinging to his arms, his apron so tattered the dogs might have been fighting over it. But she must have liked him, for when his parents met her and formally asked for her hand, wonder of wonders, she had said yes!

And so, according to the custom, they had been betrothed— the first step towards full marriage in a year's time, when he would claim her and take her home. He had never known such happiness. Ezra, the blacksmith in the next booth, teased that he was whistling and singing off-key as he worked. Then, quite suddenly and without explanation, Mary had disappeared; and he could get no comfort, not even from her parents. 'She has gone to visit her kinswoman, Elizabeth, in the hill country of Judaea,' he was told. And nothing more.

Joseph watched the dying embers cast ghostly shapes on the far wall of the cave and reflected on the bitterness he had felt for interminable weeks, three months in all. No more need to fear Ezra's teasing; like the whistling at work, it had ceased long ago.

Then just as suddenly as she had left, she returned, and with an extraordinary tale. Mary said she had found her cousin— thought to be well beyond childbearing—six months pregnant! And, if that were not miracle enough, both Elizabeth and her husband Zachariah, a priest, had had visions foretelling that the coming child would be 'a messenger of God . . . to prepare the way of the Lord', and that 'his name must be called John.' But their story was only the beginning. Mary's next words were etched forever on his brain: 'When we first came face to face, Elizabeth cried out that she felt her baby give a leap within her. Then, seeming almost possessed, she recited: "Mary, you are blessed among women, and blessed too is the offspring of your womb! Why should this honour come to me that the mother of my Lord should come to my home?" '

Joseph had been dumbfounded. In a sudden surge of anger, he had roared: 'Are you pregnant, you cheat? Then get out, and never let me see your deceiving face again!'

His eyes brimmed with tears as he remembered how startled she had looked, and how she had run crying from his presence without a backward glance. He had hurt her and he had meant to hurt, for his heart was filled with hate—hate towards whoever had forced her or seduced her; hate for life itself, with all its false hopes.

For the next few days he couldn't work, he couldn't think, he couldn't eat or sleep. What was he to do? The law called for severe penalties; he knew his rights. But in calmer moments the thought of anyone harming her was devastating. Not her, please God! Not his beloved, sinner though she clearly was. Finally, without consulting either his parents or the scribes, he had decided to divorce her as quietly as possible. There would be gossip, of course, but perhaps if she left town and lived with Elizabeth, the scandal would eventually be forgotten. That was it! He would act the next day.

Now, Joseph was a practical, down-to-earth man, and he had no use for religious enthusiasm. Not for him this business of heavenly voices, winged messengers, or calls to Messiahship. More than one would-be Messiah from the Galilee had already come to grief at the hands of the Romans. Served them right too, he used to think. But then something had happened that had shaken him to the core and changed his life forever.

That very night, about the third watch, he had been wakened out of his fitful tossing by an astounding dream. Or was it a dream? Now he no longer knew. But its truth and vividness still had the power to turn the blood in his veins to ice. Quite suddenly he had seen a being so bright he could not bear to look at it. Then a voice had spoken: 'Joseph, son of David, you are not to be afraid to take Mary to be your wedded wife. The child in her womb was formed by a miracle of God's Holy Spirit. A son will be born, and you are to give him the name Jesus, for he will save his people from their sins.'

The next morning, confused yet elated, Joseph had set in order the arrangements for the wedding. On the festive day, he took Mary to his own home with all the time-honoured ceremony and rejoicing. But he was not to be intimate with her until after the birth took place.

Joseph felt hypnotized by the dying fire and the slow, heavy breathing of the others. He stretched, debated getting up to throw more fuel on the fire—it would soon be dawn and they had to make an early start—and then sank into a final reverie.

The scene had changed, and he could see the lathered horses of a Roman patrol, their iron-shod hooves striking sparks from the cobbles of the twisting streets and terror into people's hearts. No one in Nazareth knew what this fierce clatter was about, until they saw the soldiers nailing up the emperor's edict at every corner. Once the squadron had galloped off, disappearing in a cloud of dust, the townsfolk gathered to look at the message. Those who could read spelled it out: 'By imperial edict of Caesar Augustus: a census is to be taken in this province and in every district of the empire. Each person must return to his home town, the town of his forefathers, to be registered. Anyone failing to comply before the second full moon from this date will be punished.' The usual seal and some undecipherable words in Latin were appended.

Some had greeted the news with delight—a chance for time off, for a trip, to see old relatives and friends! But Joseph's first reaction was dismay. A journey of over a hundred miles to Bethlehem, birthplace of his ancestor David, with Mary in her last weeks of pregnancy? Only her calm acceptance, and her reassurance that even Caesar must fit into God's plan for her first-born, had given him the courage.

Joseph got up, strode to the cave mouth, and watched the great orange ball of the sun edging up above the Mountains of Moab. We must hurry, he thought, and he began to rouse the others. Jericho was still a day's trek away, and then would begin the cruel climb up through the wilderness of Judaea to Jerusalem, before the last six miles to David's royal city to the south.

Meanwhile in the ancient walled city of Jericho, a lush oasis close to the Dead Sea, the winter palace echoed with King Herod's rage. He had come for warmth and peace, he bellowed, as the servants scattered before him. 'Damn it, all I ever hear about are plots and counterplots, and now my spies tell me some Eastern potentates are prowling around Jerusalem asking about the birthplace of a King of the Jews. I am the King of the Jews, and I'll kill the first man who dares say otherwise!'

He kicked the serving boy who had brought him breakfast, sending him flying on the mosaic floor. 'Wise men are they? Magi who watch the stars? Sorcerers and magicians more likely.'

Caleb, his chief informer, a small sly man with a perpetual nervous smirk, disentangled himself from the draperies where he had taken refuge. He remained well out of Herod's range, though, giving the impression of a dog who has been hit once and is reluctant to chance his luck again.

'Incompetent fool! Get those magicians down here immediately. Do you hear?'

There was a brief pause, and then Herod's twisted features gradually relaxed into the semblance of a smile. He had an idea! 'Be good to them,' he said. 'Treat them royally. After all, they are our guests.'

A powdery snow fell, blurring outlines and making the lights of slumbering Jerusalem, across the Kidron Valley, seem like a mirage. Encamped on a grassy knoll beside a grove of gnarled olive trees, the Magi sat around their crackling fire. Their servants had long ago fallen asleep, huddling for warmth against the camels that had lain down to chew the cud. The rest of the great beasts stood sullen at their tethers, scenting the night air, uneasy in this mountainous foreign terrain.

The Persian priest-astrologers, clad in exotic furs and cone-shaped hats, ignored both the hour and the harsh weather as they pored over crinkled scrolls and charts. For all their vast wisdom, they were also unaware that hidden in the bushes, well back of the circle of light cast by the fire, three of Herod's spies crouched, listening. True, the wind snatched much of their conversation away, and most of what the spies managed to hear was in an alien dialect. But the little they understood proved what earlier reports of the strangers' visit to Jerusalem had indicated.

These extraordinary men were talking about some new appearance in the heavens, which they believed heralded the coming birth of a 'King of Israel'. Small wonder Herod was said to have foamed with rage!

A faint sound like the hooting of an owl came from the valley. That would be Caleb, they thought with relief. Stealthily, with cramped, aching muscles, they slunk away to make their report.

At the very moment Caleb was telling his spies to find the Magi and send them to Herod's palace, Joseph and Mary finally arrived with their ragged companions at the outskirts of the hill town of Bethlehem.

There was no snow here, where the land lay lower than Mount Zion and Jerusalem, but the air pierced cold as they stumbled on. It had been a cruel journey—scorching heat at midday, making them long for those places in the trail where huge cliffs cast cooling shadows; bone-chilling cold at night, with nothing but the ground to lie on. And the rocky climb from Jericho, far below sea-level, to the heights of Mount Zion had exhausted them. All but one of the donkeys had been lamed by the forced pace, and now Joseph was almost carrying Mary as he struggled to keep her beast moving. Her face was one of anguish. Perhaps induced by the roughness of the ride, labour had begun.

Just then one of Joseph's nephews, who had run ahead to find lodgings, came panting out of the dark to say that the town was full.

'Did you try the large inn on the wilderness side, beyond the synagogue?' cried Joseph, with a sinking heart. 'My uncle says they know our family there.'

The lad gulped for breath. 'I went there first. They've been turning people away all night, they say. I pleaded with them, but they let me see for myself—just one huge room with everyone sleeping almost on top of each other.'

At least it would be warm, thought Joseph, as Mary gave another sharp moan. Perhaps he could succeed with the innkeeper where the boy could not.

The streets of Bethlehem were deserted, except for some Roman soldiers staggering along, clutching each other for support, as they returned from a late carouse. Joseph gave them a wide berth as he tried door after door, always with the same result: no room.

'Let's get to the edge of the village and at least pitch a tent,' cried Joseph's aunt, who, like the other women in the party, knew from the signs that the baby must soon arrive.

Joseph looked at his wife's tormented face. 'I've got to get her inside somehow or I'll lose them both!'

Moments later, at a dingy inn, the stout disgruntled landlord muttered ancient oaths when he heard the frantic knocking. By all that was sacred, would he never rest until this infernal Roman census was done? 'No room!' he bellowed, even before he had found the latch. 'No room.' He was about to slam the door when he saw Mary fainting in Joseph's arms.

'What's wrong with her? Drunk, eh?' Then he caught himself short as he noticed her white face and swollen body.

Joseph grabbed him by the sleeve. 'Please, she's going to have a child any moment now. Isn't there some shelter where she can lie?'

The landlord hesitated, pierced by a flash of compassion he had never known before. 'Follow me. It isn't much, but at least it's a dry roof over your head, and there's plenty of clean straw.' He led the way down a winding path to a limestone cave in the hillside—a humble stable. 'Not enough room for all of you,' he growled, pushing his way through an assortment of cattle, sheep, and fowl. 'The rest will have to camp in my orchard.'

Behind a fenced-off area, in a raised portion of the cavern, there were piles of hay and straw. 'You can put her there,' the innkeeper directed. 'And I'll send a maid out with some hot water right away.'

And so it was, that, surrounded by sheep and oxen, the child was born.

Less than a mile to the east, out on the bare hillside, with its sweeping view of the Judaean wilderness and the Dead Sea in the distance, a few shepherds kept watch over their flocks. The clouds had cleared, and they marvelled at the uncanny brilliance of the stars. Then, without warning, a blinding radiance surrounded and penetrated them. Frightened and trembling, they opened their eyes on a creature of shining magnificence and beauty.

'Do not be afraid,' he commanded. 'I am here to announce the most joyful news the world has ever heard. There is born this night, in the city of David, a Saviour who is Christ, the Lord! You will find the baby swaddled in strips of cloth, lying in a manger.'

Suddenly a whole legion of angels filled the heavens with their glory, singing praises: 'Glory to God in the heights of heaven, and on earth, peace to all people of goodwill!'

At first the shepherds were silent, overwhelmed. But when the vision had faded, and they had recovered from the shock, they held a brief, excited conference, all talking at once, about the startling news. One of the youngest expressed what each was thinking: 'I say we go right now to Bethlehem and see for ourselves what's going on!'

Forgetting their sheep, they ran as fast as their legs would carry them to the edge of town. There, near the inn, they found Mary and Joseph—and the baby, just as the angel had predicted, lying in a manger. Marvelling, they stammered out their story, and what the angels had told them.

A small crowd, drawn to the stable by the shepherds' arrival, eavesdropped in amazement. But Mary said nothing. She was lost in awe and wonder, as her heart weighed everything that had happened.

Once the shepherds had feasted their eyes on the mother and child, and paid their deepest respects, they went back to find their straying sheep. But as they went, they found themselves singing and praising God for what they had seen and heard— exactly as the angel had promised.

A few days later Joseph rented, at inflated prices, a one-room house in Bethlehem where Mary and the infant Jesus could rest before going on to the temple in Jerusalem. After the circumcision prescribed by Jewish law, they would then retrace the hazardous road back to Nazareth.

Meanwhile the Magi had arrived at Herod's court. They found the ailing monarch smiling like a merchant who sees wealthy customers approaching his stall in the bazaar. He had suppressed his rage. But it was all a part of his plan. He had already summoned his own experts and inquired where this Messiah was supposed to be born. They had promptly told him: 'In Bethlehem of Judaea, for it is written that "You, Bethlehem, in the land of Judah, are by no means the least of cities. For there will come out of you a ruler who shall shepherd my people, Israel." '

And so it was that, after lavishing them with hospitality, the king took the wise men into a secret chamber and asked them when the star had first appeared. Replenishing their stores of food and drink, he sent them off to Bethlehem with this request: 'Go and search carefully for this child; and when you have discovered him, send me word. Then I will come and join in your worship.'

So they departed, and that night the star, which they had first seen so long ago in the east, led them until it stood over Bethlehem, directly over the house where Jesus lay.

The exotic caravan halted outside, and small boys called out to each other as they examined the elaborate carvings and copper decorations on the camels' harness and whispered jokes about the strangers' hats. Soon a crowd gathered. But the Magi, with a single purpose in their hearts, paid heed to none of this.

Entering the house, they found the young child with Mary, his mother, and falling prostrate they worshipped him. Then, opening up their leather saddle pouches, they brought forth rare gifts of gold, frankincense, and myrrh. When they had paid their homage they left Bethlehem by the wilderness route, which by-passed Jericho. For a dream had warned them to avoid King Herod like the plague.

Shortly after their departure, an angel appeared to Joseph in a dream, warning him that Herod was scheming against the child. 'Take the young child and his mother and flee into the land of Egypt. Herod already has spies searching for the baby, and is resolved to put him to death.'

Badly shaken, Joseph jumped out of bed at once and, waking Mary without explanation, told her to get ready instantly for a long journey. Within minutes, in the dead of night, they were moving through the silent streets of Bethlehem, heading for the road south through the desert. They did not know it then, but it would be two years before news of Herod's death would reach them and they would be able to return safely to Nazareth.

Having skirted Jericho and forded the Jordan, the wise men

headed their eager camels homewards. As they rode they reflected that Hosea, one of the famous Hebrew prophets, had once written: 'Out of Egypt, have I called my Son.'

One of the Magi, the leanest, oldest, and wisest of them all, composed a poem as his camel sped through the desert night. His companions laughed with joy as they heard his strong voice carried on the wind:

> *You must return by another road,*
> *The wise men heard God say.*
> *Another road? The old road*
> *Was the known, the safest way.*
> *But the kings had been to Bethlehem*
> *And knelt as humble men;*
> *And nothing, after Bethlehem,*
> *Could be the same again.*

Christmas in the Arctic

I. Frobisher Bay

Leah Nootarak's face is as lined and creviced as a relief map of this treeless, mountainous land. But it sparkles as she smiles at the memory of Christmases eighty years ago, when she was a girl, in a hunting camp two hundred miles from here.

As I sat with her on the floor of the mission hall, with the help of an interpreter she told me: 'Christmas in our Inuit language means a time and place of joy. Early Christmas Day we would visit the white people at the mission and at the Hudson Bay post. They would throw us lots of gifts. Then we would play games in the snow. We all wore caribou clothing and lived in igloos. Our parents would give us dolls they had carved from walrus or whale tusks, and newly made mukluks or mitts. Later we all went to church. The men used to build a huge snow-house to seat about one hundred people before the wooden church was put up.'

Today, along with most of the twelve hundred Eskimo—or, as they call themselves, Inuit—who live in or near Frobisher, Leah Nootarak worships in the world's most northerly cathedral: the Anglican Cathedral of St Jude, just nineteen hundred miles from the North Pole. It is a breathtakingly beautiful, igloo-shaped church with a commanding view down the icy two-hundred-mile long fiord where explorer Martin Frobisher made landfall four hundred years ago. The interior is decorated with Inuit art and artifacts. The purple curtains behind the altar are embroidered with dozens of scenes of traditional life, the communion rail is made of two Arctic sleds set on their sides, and the pulpit is a sled standing upright on its end. The kneeling cushions are of sealskin, shaven in Baffin Island style to depict scenes from the hunt, while the cross behind the altar is made of two twisted ivory tusks from the twenty-foot narwhal.

When I attended morning church services there, the place was packed. Some babies peered from the depths of their mother's parka hoods, while others were breast-fed to prevent their crying. The numbers of young people would have made a city pastor deeply envious.

Steam boiled up as worshippers left the church and the warm air hit the bone-chilling frost outside. The 'parking lot' was a scene of furious activity as the men tried to whip their frozen snowmobiles into a sputter of life. Temperatures have nudged −40°C ever since my arrival.

I caught my first hint of the Arctic climate when the plane broke through cloud cover as we landed. The vast, rugged terrain, looking not unlike the Judaean wilderness sunk in a deepfreeze, stretched to the horizon. The time was only 1.15 p.m., and it was already evening. The air was so sharp it took your breath away, but as clear and exhilarating as vintage champagne. My beard snapped stiff with an almost audible crackle as I rushed for the tiny terminal.

Frobisher, with its twenty-four hundred white and Inuit inhabitants, may be the Toronto of Baffin Island (some roads are paved, most houses have running water and septic tanks, and the one hotel is large and comfortable) but the overriding fact of life is the cold. You can freeze to death in less than an hour, even with heavy clothing, if you become lost or unduly fatigued outdoors. It is common to talk of the Arctic cold as 'dry cold'. That may be, but it is above all cold cold—a cold with a strange intensity that tests every possible weak point.

I walked down the steep, icy hillside to the mission house, the snow crunching under my boots and the stars of the Big Dipper so close above it seemed one had only to reach up and touch them. At the home of Revd Brian Burrows and his wife Rita, the Anglican missionaries who live beside the cathedral, I dined on roast caribou (delicious) and then, over tea, talked for hours about the north, its problems and its hopes.

As the result of early missionary work, just over eighty per cent of all Inuit in the Canadian Arctic are Anglican. Today, of the roughly thirty priests, eight are Inuit, two or three more come from Canada, and all the rest from England (southern clergy, it seems, are reluctant to face the rigours of their own northland).

Brian and Rita Burrows, who have two small children with them and a third at school in Brockville, Ont., come from Coventry. Both speak the Inuit language fluently. While a handful of non-Inuit come to Burrows's English-speaking services on Sundays, his main concern is for the native people of Frobisher, the tiny nearby community of Apex, and the two remote outposts that together make up his parish. He spoke earnestly of the dramatic decline in violence, accidents, and general drunkenness since the vote to close the only liquor store here two years ago. But venereal disease is still rampant among the young people, and Eskimo unemployment often exceeds fifty per cent.

I have met three Inuit cab-drivers, and two of the Royal Canadian Mounted Police constables are also native people. But, as Burrows says, 'The people from the south take the bulk of all the jobs.' He also worries about the calibre of education at the new four-million-dollar high school and about the racism he says now exists on both sides. While the government policy, since the early fifties, of forcing the Inuit to leave their old camp life and gather into town-like settlements has created severe social problems, medical help and education are much improved.

But Inuit who wish to supplement their welfare or eliminate it entirely by hunting can do so. Lazarus, one of the cab-drivers, told me: 'In the summer, I always hunt seals and catch white whales. You can get the whales about ten miles down the bay from Frobisher. First we shoot them and then use a harpoon to land them.' At this time of the year the caribou herds come down to within forty or fifty miles of Frobisher, and a snowmobile makes it possible to leave at dawn and be back with fresh meat by late evening.

With a new sense of their own identity, many of the Inuit are again depending entirely on their native skills to earn their living. For example, I found myself later in the home of Inuit Enook Manomie, thirty-five. His wife Suzanne, who comes from Vancouver, is a graduate of the former Toronto-based Anglican Women's Training College. A hunter and sculptor, Enook was carving a huge muskox out of soapstone in the middle of his frame home when I spoke with him. He proudly showed me his supply of caribou meat and said he has taken six animals already this winter. What he cannot use himself he gives to those who cannot hunt. In his home, the old and the new mingle strangely. Strips of caribou were drying on a line strung across the room, while in the corner a TV set blared its usual fare (the CBC provides the only programming). And although there was a snowmobile outside, as we talked we could occasionally hear his dog-team fighting over scraps.

Enook's father, Manomie Sako, is one of the most famous Inuit carvers at Cape Dorset, and in the summers Enook supplements his income by helping to mine the soapstone from a quarry not far from the Cape. Before the liquor store was closed he spent much of his time drinking, but Suzanne says: 'He's a new man now. Our lives have been transformed. Often now I go hunting with him. It's great in the spring when the geese come and we can fish for Arctic char in the fiords.'

When I left Enook's house, just as when I left the Burrows's, the night sky was ablaze with the northern lights. Some Inuit children clinging to a toboggan whizzed down an icy slope beside the road, chortling with joy, and nearby, another child chanted appropriately:

> *Forty years on an iceberg,*
> *Out on the ocean wide.*
> *Nothing to wear but pyjamas,*
> *Nothing to do but slide.*
> *The air was cold and snarky*
> *And the frost began to bite.*
> *I had to hug a polar bear*
> *To keep me warm at night.*

II. Allen Island

'We do not want ever to forget the ways of our grandfathers.' That's how Ipelie, a twenty-year-old Inuit hunter, sums up his reasons for being part of a remote community that has returned to the old ways of traditional Inuit camp life.

Allen Island Camp, to which Ipelie, his family, and a group of about forty other Inuit belong, is a cluster of small cabins perched near the ice of one of the most majestic fiords on the north shore of Baffin Island. Established in 1976, it is part of a growing trend in the north as more and more Eskimos return to the land—away from the welfare, the noise, and the 'white man's ways' of such places as Frobisher Bay. Here, where the waters of the north Atlantic meet the ice-pack of Davis Strait, the mountains soar on almost every side. Some three hundred miles across the ice, the glaciers of Greenland grind to the sea.

I left Frobisher Bay for the camp, about a hundred miles to the northeast, aboard a *Star*-chartered Twin Otter plane. With me went Revd. Brian Burrows (who has been trying to visit this lonely outpost of his parish for nearly a year without success), his wife Rita, and their two small children, David and Rachel. The cargo of our small plane included two drums of gasoline for the Eskimo band and six husky pups in a large cardboard box. A bag of mail shared the rest of the space with our Arctic sleeping-bags, taken in case of a forced landing or sudden bad weather; it is not uncommon to be stranded for days by storms in these isolated places.

As we headed out over the barrens, the sun was a great fiery ball hanging just above the far horizon. Below, the mountains and jagged valleys lay in endless parallel lines, remnants of the ancient glacial age, like vast claw marks in the eternal rock. The deep whipped cream of the snow, with brown crags of wind-swept granite poking through, looked like the top of a Black Forest cake; not a tree or a shrub to be seen for hundreds of miles. We were all wearing two suits of heavy underwear under our layers of padded pants and down parkas, yet the cold was fierce, even on the plane.

Burrows was excited because he was going to conduct not only the camp's first wedding ceremony and baptisms, but its first Christmas communion as well. He told me I was the first journalist ever to visit the community.

After about an hour and a half in the air, the plane began to circle lower and lower, descending into a bowl-like amphitheatre formed by the frozen waters of the fiord and the surrounding snow-clad hills. Suddenly we could make out the huts and a knot of tiny figures waving from a small promontory. As we skimmed in on skis to the makeshift landing-strip, marked out by empty oil drums at the narrow end of the fiord, we could see two snow-mobiles, each towing a sled and followed by several large huskies, streaming along below to meet us. Working quickly, since the pilot had warned us we must be back at the plane for take-off in less than three hours (it was not the kind of terrain to attempt flying out of in the dark), we soon had our gear lashed to the sleds and were bumping over the ragged ice, the wind cutting at our faces.

There was a brief word of welcome to the children and adults who crowded down to help us over some surface water and up the slippery slope to the land, and then Burrows dashed off to make arrangements for his services.

These people live in the midst of an extraordinary, dangerous beauty. The brief daylight, which lasts only four and a half hours, floods the vast white expanse of frozen fiord and encircling mountains with a rare brilliance. The houses, covered with tough canvas and padded with insulation, look as though they too are wearing down-filled coats. Everywhere are signs of the hunt: caribou antlers, seal skins drying on wooden stretchers, and huge black Arctic ravens, waiting to pick up any scraps left by the dogs.

While there were snowmobiles around, I also saw dozens of large but seemingly friendly husky dogs. Ipelie explained: 'I have my own team of twelve dogs and it's much better than a Skidoo. They don't break down and leave you stranded; they don't need gas. One bullet gets me a seal, and then I feed them.' As he told me how he stands for hours over a seal's breathing hole in the ice waiting for a kill, and outlined his plan to take his team down the fiord to hunt for polar bear, his eyes shone. 'I like this life better than in Frobisher,' he said. 'Lots of young people feel as I do. There are no cars, roads, or noise, and even the weather is warmer because of the ring of hills. There's plenty of walrus, seal, and other game to eat. I hope to bring up my children this same way, the old way.'

Christmas, Ipelie said, will be marked by traditional games, dancing, feasting, and retelling the stories of the old days. There will be prayers too, led by a lay cathechist, in the wooden shed that is part community hall and part storehouse for the band's supply of flour, tea, sugar, and skim-milk powder.

We crowded into the shed for the wedding of Palook and Pauloosie, who have been living together for many months while waiting for a minister to arrive. The camera lens had frozen up and had to be held over the tiny oil stove for some time before it thawed enough to film the simple ceremony. Burrows next baptized four howling infants who were convinced he was up to no good, and then he held Christmas communion for the adults.

While he finished registering the newly-weds and babies in the record book, I visited one of the homes and spoke with a thirteen-year-old girl named Sheeba. She was listening to rock music on a battered radio while minding three small children. The house was simple, neat, and clean, but two huge walrus heads sat in a pool of blood on some cardboard on the floor—a study in contrasts. Sheeba told us her duties at the camp include fetching water from a spring on the hillside, cleaning the home, minding children, and helping with the skinning and cooking of fresh game. She enjoys camp life, but added wistfully: 'I would like to go to school too, but my mother says that must come some other day.' Her face lit up with smiles, however, as she described what will happen on Christmas day in the camp: 'We'll have a Christmas party, go to church, and then have a feast of Arctic char, caribou, seal, or walrus with tea and bannock. Then we give and get presents. Maybe later, when it's dark, we'll go sliding on the mountain.' Philipoo, eleven, piped up: 'A polar bear came right into the camp not long ago when the men were away and wasn't even afraid of the dogs. Sheeba's mother shot it and we had bear meat—mmmm, good!'

All too soon our time was up. People poured out of the church and houses, dogs swarmed around us, and, after much handshaking, we were off. The dogs, like outriders, flashed beside us as we lurched over the tidal ice.

The plane was already warming up, and as we swung our gear on board there was a last wave from the Eskimo drivers. Then, with a roar of engines, we headed straight for the canyon wall. But the Otter is a short-take-off plane, and we cleared the crest with ease. Allen Island lay locked in the solitude and darkness behind. Once aloft, we lunched on ice-cold sandwiches of cheese and meat and drank clear hot water from a thermos; dessert was some half-frozen oranges. Hunger and the thrill of the adventure made the simple meal taste like a gourmet feast.

III. Frobisher Bay

Living and sleeping in an igloo can be like stepping inside the meat-freezer in your local supermarket. I know, because I just spent a night in one here. It's something I have wanted to do ever since I first learned to read—that, and riding a sled or running behind a team of huskies. Both sound very romantic, but I can assure you the reality is not for the faint-hearted.

Early today I trudged out in the −30°C cold to where an Inuit hunter was hitching his dog-team to a *kamotik*, or wooden sled. I panted along behind as he drove them up a shallow valley, his thirty-five-foot caribou-hide whip cracking above their heads like a pistol. He was so accurate that with a flick of his lower arm he could make a lump of ice ten yards away jump as if it had been kicked. But the run was short. The dogs were all under a year old—most of the team was wiped out by disease last year— and the hunter said it was too cold even for them. As we turned back towards his house, they suddenly spied another building, dove under it, entangling their traces, and ending up in a howling mess. It took us about fifteen minutes to pull them all out and straighten them up again.

Once aimed for home, though, they took off like the wind, their mouths steaming and their shoulders straining. I jumped on behind and the sled-runners sang as the wind tore at my freezing face. It may not have been as fast as a snowmobile but it was certainly more aesthetic, less noisy, and without the monoxide fumes. I found myself overwhelmed with awe as I recalled that the missionaries who brought the first message of Bethlehem to these vast wastes used to travel up to six thousand miles a year by dog-team, sleeping at night in the traditional snowhouses.

The Inuit no longer use igloos as permanent winter homes, of course, but when hunting or travelling long distances they still put them up as shelter for the Arctic night. Although an experienced hunter can build one in as little as fifteen minutes if suddenly caught in a blizzard, it normally takes about an hour for one person to build an igloo properly.

With Revd Brian Burrows as my guide and interpreter, I was able to find a veteran hunter, Adamee, who was willing and able to fulfil my strange (to him) request for an igloo far up on the craggy hillside, well away from the settlement itself. I climbed with Adamee to a point about a mile from town, up on the crest of a rocky outcropping from which I could see far down the bay. Everything—islands, mountains, distant fiords—was locked in a world of white, ghostly in the Arctic twilight. The hunter, a short, stocky man in his fifties, moved swiftly up the slope, testing the depth of the snow with a fine-toothed saw. He would plunge the blade in, then shake his head if it failed to go in to the full depth of the handle. When it did, he would walk in a circle, testing again and again to find a spot where it would go in all the way on every side. Finally, right near the top, he grunted one of the few English words he knew—'Okay'—and dug out a small trench about twenty inches deep to stand in. The ice from his breath formed crystals on his moustache and the fur of his parka as he began quickly to slice out blocks about six inches thick, two feet long, and fifteen inches wide. Amazingly (to anyone used to snow in the south) the blocks were very heavy.

By the time Adamee had lifted out a ring of blocks, he had dug an oblong hole about eight feet long, the eventual diameter of the igloo. Then, using a sharp, broad-bladed knife, he scuffed up the surface of the snow in a circle and began setting the blocks of the first course in place, tilting each one in a little. This done, he jumped back into the hole and began cutting away again. This time, as he strained to lift the blocks on top of the emerging wall, he would steady them with one hand while using the knife to slant the joining edges in such a way as to prevent them from falling in on him; from an architect's or engineer's point of view, it was a remarkable feat. Soon he reached the dome, wedging the heavy blocks in so tightly they were almost horizontal, yet without the slightest risk of tumbling down.

The last piece in place—all the blocks except for the last two or three having come from what was now the floor of the igloo, well down below the surrounding snow surface and the wind—he cut a narrow door, and I slithered through on my stomach. Outside in the wind it was nearly −40°C. Inside seemed snug and warm by comparison. Later that night, though, as I dragged my heavy-duty Arctic sleeping-bag inside and prepared for sleep, the cold was incredible. I had some candles, but unfortunately I had not been able to obtain one of the small oil-heaters that the Inuit traditionally use to keep off the worst of the frost.

I removed my parka, boots, and snow-pants, and, still well-layered with sweaters and long-johns, dove inside the triple-lined Arctic bag. The stillness was almost overwhelming. Though Adamee had filled all the chinks with fine snow, I could lie on my back and see the stars through one hole in the roof. My breath formed crystals on the outer canvas of the bag and dropped on my face in a fine shower of snow every time I moved. Nevertheless, I soon felt warm enough and slept fitfully while the northern lights danced gloriously overhead. But by 5 a.m. the cold had gradually worked its way through the layers of rubber foam and canvas beneath me and had stabbed me awake.

I squirmed through the tiny doorway, and, as I made my way

down to the town and some hot coffee, looked back. I had left a candle burning on a snow ledge in the igloo and it glowed through all the cracks like some soft-lit jewel on a velvet gown. It called to mind how many artists, including the late William Kurelek, have depicted northern Nativity scenes—the Inuit mother with the tiny Christ-child, folded in furs in the igloo—and I felt strangely moved.

IV. Broughton Island

Most people would shudder at the thought of storing their Christmas dinner on the front lawn, but in this tiny community about sixty miles inside the Arctic Circle it's the natural thing to do. Not that they have front lawns, but they treat the ground outside their square, one-storey frame homes as a freezer. Everywhere you see frozen seals, caribou, and Arctic char (a species of trout) stacked up and ready for the communal Christmas Day feast.

I had left Frobisher Bay with about eight other passengers in −30°C weather. The plane, a DC3 built in 1946, took off some twenty-six hours after our scheduled departure. Even so, we had to stop once right in the middle of taking off because of heavy frost on the wings. When we taxied back to the terminal we were treated to the unusual sight of flight attendants climbing up on the wings with large industrial brooms to sweep them off. A bearded Cockney, who kept us chuckling most of the trip with his running commentary, cracked: 'Imagine that. They can put a man on the moon and these blokes have to use a ruddy broom!'

Then, after a ninety-minute flight up and over Cumberland Sound to Pangnirtung, the plane blew the right tire as it landed on the icy runway. The pilots here are the best in the world, however, and we finally limped to a safe halt.

After several hours a Twin Otter flew up from Frobisher with a spare wheel, and then carried me and several Inuit passengers up the long fiord and through the Pangnirtung Pass, over the Penny Ice Cap, to Broughton Island. Below us lay one of the most spectacular stretches of mountains and canyons on the face of the earth. For all its wild beauty, I had the feeling that man has no place here, and it was vaguely reassuring to see the sign near the cockpit saying the plane had an emergency radio beam to help in locating it if we went down. An hour later, we were sweeping in a wide arc out over Baffin Bay, literally at the top of the world, as we prepared to descend to the six- by twelve-mile, mountain-ringed island known as Broughton. Here, north of the sixty-seventh parallel, there is no sun and very little daylight during December and January. About four hundred natives and seventeen whites make up the entire population.

I was bunked in a tiny glorified cottage, jokingly known as the Broughton Hilton, run by a Welshman named Tony Moss-Davies and his Inuit wife Geela. We ran out of water the very first day—it is delivered daily to all the houses at six cents a gal-lon—and had to dash in the sub-zero weather to another build-ing to wash. Two days later, the sink there froze up too. Meals were served in Broughton's only restaurant, owned by Geela Moss-Davies, and usually attended by a large crowd of curious Eskimo children who seemed fascinated by any stranger, espe-cially one of my size. Background music consisted of a juke box, three well-used pinball machines, and the crackling of a radio—the only, and very uncertain, contact with the rest of Canada.

Revd Jonas Alloolloo, a thirty-year-old Anglican priest who is one of eight Inuit ministers serving the eastern Arctic, lives here. Educated first in Churchill and then for two years at the Univer-sity of Manitoba, he graduated from the Arthur Turner Train-ing School, a college for Anglican Inuit clergy at Pangnirtung, in 1975, and has served the ninety-nine-per-cent Anglican commu-nity of Broughton ever since. In addition to his duties as a priest, he maintains his Inuit identity by hunting, mainly for seal, 'at least once a week'. (He says it also helps to stretch his stipend.)

Early the next morning, I put on all the clothes I had with me and mounted the sled behind Alloolloo's snowmobile. He had a grub-box lashed to the rear of it, caribou hides on the floor, and a spare can of gas. I sandwiched myself onto it and held on for dear life as he headed out across the crazily tumbled ice of the fiord. The temperature was about $-30°C$, but the wind factor as we sped along made it much colder than that. Frost bit at our faces and seeped into any available crack.

We travelled out for thirty miles on the ice, skirting the soar-ing peaks of the mainland which shimmered in the half-light. The mountains looked as though they had been dusted with icing sugar—there is very little snowfall here in winter and scarcely any vegetation in summer. It is, in fact, a frozen desert.

We had to stop frequently, walking to restore circulation. Finally we arrived at the mouth of a deep fiord where there was fresh ice, and Alloolloo, rifle in hand, began looking for the small dimples on the surface that indicate seal blow-holes.

Seals surface for air at intervals of ten minutes or so. The hunter stands motionless near the hole, his parka-hood thrown back to hear. The moment the seal enters, he fires a shot directly through the thin wall of ice, killing it instantly. While several hunters nearby were successful in getting some meat for Christmas, it wasn't Alloolloo's day, and he finally packed up his rifle. By the time we set out for home it was pitch dark; we had thirty miles to go, and the cold was worse than before.

We stopped after about an hour and decided to boil water for soup. Alloolloo got out his battered Coleman stove and thawed it out by holding the generator in his hands. He then filled it with gas from his tank (contrary to all the rules), poured more gas on the burner, and lit a match to warm it up before lighting it properly. Eventually it worked, and we had one of the most memorable meals I have ever enjoyed: soup and hard-tack biscuits eaten as we stood on the ice of the Arctic Sea. By the time we at last saw the lights of Broughton, twinkling like bright sequins in the far distance, I was sore from the pounding of the sled and more than half-frozen.

Later Alloolloo talked to me about Christmas in Broughton, and about Inuit aspirations and problems. He pointed out the difficulties Inuit parents have in adjusting to settlement life. 'Inuit in the camps never had to discipline their children. Youngsters had two role models to follow—their hunter-father and their mother. Here, however, there are all kinds of possibilities and the children become confused. Often vandalism can be the result of their frustration.' According to him, the natives of the Baffin region are very keen on the unity of Canada, and he said that all of them support the stand of the Eskimo Brotherhood of Quebec against the separatist policies of the PQ government. Like all the Inuit I met here, Alloolloo is an unflaggingly optimistic, practical man. He loves his work, loves this land, and believes there can be a bright future ahead. Having attended service in his little church, with its quaint steeple rising against the mountainside, I could imagine him as he would be on Christmas Day when the pealing bell once more calls his people to worship. His quiet conviction, that the Christ who was born in

Bethlehem can be born anew in the hearts of his people today, carries with it a quiet and reassuring note of certainty.

V. *Pangnirtung*

James Nashak shook the chunks of ice from the fur of his parka-hood and pointed proudly at the pile of large frozen fish on his sled. He had just returned from a trip up the fiord to a small lake where Arctic char abound. Tied on top of his gear was the long harpoon with which he had managed to spear twenty-eight fish, luring them under the hole in the ice with a flashing ivory ring on the end of his line.

Nashak, born thirty-one years ago in a remote camp on Prince of Wales Island, far to the north of Hudson Bay, is one of a new breed of Inuit. A hunter to the tips of his sealskin boots, he is at the same time training to be a priest at the most northerly theological college in the world.

Nashak and three other Inuit—Moses Kyak, Bobby Nakoolak, and Richard Hunter—form the current class at the Arthur Turner Training School for Anglican Eskimo priests here at Pangnirtung. Founded in 1970 by the late Right Revd Donald Marsh, then Bishop of the Arctic, the school has already produced eight Inuit priests including Revd Jonas Alloolloo with whom I went seal-hunting at Broughton Island. For the first time since missionaries arrived in the north, Inuit priests now outnumber white clergy in the eastern Arctic.

Pangnirtung—the name means 'place of many caribou'—the tiny settlement of about nine hundred and fifty Inuit and sixty whites where the school is located, sits on a rocky shelf on one wall of a long, spectacularly steep-sided fiord. The main street is really the airstrip, which runs along the foot of the sheer rock-face and puts your heart in your mouth the first time you sweep in for a landing.

Daylight at this time of year is limited to about three hours, and the residents will not see the sun itself until some time in mid-February, when it will gradually lift over the granite mountains that guard the mouth of the fiord. But the slanting rays of sunshine do catch a few peaks of the surrounding ice fields just before darkness falls, illuminating them in an almost indescribable beauty. Most people imagine the Arctic as a flat snowy desert. Here, though, the mountains along the fiord and inland on what is known as the Pangnirtung Pass rise more than a mile high, with some of the most awesome cliffs on the face of the earth. Many of them have never been climbed—and some never will be. More and more climbers are coming here in summer for this very reason; just a few months ago, Sir Edmund Hillary, who conquered Mount Everest, worked out here with his crew before leaving for Nepal and the Himalayas.

The Inuit name for the region, now declared to be Canada's number-one Arctic national park, is Auyuittuq: 'land of the big ice'. At the centre is the Penny Ice Cap, over a mile deep, which chokes the adjoining passes with its glacial tongues. Avalanches of both rock and snow are common here, and at times the wind roars down the Pangnirtung Pass over the settlement at more than a hundred miles an hour, bowling over houses and other buildings in its ferocity. Totally treeless and gripped by −40°C cold, the land seems barren of life. And yet, miraculously, herds of caribou thrive, digging down to the moss with their razor-sharp hooves; the Arctic fox and wolf prowl for ptarmigan (a type of partridge), Arctic hares, and lemmings. The white owls swoop for prey in the twilight; the huge, croaking ravens flap around the settlement or perch on poles; and the waters of the fiord and nearby Cumberland Sound team with char, seal, and magnificent whales.

With unemployment running at about eighty per cent, most of the community is on some kind of government welfare assistance, according to Revd Michael Gardiner, the resident Anglican minister. A wiry Englishman, Gardiner now varies his usual routine by talking about community problems on a local open-line radio show run by one of his choir members, Eliyah Nowdlak. The broadcast booth is a plain room in what was once the mission house. In an interview, Gardiner pointed out that there is considerable discussion among the young people about social issues such as the value of marriage. Some pre-marital sex was always tolerated in the hunting-camp life of the old days, but once a choice of partner was made, fidelity was the rule. There was even some 'trial marriage', which Gardiner says was 'not necessarily a bad thing'. But once the Eskimo had been brought into a settlement by the government, their patterns have changed. Promiscuity among the young is a major problem, with venereal disease rampant in many places, especially in Frobisher Bay.

The custom of simply living together is following trends in the south.

Yet the Inuit here—one hundred per cent Anglican—continue to go to church in great numbers, not just on Sundays but through the week. Young people are very much in evidence in the church, and Gardiner says their interest in religion is still very keen. His church has programs of home prayer-study, Bible groups, and youth activities that far surpass those of most Toronto congregations. It would be wrong, however, to conclude with some observers that their deep religious commitment is a matter of 'simple natives' just accepting what they are told. The Inuit is anything but uncritical in his approach to religion, or anything else. The land, which is unforgiving to those who act without thought, has taught him to be intensely practical, profoundly realistic. He accepts the 'fact' of God and his care—the core of the Christmas message—as an essential part of a life close to nature and the elements. 'The Inuit have always believed in the intervention of the supernatural in their lives,' says Gardiner. 'They're on a different time cycle from people down south, closer to real things. Each one can talk personally of a time when God saved them from starving or freezing or being lost in a storm.'

VI. Pangnirtung

Here on the roof of the world, Christmas Eve comes full of strange ambiguities. For the Inuit of this frozen land on the edge of the Arctic Circle, as for all of us, hope springs afresh in the midst of doubt, fear, and often stark tragedy. It was the same at that first Christmas in Bethlehem.

In the northern part of Baffin Island, there will be total darkness tomorrow as hundreds pack the tiny churches, and then feast on caribou, walrus, seal, and Arctic char. The moon will shine at midday, leaving the icy peaks all sparkling silver and glinting on the frozen sea. Here at Pangnirtung there will be a brief twilight as the bells peal out and the smoke from the cabins goes straight up into the turquoise dome of heaven. Clouds of steam will wrap the worshippers as they leave the church and the warm air hits the frost outside.

For me, visiting these remote settlements and meeting the

people has been exhilarating—an insight into our Canadian identity and heritage. But it also has been a tough adventure, tougher in many ways than my gruelling one-hundred-mile hike from Nazareth to Bethlehem. Yet as I pack and wait somewhat anxiously for a plane to take me out and home, a host of unforgettable scenes flash through my mind. One was a version of Christmas I saw pinned up on the wall of Pangnirtung school, the work of a six-year-old. The drawing showed an igloo with a star shining down, a polar bear and some dogs, and a sled in front. In the doorway sat an Eskimo mother and father with a small baby wrapped in furs. The story was in Eskimo syllabic script with the English written below. This is what it said: 'Mary and Joseph were alone when Jesus was born. There was no good, comfortable place for them to settle in. Joseph built an igloo for them because that was the only possibility for that moment for their great need. There were no other Inuit around. Only some animals were around. With only the *kamotik* [sled] to use for transportation did they go to see other Inuit friends and to show them their new-born baby, Jesus.'

Then there was James Kilibuk, seventy-five, playing with his great-grandson Christopher, who will be one year old tomorrow, on Christmas Day. Kilibuk, born on Blacklead Island, across Cumberland Sound, was a Hudson Bay cook and guide for over forty years. His face has scarcely a line in it and it shone with joy as he cuddled the child, whose tiny fist clutched a seal-bone teether. The settlements here are full of infant children and an extraordinary love flows between them and their parents. I was reminded of Carl Sandburg's saying that the birth of a child is God's opinion that life is worth living and should continue to go on. That, in essence, is what the Christmas message is all about.

Practically all the people I met in the Arctic either had a story to tell, or were stories in themselves. There was Richard Hunter, forty-one, from Labrador, who is training to be a priest here— the first Inuit minister for the whole of Labrador. Like most of the Labrador Inuit, Hunter is a Moravian. The first Moravian missionaries (Moravia is now part of Czechoslovakia) came to Labrador in 1707 and many were killed by the natives. Hunter is thus the product of almost three hundred years of Christian influence there. He told me: 'As a boy, I used to wonder why there were no Inuit ministers. I thought that the Inuit must be too bad to be pastors and that following God was too holy for us. I believe that my being ordained will have an enormous impact on my people.'

Johanasee Qappik, forty-one, a hunter and a member of the choir at Pangnirtung's only church, told me of how his life had been changed by a 'miracle'. Two years ago he was flying on a DC3 plane from the top of Baffin Island to Pangnirtung. Weather prevented the plane from landing at either Broughton Island or Pangnirtung, and so the pilot was forced to try for Frobisher Bay, one hundred and fifty miles to the south. But he ran out of gas about fifty miles from the airstrip, and had to make an emergency landing in the total darkness on the mountainous tundra. The plane bounced off one crest and finally came to a halt just short of a gorge on the only flat ground for miles. People called it an amazing stroke of luck, but for Qappik, the rescue after three days of freezing and hunger was a sign of God's action and care. He said: 'I suddenly realized that God's power can still be known today. Since then, Christmas for me has always been the greatest time, the time we celebrate God's concern for creation and all mankind.'

There were many moments of humour too: the sound of a resonant voice singing 'Jingle Bells' in Eskimo on the radio; the white Hudson Bay clerk who said that if Santa Claus and ten reindeer ever came down in Pangnirtung fiord there would be ten dead reineer in a hurry—'The Inuit wouldn't let that many caribou get by.' Not to mention trying to eat frozen sandwiches without taking my heavy mittens off during an eight-hour trek to hunt seals with an Inuit minister.

Most of all though, I was impressed with the life of the church in the north. Mission work has often been the target of would-be northern experts who usually fire their salvoes from the security and warmth of a retreat in the south. This is not to say the churches have made no mistakes. They have in the past, and will probably continue to do so. But schools, hospitals, and dental care in the Arctic all began with the missionaries. And when the native people fight to save their culture today, part of that culture is a heritage of written language given and preserved by the church (the Inuit syllabic system of writing was adapted by an Anglican clergyman from work already done for the Cree by a Methodist minister).

If most whites in the Arctic come for short periods, aiming to make their money and get out, some clergy have devoted their lives to the north—Father Joseph Choque, the Roman Catholic priest at Frobisher Bay, for example, and Revd Michael Gardiner, who has spent twenty-two years at Lake Harbour and Pangnirtung. What is more, while few if any Inuit can yet be found in the key positions in other spheres of influence such as government and business, Inuit clergy are now taking the lead in what was once an all-white hierarchy.

My final moments at Pangnirtung were tense as I woke on the day of my departure to find the air filled with thick ice-fog. I couldn't see the peaks four miles across the fiord at all. Since it is nothing to be delayed by weather here for several days or even weeks, I was relieved to see an Austin Airways Hawker-Siddeley loom out of the mist and land just after noon. The crew dumped about twenty Christmas trees on the frozen tarmac, unloaded some fresh produce for the Hudson's Bay store, and told me to climb aboard quickly. As we roared down the runway and 'felt' our way by radar up between the hidden cliffs towards the vast expanse of Cumberland Sound, Pangnirtung slid back in a cloud of enveloping fog. I would be home in time for Christmas Day in Toronto after all.

The Easter event

Easter is at once the basis of the Christian faith and a challenge for it. Anybody who takes the trouble to read the accounts of Jesus' Resurrection in the four Gospels will discover what scholars have known for centuries: there are extraordinary differences, discrepancies, and even outright contradictions in the texts. Attempts have been made to combine, harmonize, or explain these problematic details away, but none of them works unless one is prepared to be intellectually dishonest.

According to Luke, all the events, or Easter phenomena, occurred on Easter Day itself: it was on the evening of Easter that Jesus led the disciples to Bethany, just outside Jerusalem, and there was taken up into heaven. But in Mark's version the disciples were told to leave Jerusalem and go to Galilee, where Jesus would meet them—a journey of several days. According to Matthew, they went to Galilee and met the risen Lord, by prearrangement, on a mountain; it was there, he says, that Jesus gave them his great commission to go forth into all the world, before his ascension to the Father. Yet John's Gospel, in its present form, has Jesus take his final leave of the disciples on the shore of the Sea of Galilee, some days after the Resurrection.

Rather than casting doubt on the reality of Jesus' Resurrection, however, such discrepancies are seen by many critical scholars as confirming it. What is supremely obvious is that no one felt any need or desire to 'cook the books' or smooth out inconsistencies when the oral gospel tradition was written down. Witnesses to an incident or series of events before a judge in a court of law seldom agree on every aspect. Indeed, one would probably suspect collusion if they did. The killing of President John F. Kennedy took place before the eyes of a vast crowd in the streets and millions of television viewers; no set of circumstances in our time has been so painstakingly scrutinized, sifted and analysed. Yet there is still no overall account of the assassination that meets with anything approaching unanimity. The debate goes on and on.

The point on which there is total unanimity in the Gospels—and it runs right through all the earliest strata of the New Testament—is the bedrock belief that Jesus, whom they had seen done to cruel death, was indeed alive again. This belief is evident in the earliest testimony to the Resurrection, written at least a decade before the Gospels: Paul's first letter to the Corinthians. Writing about twenty years after the death of Jesus, Paul says: 'For this is the teaching which I handed on to you at the beginning and which you have received, i.e. that Christ died for our sins according to the scriptures; that he was buried, and that he was raised up on the third day . . . that he was seen by Cephas [Peter] and then by the Twelve; then he was seen by upwards of five hundred brethren at one time of whom many are still alive today, though a few have died. Then he was seen by James, then by all the Twelve. . . .' (1 Cor. 15:3-6.) What is most significant about this is the fact that witnesses were still alive to confirm or deny the declaration at the time Paul made it. Peter is the most obvious one, but Paul himself alludes to many others.

There have been many and varied attempts to explain away this fundamental conviction that Jesus had been raised by God from the dead—hallucination, delusion, deliberate fraud—but none of them really does justice to the case. The growth of a tiny, fearful, defeated group into a movement ready to challenge the world implies a tremendous, even miraculous, cause. People do not go out and lay down their lives for what they know is a forgery. Nevertheless, it is worth noting that while the New Testament proclaims the Resurrection on almost every page, the Gospels tell of no one who claims to have witnessed the actual event. The Resurrection itself, however it happened, is described nowhere except in the unauthentic or apocryphal Gospel of Peter (about AD 150), which tells the story in great detail. The difference in atmosphere between the Gospels and this work, however, is so great that anyone can spot its naïvety and imaginative embroiderings.

In an age when many are looking for absolute certainties, it is tempting to expect 'proof' of Jesus' Resurrection in the Bible. Yet while there is plenty of historical evidence to be weighed, no hard and fast proof is attempted—or indeed possible. What we are faced with ultimately is the consuming faith of those who had seen Jesus in the flesh and who witnessed that he had conquered the tomb. The only appropriate response to that event is either faith or sheer unbelief. This faith is not irrational, although it has elements of the non-rational in it. Pascal was right: 'The heart has its reasons that reason knows not of.' If the Resurrection were 'proved', there would be no room for risk, for trust, for the adventure that has marked Christian living down the ages. When a Christian says he knows that his redeemer lives, he is not using 'know' in the way a scientist does when he says he knows water runs downhill. This kind of knowledge belongs to the heart as well as the mind. It is the kind of knowing that lovers speak of when they say they know that they are loved.

Easter
and the
new creation

Life can begin again! That is the central message of Easter, on
which all the rest is commentary. Rebirth is possible, both for the
individual and for society as a whole. And this is why Easter
always belongs to all people, not just to those who call themselves
Christians. For behind both the religious festivities and the secular rites—the giving of Easter eggs and flowers, the wearing of
new spring clothes—lies a truth of urgent and universal significance. Like the earth itself, after the icy trials of winter humanity
has a need, a longing to be reborn. There is nothing pious or
sentimental about this need. It is rooted in a sober, even frightening, awareness of present realities.

There was a time when prophecies of impending doom were
largely the stock-in-trade of religious fanatics, strange figures in
the street carrying signs or banners: 'The end is at hand! Prepare to meet thy God!' Now doomsday is no longer the monop-
oly of those once widely regarded as the 'lunatic fringe'. On all
sides come warnings—from experts in economics, ecology, population planning, global food strategy, nuclear and other technology, as well as the social sciences—that time may be running
out for 'spaceship earth'. Speaking of nuclear holocaust, the
great Swiss psychiatrist Carl Gustav Jung sounded the warning
as early as 1957: 'It needs only an almost imperceptible distur-
bance of equilibrium in a few of our rulers' heads to plunge the
world into blood, fire, and radioactivity.' In his book *The Undis-
covered Self*, from which this statement is quoted, Jung issues an
eloquent plea for a rebirth of humanity based on a rebirth of
each individual through radical self-knowledge and a commitment to love. He writes: 'It is, unfortunately, only too clear that
if the individual is not truly made new in spirit, society cannot be

either; for society is the sum total of individuals in need of redemption.' The Resurrection is a symbol of this rebirth for all humanity. As such a symbol, it is not merely an empty sign. Easter, born in the miracle of spring and in the story of human triumph over grief, despair, and death itself, has energy and power to change humankind. It holds out the affirmation that, just as the rotting seed pushes new shoots up through the thawing earth, so love can break through hatred; caring can take the place of greed and cruelty; and personal failure, moral or otherwise, can give place to victory.

For Christians, of course, Easter is more than a symbol. But while singing the Easter anthems and rejoicing in Christ's 'victory over death', many have sometimes overlooked the central message in it all. The New Testament authors make it clear that the story of Jesus is not just another tale of a god or hero who overcomes death. Antiquity had plenty of such 'divinities'. The point is that in Jesus and the Resurrection they saw the beginning of a new humanity. Jesus is seen as a second chance for the race. The story of Genesis is being re-enacted in a fresh start for mankind. This is why John's Gospel leads off with: 'In the beginning was the Word.' He wants to remind his readers of the first words of the Bible: 'In the beginning, God created . . .'. For the same reason he tells of the risen Christ 'breathing on' his disciples as he gave them the gift of the Spirit. John has in mind the old story of the creation of Adam: 'And God breathed into Adam, and Adam became a living soul.' For Paul, being a Christian does not mean belonging to a new religious cult or performing certain rituals, but becoming a 'new man'. He believes that the dawn of a new day for humanity has arrived and that even nature will one day be wholly renewed.

Conveyed in almost the last lines of the New Testament is a prophetic vision not only of a new humanity but also of 'a new heaven and a new earth'. Seen in this light, the Bible's message of Easter has much in common with the current secular call for a new kind of human being and awareness, especially in the face of the nuclear risk: the two lines almost converge. This does not in any way mean that all others must, or are likely to, become Christians. What it does mean is that the churches have a message that—if they can free it from theological jargon—is relevant to modern thinking. Meaningful conversation about the central quest for human renewal is possible. All sides, not least the churches, have much to learn from this kind of dialogue.

Hiroshima

The site of the first crucifixion of humanity by an atom bomb remains forever fixed in human history and consciousness. At Easter particularly, Hiroshima looms as a symbol either of global resurrection or of that final apocalypse in which we will all be cremated equal. The choice is ours: either hope renewed or Armageddon to come.

Certainly no one can ever come to Hiroshima and remain the same. Here knowledge of the face of evil moves from the cool recesses of the mind to burn in the soul itself. Most devastating of all is the awareness that the nuclear weapons now in the arsenals of the superpowers have warheads whose lethal power makes the bomb that fell here in 1945, on the order of President Harry Truman, seem a mere firecracker by comparison. Crude estimates put the combined explosive force of the fifty thousand nuclear devices in the hands of the Americans and the Russians at one and a quarter million times that of the one that obliterated Hiroshima. What began as a search for security under the slogan of deterrence has now escalated to the point where both sides are talking of first-strike capability, of winning limited nuclear wars, and of 'acceptable levels' of casualties. The world budget for armaments is now about five hundred billion dollars a year, and yet there has never been a greater risk of holocaust and extinction. Logic and reason and humanity have abandoned the throne, and naked insanity rules in their stead.

Is there any glimpse of hope beyond this stark terror? To find out, I came to Hiroshima, a city whose tragedy remains a blot on the conscience of mankind. Today, the Saturday before Easter, 1982, as dawn breaks in Hiroshima's Memorial Peace Park there is at least the promise of a cloudless sky. The petals of the cherry blossoms spiral silently down as if to caress this hallowed ground, and the birds are singing their hearts out. All is exactly as it was on 6 August 1945, the day when, without warning, at precisely 8.15 a.m., there was a blinding flash two thousand feet above the spot where I am standing—and Hiroshima became a writhing city of death.

This fan-shaped town, situated on six islands in the delta made by the Ohta River as it runs into Hiroshima Bay, was convulsed by an earth-shaking roar, and became a sea of fire. The Four Horsemen of the Apocalypse had been turned loose. Those who died in the first onslaught—about one hundred thousand men, women, school-children, round-faced toddlers, and new-borns alike—were the lucky ones. Most of the additional hundred thousand casualties were doomed to die in agony from ruptured organs, horrendous burns, or the slow hell of radiation sickness. In the Atom Bomb Patients Hospital, some two hundred survivors are still suffering their living death, their bodies wracked by leukaemia, various malignancies, and burns that have yet to heal after nearly thirty-seven years. One of them, an eighty-year-old man, told me through an interpreter of trying to flee from the raging inferno that followed the explosion, and of meeting survivors searching for a hospital. They did not know that eighty per cent of all doctors and nurses had been killed, and that only one hospital was left standing. He said they were all naked or in rags, with cuts and horrible burns over most of their bodies. Their hands and faces—flung up in protection from the blinding blast—were so badly burned that the skin was running off. They were staggering along with their hands stretched out before them as if pleading with God, the universe, the pitch-black sky, for help or an answer to their mute question: Why?

One reporter told of a group of soldiers, begging for water, whose eyes had liquified and were running down their faces. The heat of the blast at its centre was from 3,000 to 4,000°C. Granite rocks almost a mile away still show signs of surface melting. The shadows of those people completely vaporized or blasted away remained etched like photo images on walls and stairways.

As the sun, rising out of the Pacific, catches the green, cone-shaped hills that encircle Hiroshima on three sides, the vast park is now bathed in soft light. I can see the arched cenotaph, with its list of the two hundred thousand known dead, and behind it the eternal flame and its reflecting Pool of Peace. Past that, between the lines of cherry trees, is the mound containing the bones of thousands of unidentified dead: and, to one side of that again, the wreath-bedecked sculpture in memory of all the children who were victims. One of the three bronze sculptures of children affixed to the marble is a naked girl, her arms flung out as if on a cross. I am alone in the park, except for a few joggers. Movingly, each one, when he or she comes to the memorial cenotaph, stops and, with bowed head and hands together, is lost for a while in silent meditation. The stark inscription says quite simply: *'Let all souls here rest in peace. For we shall not repeat the evil.'* As Mayor Takesh Araki explains, these words are more than a prayer; they are a solemn promise: 'These words are the pledge we have given to the A-bomb victims. In them we appeal for the abolition of nuclear weapons and the renunciation of war.' The children's monument is festooned with multicoloured streamers made of tiny paper 'cranes of peace'—each one carrying a prayer of remembrance for some child who was incinerated, whether in one of the ninety thousand buildings destroyed, or simply on the way to school. In the background of it all is the skeletal ruin of the Atom Dome, the former industrial exhibition hall that miraculously survived although it was only a hundred and fifty yards from the hypocentre (the spot immediately below where the bomb went off).

To Canadians all of this may seem remote, perhaps even irrelevant. But today the superpowers are, as *Time* magazine recently put it, 'thinking the unthinkable', and the possibility—many would say the inevitability—of nuclear war either by accident or by design looms ahead. None of us would escape its consequences. Scientists have repeatedly pointed out that the detonation of a one-megaton bomb over Metropolitan Toronto would kill more than six hundred thousand people; another eight hundred thousand would be agonizingly injured. The flying glass and debris carried by winds of more than six hundred miles an hour would mow down citizens as far away as Mississauga. Blindness and retinal damage from the flash would occur as far away as Aurora and St Catharines. More than ninety-one thousand would be hideously burned—more than the number of intensive-care beds in the entire world. All the major hospitals themselves would be levelled and about three-quarters of the city's doctors and nurses killed. Dr Bernard Lown, president of International Physicians for Prevention of Nuclear War (IPPNW) warned in Toronto in 1981: 'Modern medicine has nothing to offer—not even a token benefit in a thermo-nuclear war. Nuclear war is not survivable . . . truly the living will envy the dead.' Just yesterday the English papers here carried reports from the current meeting of the IPPNW in Cambridge, England. The two hundred physicians, including Dr Frank Sommers, a Toronto psychiatrist who is founder and head of Canadian Doctors for Social Responsibility, predict that a nuclear war in Europe would kill more than one hundred and fifty million, and that most survivors would die of their injuries, radiation sickness, or starvation. On the eve of leaving for the Cambridge conference, Sommers told me in a phone interview that since coming to Hiroshima two years ago he has dedicated himself to organizing Canadian doctors against nuclear war. 'I have a growing conviction that this is the life or death issue for every person on this planet now,' he said. 'We are in a crucial point of transition for humanity where what Freud called the *thanatos* or death-urge starkly confronts the *eros* or life-urge. Our very extinction as a species is at stake.' Hope, for Sommers, and for the rising tide of those around the world who feel that nuclear holocaust not only must be avoided, but can be, lies in the fact that if enough people drop their passivity or work through their deep depression and repressed fears about the bomb—'if they undergo a personal conversion'—they can bring about a worldwide shift in direction. 'Millions in the USSR are just as scared as we are—their flesh burns at the same temperature as ours—and thousands of their doctors are organizing just as we are,' he said.

Yesterday I stood and looked out over Hiroshima with Dr Harry Jennison, executive director of the American Academy of Pediatricians. A member of the more-than-ten-thousand-strong American Association of Physicians for Social Responsibility, Jennison said his stomach was still reeling from viewing a film at the Hiroshima Peace Centre, which showed doctors' attempts to deal with the tens of thousands of Hiroshima casualties just after the blast. He noted how the growing anti-nuclear movement is cutting across all party and credal divisions. 'You cannot be a doctor, especially a children's doctor, and not see this as the paramount issue of our time. All the advances of modern medicine become folly once you commit the insanity of thinking anyone can win a nuclear war.' Jennison said that up until two months ago he felt very pessimistic about the risk of nuclear war, but that he now senses a 'cautious new optimism' because church leaders, lawyers, and ordinary citizens across the United States are organizing to cry 'No, no, no, never' to both the Kremlin and the Pentagon. His words echoed what Revd Harvey Cox, Dean of Divinity at Harvard and a leading American social commentator, told me just before I left Canada on the long journey here: 'Ever since visiting Hiroshima four years ago, my life has been changed. Standing at the cenotaph there, I felt rooted, paralyzed, unable to leave. What had before been just a mental awareness of the bomb hit me in my chromosomes. I realized this was the spot where everything had changed. I knew in my innermost self that Hiroshima was the first step towards a capability to annihilate the species and the earth itself.' He said: 'The real news now, though, is that an enormous effort is being made by all ranks of people everywhere to step back from the nuclear brink. That's an Easter message for mankind!'

This chain of events, thank God, is beginning to take place in Canada too. The leaders of the churches, most notably the Roman Catholic bishops and the Moderator of the United Church, have called on all their people to fast, pray, form networks, write their members of parliament, and do all in their power to let those in authority know that enough is enough. One of the most significant aspects of the growing anti-nuclear movement all over the world is that it no longer belongs to the 'peace-niks', would-be radicals, 'pinkos' or crypto-Communists. No one is calling for appeasement, cave-in, or total disarmament by one side alone. Members are talking about immediate practical goals such as a nuclear freeze, or a ban on testing cruise missiles in Alberta. As Senator Edward Kennedy said in explaining his call for a freeze in the face of then-State-Secretary Alexander Haig's insistence that the US must have more nukes before it can have less: 'When an elevator is going up and you want it to go down, the first thing to do is to push the button to make it stop.' The point is that nobody wants a nuclear war (although the military-industrial complexes in both the USSR and the US obviously profit from escalating fears of one). But unless there is a quantum leap forward in human thinking, unless at this Easter there is a sufficiently massive resurrection in the hearts of the true silent majority of the world who have remained passive in the face of this threat for too long, a nuclear Armageddon seems inevitable.

As the Bible says, 'I have set before you this day life and death. Therefore choose life!' In the tabernacle of the Roman Catholic Memorial Cathedral for World Peace in Hiroshima, there is an inscription, sent and paid for by the people of Bonn, West Germany. It reads: 'Out of the ruins of man's guilt springs the triumph of the risen Christ and his peace.' That can be the symbolism and the Easter message of Hiroshima for all mankind, including generations yet unborn. 'And let all the people rise and say, "Amen".'

Speaking out

Absolute certainty and sexual morality

In the introduction to this volume, I suggested that it is folly to search for infallible answers in the realm of theology. The same is true of moral questions. Apart from the single imperative of love, in the fullest Christian sense—love of God, love of neighbour, love of self—the Christian religion offers no absolute certainty on most of the serious moral issues of our time. Jesus said very little about sex and marriage, and nothing whatever on such topics as abortion, homosexuality, surrogate motherhood, or genetic engineering. With hardly anything to guide us but the law of love, we have been left as co-workers with God to work out our own salvation 'with fear and trembling' (Phil. 2:12). This does not mean that we should carelessly throw aside traditional church teaching in the area of sexuality. What it does mean is that none of the elaborate and often rigid, misery-producing dogmas that have accrued over the centuries is engraved in sacred stone, never to be re-examined. God's spirit is alive and at work in his world, and new insights dictate new ways.

On homosexuality

For example, homosexuals—who historically have suffered so much from the allegedly righteous—are now being seen in a new light. Scholars have a new understanding of the biblical passages dealing with homosexual love. Most of the prohibitions against it stemmed from a desire to add to the tribe, on the one hand, and a fear of idolatry on the other. Moreover, prostitution, both male and female, played a prominent role in the worship at pagan temples throughout much of the ancient world—

to be one with the prostitute symbolized union with a particular local deity. Thus many modern scholars consider the sin for which Sodom was punished (Gen. 19) to be not homosexuality, but violation of the rule of hospitality. Similarly, they see Paul's railings against homosexual acts as based upon his condemnation of the idolatry associated with such conduct in Corinth and elsewhere.

At the same time, the social sciences have discovered that the vast majority of homosexuals do not choose their orientation: it chooses them. Whatever the causes, the condition seems to be a constitutive one, and the success rate for psychiatric and other attempts to change it has been minimal. In spite of traditional teaching, many leading Roman Catholic, Anglican, and other moral theologians now argue that homosexual love can be moral provided it meets the same criteria that the rule of Christian love demands of any heterosexual union: commitment, mutual consent, and a life together that enhances the humanity of both. Most of the major churches now have official associations for homosexual clergy and laity, to provide common support and, in some cases, pressure for a change in church attitudes.

The United Church of Canada in its courageous study guide on human sexuality has gone further than perhaps any other North American church in attempting to find a Christian sexual morality more in tune with today's realities. Entitled *In God's Image—Male and Female* and drawn up by a special commission on family life and human sexuality, the report says that premarital sex is not automatically sinful, that masturbation and sexual fantasizing are part of most people's normal experience at some time or another, and that it sees no objection to the ordination of homosexuals provided they meet the other rigorous requirements for any ordinand. The report is not yet official policy, and its study across the country has touched off a vigorous emotional debate among the two million members of the denomination. The opposition has called it the 'work of Satan', and there have been threats of resignation on the part of clergy and laity alike. The parallel document for Roman Catholics is the published report of the Catholic Theological Society of America, *Human Sexuality: New Directions in American Catholic Thought* (1978). In this thorough-going examination of both the theological issues and the latest information from the social sciences, the authors move far beyond the current teaching of their church. Regarding homosexuality, they state: 'It bears repeating . . . without condition, that where there is sincere affection, responsibility, and love—God is surely present.' The document is, of course, highly controversial and was directly repudiated by Pope John Paul II during his 1979 tour of the United States. Personally, I find in both these studies encouraging signs of a more Christian approach to sex in the decades ahead.

On birth control

It is ironic that in spite of the churches' age-old preoccupation—one could almost say 'obsession'—with sex, most churches at the official level have failed to formulate a positive theology of sex and the body. Few aspects of their combined teaching have done more harm, twisted more lives, or heaped more unnecessary guilt on millions of people than their generally negative approach to this very basic element in human life and development. Based on body-denying Greek philosophical ideas, the churches' teachings about sexuality have elaborated rules that often rob a God-given gift of its natural joy.

My good friend Rabbi Abraham Feinberg, in his book *Sex and the Pulpit* (1981), suggests that the negative obsession with sex was a direct ploy for control over church members through their most vulnerable instinct. He could be right, but I think it is less cynical to theorize that like many well-meaning yet horrendous human acts, such teachings originated in a sincere but mistaken belief that you can protect people from harm by forcing them to do what you want. The idea was to help preserve family life and the sanctity of marriage. Yet many current religious 'thou-shalt-nots' regarding human sexuality actually work to destroy this very set of values.

A glaring example of this is the stand of the present Pope and the Curia on the 1968 encyclical *Humanae Vitae*, which condemned the pill and other artificial forms of birth control. The refusal to change on this controversial ruling—made despite the fact that most of the scholars and other members of Paul VI's own commission were opposed to it—hardly matters any more in North America and most of Europe, where an overwhelming majority of Catholics ignore it completely, often with the support of their clergy. But in Latin America, where fifty per cent of the total Roman Catholic population of the world will soon reside, or in other Third-World countries of Africa and Asia, millions of couples have seen their married life torn apart by the constant fear of unwanted pregnancies. True, condoms, the pill, and other family-planning devices do interfere with natural processes. But so do the technologies of most modern medical practices, from organ transplants to blood transfusions. Yet these have not been proscribed as contrary to the so-called natural law of the church.

Overpopulation, as even Roman Catholic priests in offices not five minutes away from the Vatican will tell you, is a major cause of famine, poverty, and war. Yet when I accompanied the Pope on some of his tours, particularly the Mexican trip, I was repeatedly shocked to hear him admonishing struggling peasants to use only 'natural' family-planning methods. Since all such methods are still highly unpredictable—including the now-favoured method of Dr John Billings, which charts fertility by observing the woman's temperature and the changes in her vaginal secretions—and since vast millions of the world's Catholics have virtually no access to proper instruction in such procedures, John Paul's precepts are ultimately cruel, and a cause of growing injustice. More and more, they are destroying the very family life they are meant to protect and enhance.

On marriage and divorce

In the realm of marriage and divorce too, religious rigidities undermine the sacrament they were designed to protect, causing undue guilt and hardship for countless numbers of the faithful. This is not to say the churches must give up their ideal of marriage as binding one man and one women together for their lifetime. But just as there is forgiveness and restitution for all who, in their human weakness, fail to attain other ideals, so it should be with failed marriages. To put it another way, what possible grounds, biblical or otherwise, can a church have for making failure at one marriage and the wish to begin another the 'unforgivable sin'? The 'sin' is apparently not the failure of the first marriage: most groups have no proscription against civil divorce per se, although the couple will often be made to feel like religious lepers. The real problem arises when one or both of the divorced pair decide to remarry and try to build new lives—even though this fresh start would seem to suggest the kind of personal 'resurrection' that the New Testament depicts as the Christian response to failure.

While the Eastern Orthodox Churches, the Anglican Church in Canada, and the United, Lutheran, and Presbyterian Churches will marry such couples in church, the Roman Catholic and certain fundamentalist Churches will not. Canadian Anglicans who are divorced and wish to remarry must first be approved by a Bishop's Court. Opposed by many priests, it is in my view a humiliating procedure, in which the couple must set out in writing (after the trauma of the civil divorce) all the reasons for the breakup of their previous marriage(s), their full financial situation, and their intention to attend church regularly in future.

For Roman Catholics the problems here are enormous, and surrounded with what can only be called outright hypocrisy. Divorced persons can be married in church and come to full participation at mass only if they can persuade an official marriage tribunal that the first marriage was not a true Christian marriage at all. Before the Second Vatican Council, an annulment would be granted only if it could be proven either that the first marriage had never been consummated, that one or the other party had been forced into it, or that the two parties were closely related. With the admission of new psychological criteria, the basis for annulments has broadened and the process is much easier—so much so that on the eve of the 1980 World Synod of Bishops on the family, the late Cardinal Pericle Felici, a giant in the Curia, said that annulments were becoming a form of divorce 'Vatican style', especially in North America. Yet there are huge backlogs at most tribunals—couples may have to wait as long as five years to be fully processed—and the costs can be very high, since experts such as psychiatrists must be called to testify.

The vast majority of divorced Catholics who remarry avoid the annulment proceedings altogether and are wed at city hall or in other churches. They refuse to go through the charade of claiming they have never been really married before when they know very well that they have. The obvious fact is that it is possible for people to be apparently—at least to outsiders—happily married for years, to have children and to raise them, and then to find that love has failed and they have grown irreconcilably apart. Since Catholic marriages end in divorce at the same rate as those of the general public, the number of people we are talking about here is very large. What adds to their burden of guilt and hurt (as if there were not enough of both already during the divorce) is the official church position that those who remarry without an annulment are not truly married but 'living in sin', and therefore should not receive the Holy Communion at mass.

The hundreds of bishops attending the 1980 synod, where they argued for more compassion towards such church members, were stunned by Pope John Paul's response. On the final day, in a speech that could well have been written before the synod began, since it budged not an inch on any of the bishops' concerns (their actual recommendations have yet to be made public and probably never will be), the Pope said that Catholics who remarry without an annulment must 'live as brother and sister' if they want to receive the sacrament of the Eucharist. In brutal terms, this would mean breaking up a second marriage and family in order to be reinstated into full fellowship—a kind of Pharisaical rigidity taken to its absurd conclusion. It is the precise opposite of what Jesus laid down when he said: 'The sabbath was made for man, not man for the sabbath.' To paraphrase: 'Marriage was made for man, not man for the sake of marriage.' Small wonder that organized groups of separated and divorced Catholics are mushrooming up around the world. They need all the mutual support they can get. Small wonder too that many priests, showing more Christian spirit than their leaders do, are telling such couples to follow their own consciences and come to take the bread (and wine, where offered) if they want to.

My conviction is that the proper Christian response to the increasing phenomenon of divorce is to maintain the ideal of marriage through better preparation for it and more church-sponsored support for those already married. But when a breakup occurs, everything should be done to assist the separate parties and their families, and to smooth the way should they wish to attempt a fresh start in a second marriage performed in and by the church. Surely here, as in all aspects of life, Jesus' message that life can begin again needs to be proclaimed and acted upon.

On living together

None of the churches has really come to grips with the growing number of couples who are living together 'without benefit of clergy', as people used to say. A special committee presented the Anglican Bishops of Canada with a very positive, realistic report on the subject in June 1980, but they have managed to sit on it ever since. The report made it clear that while the church could not approve of 'trial marriage' or a promiscuous series of irresponsible, impermanent 'shacking-up-together' arrangements, it should recognize some common-law marriages as being just as valid as those performed in a regular way.

The truth is that in the final analysis couples marry each other. The church doesn't marry them; it simply recognizes what has happened, asks God's blessing upon it, and seals the marriage in a societal way. Some people—many, in fact—intend to take this final step as soon as it becomes legally possible for them to do so. Others, for a wide variety of reasons, have a commitment to stay together but do not see church marriage as a necessary or desirable option. I concur with the report's suggestion that these couples should receive the full recognition and acceptance that the churches accord those officially married in a church. The marriage certificate itself, or a fine church wedding, is no guarantee that the relationship is any more or less Christian than that between a man and woman living common-law.

On abortion

I have often written on the issue of abortion, at present one of the most emotionally charged topics of debate in Canada and elsewhere. Like free will, it is not a subject on which one can hope to say much that is original. All the arguments have been presented by now—usually with more heat than light. I want to state, first, that I am pro-choice, and, second, that this is something quite different from saying one is pro-abortion, even though there are those who, in blind enthusiasm for their cause, refuse to make this key distinction. I don't for one moment believe that anyone who knows a particle about the subject likes or favours therapeutic abortions in and of themselves. Abortion for whatever reason is a nasty business, and a fetus is not simply a clump of tissue. To say otherwise is to pretend that there are no moral values at stake in this debate at all. There are indeed.

A fetus, even at the earliest stages, is a human-life-in-process, and the taking of any life is a serious matter. However, emotional words such as 'murder' are wholly inappropriate, and only get in the way of rational discussion. If abortion before the fetus is viable is murder, then logic demands that any doctor who performs such an operation be charged with first-degree murder and given the mandatory life sentence for such a crime. Few of even the most ardent anti-abortionists are prepared to go that far. What we are faced with in any decision to abort is not one life, but two. We are dealing, on one hand, with a fully developed adult human who has a history, commitments, relationships, and a life partly lived, with all the responsibilities these entail. On the other, we have an as-yet unformed, unknown life, in the process of becoming. We have a duty to both; but the duty to the actual person of the mother is the greater. If for any reason other than the merely frivolous, the mother-to-be does not want to bring a fetus to term—if her health, economic situation, relationships, or any other part of her life promise so much stress that the child is not a wanted child—no one, in my view, should have the authority or the power to coerce her into bearing it. This position is pro-life because it opts, as the lesser of two evils, for the life of the mother. It is pro-family because no family can endure when it is built upon coercion, undue anxiety, and unwanted babies.

The view of religious communities who oppose abortion— from Roman Catholics to fundamentalists to Orthodox Jews— should not be permitted to dictate policy to the majority of citizens. With total freedom of choice, the decision to have or not to have an abortion must be faced morally since it will be a matter of personal responsibility. No one can be forced to have an abortion; therefore those who are convinced it is always wrong can follow their own consciences freely. Current Canadian law should be changed to permit abortion clinics so that others can follow theirs as well. The present system, under which only hospitals with abortion committees can perform abortions, is manifestly unjust to thousands of women in areas where no such service is available.

The Bible says nothing about abortion, but the kind of respect for human freedom enunciated by Jesus seems to me to rule out coercing any sane, intelligent woman of goodwill to act in a manner contrary to her own deepest convictions and wishes. In an ideal world, one in which the kingdom of God had already arrived, there would be no need to discuss this tragic business at all—tragic no less for the doctors who have to perform abortions than for the parents, families, and friends involved. But given life as it is, with all its ambiguities and its tendency to present us not with a clear choice between good and evil, but with the necessity of finding the lesser of two (or more) acknowledged evils, the need to wrestle with abortion is urgent. The biggest problem of all is that the two extremes in the dispute—often through either blind rigidity or naïvety—have succumbed to the temptation to opt for simple black-and-white solutions propped up by equally simplistic slogans. The abolitionists want the rights of the unborn so entrenched in the Charter of Rights that any abortion would be illegal. Similar amendments to the US Constitution are being vociferously pushed forward by strange coalitions of religious and other groups who have never had any use for one another before. On the other hand, those who call for 'abortion on demand' wrongly give the impression that abortion is an ordinary kind of therapy, like having an appendix out or a tooth pulled.

Both extreme views are wrong. On closer examination, each represents an attempt by its supporters to enshrine their own belief systems—religious or otherwise—and impose them on the rest of society. Encouraging people to think of a fetus, even in its earliest phase, as no more than a lump of jelly or a group of quickly multiplying cells is to trivialize human life and raise questions about its protection in other cases—in old age, for example, or extreme illness. Moreover, using abortion as a means of birth control is clearly abhorrent to the majority of thinking citizens. But to make all abortions (including those of children who become pregnant or women who are victims of rape or incest) illegal is a form of legalized violence against women.

What is interesting is the way in which those with rigid views on either side can bend or change when faced with this moral dilemma themselves. That is why a recent document on abortion, released as a study paper for the Anglican Church, begins with a case history. The girl, seventeen, was a grade-twelve student at a school in the suburbs of a Canadian city. She was six weeks pregnant by the boyfriend she had been dating for a year. She had gone to a birth control centre and the two of them had decided on condoms, but were careless about their use. Both teenagers had received minimal sex education at school and none from their parents; yet since the girl asked few questions at the birth control centre, her counsellor assumed she was fairly knowledgeable. When she told the news to her family, the recriminations were fearful. Her parents were in full sympathy with the right-to-life movement on deeply held religious grounds. But within three weeks they had come to realize that their daughter's health and career would be jeopardized by bearing a child. In their view, she was simply too immature to handle motherhood, and after consultation with the family doctor, an abortion was arranged. Now, although the parents continue to voice their opposition to abortion, it is with some deeper sense of the brokenness of the human condition and the greyness of most moral and spiritual issues. The authors of the report— obstetricians and members of the primate's task force on human life—point out that of the sixty-five thousand, seven hundred and fifty-one legal abortions performed in Canada in 1980, almost thirty per cent of the patients were under the age of twenty. 'The social, economic, psychological, and physical conditions of many of these women were far worse than those of the girl cited,' they said. They note as well that they share her parents' moral and religious objections to abortion, but 'nevertheless acknowledge that these need to be tested against other moral and religious convictions we have about the quality, sancity, and freedom of human life in a complex modern world where sex and pregnancy are only part of the life situation.'

The Anglican report endorses the current situation in Canada, in which abortion can be obtained from hospitals where a three-doctor therapeutic abortion committee decides that the woman's life or health would be at risk in bearing a child. But the authors point out that many, especially the poor, cannot avail themselves of such help because of financial or geographical factors: only one in four general hospitals even has a therapeutic abortion committee—two hundred and sixty-nine in Canada. The report recommends free-standing clinics, outside of hospitals, as a way of providing more equal access. An evaluation of present facilities should be made lest anyone be denied access to legal abortion by such irrelevant factors as locale or poverty, it says. The most logical and urgent part of the report is its recognition that the only serious way for those concerned about abortions to diminish or abolish them is through an all-out contraception-education program 'at an early point in high school when the subject of health is still compulsory.' For example, the authors point out that, contrary to public opinion, 'access to sex education is extremely limited in Ontario'. There is no special budget for developing adequate curricula or teacher training, they say. Surely to oppose abortion on the one hand while on the other fiercely opposing sex education and the very contraceptives that could prevent unwanted pregnancies, as many religious groups do, is an illogical, often tragic, mistake.

The United Church of Canada has the most liberal stance on abortion of any major denomination (though there are many members who oppose this official position). Its General Council is on record as arguing that abortion should be removed entirely from the Criminal Code and treated as a matter between the woman, her partner, and the doctor. At the official level most other major denominations, while torn by the topic, support the present law. (It should be noted that although Orthodox Judaism is generally opposed to abortion except in extreme cases, it parts company with those groups that insist abortion is murder: in the classic Jewish tradition, the fetus only becomes a full person at birth.)

On mandatory celibacy

During my parish ministry and in the years since, I have often marvelled that what the Holy Spirit cannot get the churches to do, economic realities or other necessities very often can. It took soaring energy costs and rising construction expenses to make them take a different approach to the design and use of their buildings, for example. I predict that a similar phenomenon will sooner or later be experienced by the Roman Catholic Church in regard to its rule of obligatory celibacy for priests. Once the world-wide crisis caused by the increasing shortage of clergy reaches its peak, we will see an end to what is, after all, a man-made tradition that has wreaked hardship and much suffering over the centuries. To compound this shortage, some Catholic authorities say, their church is no longer drawing the quality of

young men once so readily available. As Cardinal Joseph Berna-
din of Chicago stated in 1980: 'We are not getting the best people in terms of intelligence, commitment, or generosity.' This
assessment has been echoed since then by Catholic educators
here as well.

Celibacy for clergy is not commanded in the New Testament—in fact, bishops in the earliest church were expressly bid-
den to have just one wife (I Tim. 3:2)—nor was it the rule of the
Roman Church for the first ten centuries at least. Peter was himself a married man, as were probably most of the other disciples.
Many of the women who followed Jesus and his disciples about
the country on their travels and 'ministered to them' were
undoubtedly the disciples' spouses. Jesus himself was unmarried
as far as we know (in spite of various modern speculations on the
matter), but there is no incontestable proof. He was called 'rabbi'
by the crowds and others in the New Testament and it was
foreign to the rabbinical tradition for a rabbi to remain single.
Certainly it would in no way affect my Christian beliefs if it were
somehow discovered that he had been a normally married man.
In any case, the rule of celibacy was never adopted by the Eastern Orthodox Churches except in the case of bishops, and even
today the Ukrainian Catholics, part of the Roman Catholic
Church since 1596, still have married clergy in Canada and elsewhere.

My observations, based on personal knowledge and a close
reading of the relevant literature, indicate that celibacy is not
just the major reason for the decline in numbers of priests, but a
serious problem for many already in the priesthood. A number
of studies have shown that inner turmoil over sexuality, combined with loneliness and a general sense of loss, consume the
energy and creativity of many priests. Alcoholism, drug addic-
tion, and emotional breakdowns take a heavy toll. Shocking as it
may seem, some priests are simply unable to fulfil their vows and
as a result either become involved in affairs, usually with parishioners, or have secret 'wives' whom they promise themselves
they will marry openly if and when the rule is finally dropped. I
have been called a number of times at the *Star*'s religion desk by
women involved with priests who want to know when I think the
Vatican will permit such marriages. Given the unyielding attitude of the present Pope, my advice to them has been: 'If you
are really serious about getting married, you had better turn

your affections elsewhere'. This aspect of the current crisis is a story that has never yet been fully written (apart from sensationalist treatment in the occasional commercial film).

One of the major documented reasons the Catholic Church is having special problems recruiting nationals as clergy in Africa and many other Third-World countries is the feeling in those cultures that it is against nature for a man not to take a wife and raise children. The incidence of priests having mistresses in such situations is also reportedly much higher: their flocks think more rather than less of such priests. In these cases, church law and nature or tribal custom are all taken care of. But such double-think exacts a toll of guilt from the more conscientious and sensitive. They are being forced to live a lie, and the tragedy is that it is entirely unnecessary. The rule of celibacy belongs not to essential church dogma—as Thomas Aquinas showed (Su. Theol. II, iii, q.ii, a.11)—but to church discipline. As such it can, must, and will be changed one day.

Those who think that my critique is biased because I am not a Roman Catholic (although my two younger girls were both educated in separate schools at my expense) should read *Ministry: Leadership in the Community of Jesus Christ* (1982) by the renowned Roman Catholic scholar Edward Schillebeeckx. He cites celibacy as the chief source of the current troubles in the priesthood, including the fact that about fifty per cent of all parishes and missions in the world are now without a resident priest. The Dutch theologian also points out that celibacy became official church doctrine only in the twelfth century, and argues that it is based on antiquated opinions about sexual intercourse being somehow dirty and sinful. He states further, and rightly, that celibacy can only be an effective, credible sign of single-minded devotion to God if it is plainly an option for the clergy, side by side with that of marriage. Numerous other Catholic theologians and prelates, as well as thousands of rank-and-file clergy, agree with him.

Incidentally, there are many thousands of priests who, although they left the active ministry to get married, would be very happy to take up their role again if the rule were changed. In the United States, a large group of married clergy called CORPUS has been advocating this move for some time.

A decade ago the late Charles C.E. Field, a professor at Trinity College in Toronto, did a three-year study of the training of ministers in which he concluded, among other things, that the majority of candidates were 'passive-dependent' personalities. And in 1977, an American psychologist said his tests on ordained clergy showed a similar pattern. Dr Mark Kane of Adelphi University's Institute of Advanced Psychological Studies set out his findings in *Lions of God, Lambs of God*. Extensive tests with fifty Roman Catholic priests and fifty Protestant ministers living in the New York area showed that clergymen have a greater degree of dependency and passivity than people in most other fields. The most significant aspect of this study was Kane's discovery that Roman Catholic priests showed a much greater sense of dependency and passivity than the other ministers did. He concluded that the requirement of celibacy is a major villain in the situation because, in his view, it keeps more independent personalities from offering themselves as candidates.

Sex, violence, and the Bible

Nudity, rape, gang-rape, incest, masturbation, polygamy, concubinage—it's all there, along with plenty of normal marital intercourse. So is raw violence, everything from torture to murder, even genocide, much of it performed in the name of the Lord. The book in question is not some cheap exploitative novel, but the Bible. That is why the so-called moral majorities in both Canada and the United States who want the 'dirty books' out of the schools should stop and think before their urge to censor carries them too far. For by their own criteria, the Bible itself could be banned.

Groups such as the ten-thousand-member Renaissance International, headed by Revd Ken Campbell of Milton, Ont., have targeted books in school librairies—some of them by leading Canadian authors—for attack, while one local school board has recently given principals the power to remove offending books from the library shelves. Meanwhile, in the United States a new coalition has been formed to monitor and attack explicit sexuality on television. Reports indicate that it is made up of TV-evangelist Jerry Falwell's Moral Majority and the National Federation for Decency, headed by Methodist Donald Wildmon of Tupelo, Miss. Falwell, a major spokesman for the burgeoning religious right, regularly flays immorality on television both from his pulpit and on his own TV program, The Old-Time Gospel Hour.

Ken Campbell has often accused Ontario school boards of allowing 'pornographic' material on school reading-lists and ignoring the Bible. But the book and film banners themselves have ignored many erotic and violent passages in the same book.

The eroticism of the beautiful love poem The Song of Solomon, for example, is frequently handled by declaring—with no proof or evidence whatever—that it is an allegory of Christ's love for his church, while violence of the bloodiest kind, such as the wholesale slaughter of various tribes by the Children of Israel, is justified as being performed at the Lord's command. The rendering of the King James Version helps to mask some of the reality because of its lovely archaic language: Genesis 4:1 tells us Adam 'knew' Eve, whereas the New English Bible explicitly states that 'Adam lay with his wife', and refers to the sons of the gods having 'intercourse' with the daughters of men. Yet careful reading even of the King James Version would shock the ultra-sensitive if they applied the same standards they insist on for secular works. But the shock does not hit them, partly because of the habit of suspending judgement while reading the Bible, and partly because of the selective reading pattern that focuses only on what is 'edifying'.

Those who insist that all books, films, and programs must reflect 'Judaeo-Christian values' must feel some discomfort at young people's reading the intriguing story (Gen.12:11 ff.) in which the patriarch Abraham goes down to Egypt. Knowing how very beautiful his wife is, he is afraid the Egyptians will lust after her and kill him to get her. 'Tell them you are my sister,' he instructs her. She does so, and as a result is admired by the Egyptians, praised to the Pharoah, and then taken to become a member of his harem. True, God sends plagues on Pharoah as a punishment and he eventually gives her up. But Abraham—who was given many gifts by the king for bringing his 'sister' or, in blunt language, pimping for her—does not see the evil of his deceit. In chapter 20, he pulls the same trick, which his son Isaac then uses in chapter 26. The ploy became standard procedure!

Most of these early biblical characters, including Abraham, had not only more than one wife, but several mistresses or concubines as well. In chapter 16 we learn how Sarah, who was initially barren, told her husband Abraham to have intercourse with her slave girl Hagar. Later, as a result of a feud between the two women, Hagar is cast adrift in the desert with her infant son Ishmael. However normal the practice at that time, there is little doubt that by today's standards Hagar was the victim of rape, since as a slave she had no choice. The story of Lot (19:1 ff.) is another strange one. Two angels come to the door of his house and are given hospitality. But a crowd of men of all ages, citizens of Sodom, gather outside shouting for Lot to bring them out in the street 'so we can have intercourse with them'. Lot, quite rightly, is indignant and firmly refuses. Those who use this passage to justify condemnation of homosexuality, however, neglect to note his counter-proposal to the lusting horde. Abraham's nephew tells the crowd he has two virgin daughters they can have instead: 'Let me bring them out to you and you can do what you like with them.' (19:8.) Fortunately for the unsuspecting girls, the angels intervene and God destroys Sodom.

From suggested gang-rape and sodomy, the narrative moves on to incest and 'rape' by females. In the same chapter (19:30 ff.) we learn that after his wife was killed by being turned into a pillar of salt, Lot lived in a cave with his two daughters. Here is the account in the King James Version: 'And the first-born said to the younger, "Our father is old, and there is not a man in the earth to come in unto us after the manner of all the earth: Come, let us make our father drink wine, and we will lie with him, that we may preserve the seed of our father." And they made their father drink wine that night; and the first-born went in, and lay with her father; and he perceived not when she lay down nor when she arose.' The trick is repeated the next night with the younger daughter, with the result that 'both were with child by their father'. There is no word of censure in the text.

Also in Genesis (chapters 29 and 30), Jacob is asked by both his wives, Leah and Rachel, to have intercourse with their respective slave girls. Both bear a number of children. In a very odd and intriguing story, Rachel, Jacob's favourite, wants some mandrakes (narcotic-producing plants used traditionally in love potions and to induce pregnancy) that one of Leah's sons has found. She thus makes a deal with her rival: in exchange for the mandrakes, she says Leah may have Jacob for the night to sleep with. Subsequently, Jacob decides to leave his father-in-law's territory and strike out on his own with his wives, concubines, and herds. However, Rachel steals her father's household goods, and when he comes in hot pursuit to retrieve them by searching Jacob's camp, she sits on them in her tent and lies to her father. She tells him she is menstruating—'the way of women is upon me'—and so cannot rise.

A full saga of sex, violence, and massive deceit can be found in Genesis 34, in which Dinah, one of Leah's daughters, is raped by

Shechem, a Hivite. Shechem offers to marry her with full dowry but is told he must first be circumcised, together with all his tribe. All the Hivite males are then circumcised to meet this condition. But 'on the third day, when they were sore', two of Jacob's sons (no doubt with servants to help) take their swords and massacre all of them in their weakness.

This is only a hint of the violence to come in later books (for example, the slaughter of the Amalekites, I Sam. 15:1-8), not to mention the 'cursing Psalms' or, in the New Testament, the Passion and crucifixion of Jesus himself. To say all of this is not to attack the Bible or weaken its authority. It is to take it with full seriousness 'cover to cover'—just as some would-be book banners or censors claim they do. To talk naïvely about giving the Bible to students or children in place of books that fail to 'uphold Judaeo-Christian values' is to trivialize it and fail to recognize the full gamut of the human sins, emotions, and actions it contains.

In an interview, Campbell said he was raised with the Bible as the dominant literary influence in his life, and could not remember ever being negatively influenced by either the language or the manner of describing sexual acts. 'However, how much that was due to the nature of the King James Version's language I can't tell,' he said. The evangelist said he has no use for those who water down the strong sex ('The Song of Songs is one of the best handbooks on marriage I know') and violence in Scripture, because the Bible is dealing realistically with human life: 'Let's face it; the impression some evangelicals give of the Judaeo-Christian world-view as a rosy-tinted, Pollyanna approach to life is a caricature.' Nevertheless, he admitted that he believes certain sections should not be read or discussed uncensored in the hearing of the young, noting that he was once embarrassed by taking part in family worship when the father of the house read a passage from Deuteronomy stating the penalty for the woman who interferes in a fight between two men by seizing the 'privates' of one. 'With small children present, it was most inappropriate,' he said. In my view, Campbell has yet to fully work out the problem of this 'inappropriate' side of the Bible—and he is not alone.

The churches as a new political force

Most informed Canadians have been first astonished, and then either inspired or enraged—depending on their viewpoint—by the way the Roman Catholic and other major traditional churches have been speaking out on political and social issues since the early 1960s. No longer do the clergy rest within their cloisters or hide behind their pulpits, six feet above argument and rebuttal, attending to the spiritual wants of their private flocks. Especially at the top levels of leadership, their whole agenda has radically changed.

In the past when the hardier clerical types ventured into the public domain, with a few notable exceptions, they were out to fault the more obvious evils of gambling, drinking, profanity, and illicit sex. Now literally nothing is secure from church analysis and action. Church people are still prepared (of course) to render to Caesar the things that are Caesar's and to God the things that are God's. It is just that they no longer accept Caesar's view that everything important in daily human life, everything practical, belongs to him, while only the peripheral, ethereal, or so-called 'spiritual' things belong to God. Not unnaturally, Caesar is upset by this turn of events. Things were rolling along just fine for the powers-that-be before all this activism nonsense began.

In the United States, the recent Pastoral Letter of the American Conference of Roman Catholic Bishops on nuclear weapons has dismayed the Pentagon and the President—and touched off an international furore. And in Canada 1983 began with one of the biggest religion stories ever carried by Canadian media: the New Year's statement on our economy by the social affairs commission of the Canadian Catholic Conference of Bishops. The bishops' 'ethical reflections' on the economy took sharp issue with government policies to fight inflation, and labelled the unemployment situation an unacceptable moral evil. Months later, the controversy over this unexpected incursion into the nitty-gritty of the market-place—especially the bishops' suggestions that Western capitalism did not come down from heaven with the Ten Commandments and may need drastic revision in the interest of justice—is still spawning heated editorials, articles, and grassroots debate. The prelates have been accused of everything from breaching the separation of church and state to trying to baptize Marxism and Marxist rhetoric. Government and corporation economists attacked them as 'naïve' and 'meddling'. However, to date almost every independent economist in the country has praised the statement's main thrust: that people matter more than profits. Leaders of the Anglican and Protestant Churches have rallied behind the bishops solidly, as have labour leaders and a whole range of academics in the social sciences.

I leave it to others to discuss the bishops' specific economic proposals. They seem eminently moral and workable to me, but any expertise I possess lies elsewhere. What matters to me is that the bishops' action be seen in its proper context as part of the much wider and deeper social activism now characteristic of all leading denominations. Roman Catholic social teaching goes back at least to Pope Leo XIII and his famous 1891 encyclical on social issues, *Rerum Novarum* (of new things), but it took a great leap forward at the Second Vatican Council, called by Pope John XXIII and begun in 1962. On the Protestant side, the World Council of Churches, now made up of more than three hundred independent churches world-wide, has been moving steadily towards greater social and political involvement ever since it was founded in Amsterdam in 1948. Those who feel threatened by the so-called politicization of the churches and love simple slogans see this activism as the result of a massive Communist plot. The truth is more complex and less amenable to paranoia.

Before setting out the real forces at work here, it is worth noting that the Canadian bishops' New Year's broadside was very much in tune with what they have been saying for several years now in their annual Labour Day messages and elsewhere. What is more, the clerics prefaced their statement by noting it was wholly derived from two sources: the 'preferential option for the poor' made clear in the Bible, which has been affirmed by World Synods of Bishops, and was fully adopted at Medellín, Colombia, and Puebla, Mexico, by the Catholic bishops of Latin America; and the 1982 encyclical *Laborem Exercens* (on work) of Pope John Paul II. You can't get more Catholic than that.

The prime reason for the present stance of the churches (surprising as this must seem to the critics) is a fresh understanding of the Old and New Testaments and of Jesus himself. The struggles for freedom and equality that have marked the past thirty-five years—from those of colonial nations to that of blacks or of women in North America—have led many Christians to read their bibles in a new light. The theme of liberation, both personal and social, is now seen as the unifying note throughout the Bible, from the exodus out of Egypt (a highly political event) to the great prophets, to Jesus, to the apocalypse itself. There is no way you can read Amos or Isaiah now and say that the churches must stick to 'smells and bells' or the cure of the soul alone. It is impossible to read the Gospels seriously and then be content to go around uttering pious blessings on the social status quo. You can't accept a God who creates the world and then reveals himself in and through human beings, without knowing that there can be no false barrier between what is religious and what is not: there is a religious or 'depth' dimension to every part of life. Those who feel that economics or Indian land claims or racism or nuclear war are outside the purview of the church should read Luke 4:17, where Jesus, quoting Isaiah, sets out his 'political platform'. They might also scan Matt. 25:31 ff.: the gospel is about the salvation or liberation of the whole person in community with others; Jesus opts for the poor, the outsider.

This is why the major Canadian churches have coalitions on everything from the social responsibilities of big corporations to human rights in Latin America. This is also why the World Council of Churches gives humanitarian aid to some liberation groups in southern Africa. The WCC's controversial Program to Combat Racism (PCR) is active because to be credible the churches could not go on forever talking about how nice it would be to end racism. They had to do something, whatever misunderstanding and calumny might result. But once you see the oppressed and the marginal as your principal responsibility as a Christian, you begin to see evil in a different way. Especially in the poorer developing nations, it quickly became evident that disease, prostitution, hunger, poor housing, illiteracy, and the rest were neither accidents nor natural phenomena. They were the results of specific systems and social structures, either local or international, that were unjust. The churches began to realize that side by side with personal sin there is corporate sin.

In the past a narrow individualistic view of the gospel let the real sources of the gravest injustices off the hook almost entirely. For example, you could be the God-fearing head of a multinational corporation and kneel devoutly in prayer each week without thinking that across the seas you were part of a web of oppression crushing the poor. The churches have seen clearly that to deal with hunger and other Third-World needs—or unemployment at home—the old bandaid approach of traditional charity and relief is not enough. The system itself must be changed, including such things as world trade agreements and the overseas investment policies of banks and other institutions. The overriding political, social, and moral problem of our time is that of the arms race and the possibility of the holocaust of all humanity—perhaps even of the planet itself. From the Pope to the six Canadian church leaders who met with Prime Minister Trudeau just before Christmas 1982, religious voices are being raised in protest. And rightly so. To claim anything whatever to do with the Prince of Peace and not to agonize over the current nuclear madness is to commit a form of blasphemy. The unique global peril is calling forth a unique Christian response. For these leaders not to speak out at such a juncture would be to abrogate any claim to moral or spiritual leadership whatever.

One final word. Critics who deplore or mock the churches' speaking out on socio-economic problems ignore one basic fact. There has never been a period when religion and politics were not closely intertwined. The churches have always been political even when they most loudly proclaimed their neutrality and 'innocence'. In truth, the awareness of this reality has been a part of the current trend. Leaders of various denominations have seen that up until fairly recently they worked hand-in-glove with the dominant forces of society. Whether inadvertently or deliberately, they shored up the ruling classes and blessed them in all their ways. In some situations, by saying nothing they gave clear approval and assent, just as those evangelists do who gladly go to (and are equally gladly welcomed by the authorities in) such places as South Korea, or Guatemala, or, indeed, Moscow. The most obvious example is the case of the Roman Catholic Church in Latin America. For centuries the hierarchy there sided with the ruling juntas or oligarchies and educated their children in their schools and colleges. Cardinals and archbishops were given honorary titles in the army and received Vatican medals in return. Most of these practices have now changed, but today the church there is radically split over the issue of activism, some bishops siding with the priests and nuns who work with the poor, the others blessing the helicopters sent in as part of American military aid—as in El Salvador.

Many, especially those most affected by the critique of the churches and their new activism for the oppressed, wish the whole matter would go away. Some church members have quit, withdrawn their financial support, or organized into a kind of opposition party. However, judging from the current leadership in the Anglican, United, and Roman Catholic Churches in Canada in particular, we have only seen the beginning of this process. I predict that the socio-political involvement of these and other main-line churches will not only continue but grow even bolder and more vocal in the months ahead.

A postscript: This opinion was confirmed by the strong stand on social justice taken at the Sixth Assembly of the World Council of Churches in Vancouver, July-August 1983.

Are the churches moving left?

When Moses told the Pharoah to 'let my people go', he did not know he was founding a liberation theology that twentieth-century critics would brand as subversive and Marxist. When the prophet Amos challenged the rulers and the economic injustices of ancient Judah and Israel in the name of God, he did not know that similar activities would one day be labelled unpatriotic or Communist. When Jesus read from Isaiah in the synagogue in Nazareth and met with open hostility, there was nothing to indicate that he knew this would be the fate of those who followed him and took a similar tack in the 1980s. But no doubt he did: after all, he knew it had cost Isaiah his life, and would cost him his as well. Humans have always destroyed the prophets—those who disturb the status quo—and made heroes of them afterwards.

It is worth hearing the words that Jesus read: 'The spirit of the Lord is upon me, for he has anointed me to make known (by word and deed) good news to the poor; he has sent me to proclaim release for prisoners, sight for the blind, freedom for the oppressed—to make known the acceptable year of the Lord.' (Luke 4:17.) The safe way to 'hear' this passage is to make it refer only to so-called spiritual realities. You can then sit in a racist church in South Africa and really believe that these words have no application to the gross evils of apartheid; you can relax in a church in Canada and hear in them no relevance for the more than a million unemployed outside. In fact, you can take the whole of Christianity—even Jesus' clear words about peace and peacemakers—and twist it so that it deals only with the soul or one's own private pipeline to God. The problem is that no one, not even Jesus, gets crucified for that. It disturbs no one; offends no one; nor does it question any established order. But once you take Jesus' words seriously; once you stop the dodge of spiritualizing everything and realize he might have meant it when he sided with the poor, the outsiders, the marginalized, and the sinners, you incur a great deal of risk—as the traditional churches are now finding out.

For those who have suckled longest and most safely at the breast of any existing system, social or economic, will always fight tooth and nail to resist change or challenge. Whether the structures that support them are just or unjust is irrelevant to their response. We all share in this instinct. The threat need not even be a real one: all that's required is for it to be perceived as such. In earlier times (and in many parts of the world still today), the instant reaction was one of violence. In the West, however, smearing or killing the upstart's reputation works just about as well and is decidedly less messy. This is precisely the process at work in the current campaign to discredit the World Council of Churches (WCC) on the one hand and the Roman Catholic Church—particularly here and in Latin America—on the other. The WCC, made up of more than three hundred independent churches from Pentecostal to Eastern Orthodox, has been the target of a well-orchestrated, well-funded slur campaign for years. But the criticism has stepped up sharply in the early 1980s. In the case of the Catholics, it was at first reserved for certain 'maverick' priests, nuns, and religious, mainly in Third-World countries. The American bishops' stand on nuclear arms, however, and the Canadian bishops' intervention over the economic system, have provoked a wider attack. And when the American prelates bring out their own critique of the United States' economy in 1984, the rising fury will know no bounds.

What the critics of these activist churches have said, are saying now, and will continue to say, is that both the WCC and the Roman Catholic Church have taken vast strides to the political left and have aligned themselves with the forces of Marxist revolution. Most of the charges are made by way of innuendo, guilt through association, and quarter-truths rather than by outright accusation. For example, it is revealing that the more hysterical of the responses to the Canadian bishops' New Year's statement went on about the clerics' alleged 'Marxist rhetoric' and 'Marxist analysis' (one Toronto columnist's meanderings bore the headline, 'Bishops Get High Marx') without citing any instances of the same. Apparently the bishops' chief 'sin' consisted in daring to wonder aloud whether our present form of capitalism really is working to the greatest benefit of the greatest number; to suggest, for example, that a system which has allowed one and two-fifths million people to be out of work while others make large profits is perhaps less than perfect. But if it be leftist or even Communist to criticize capitalism or the Western way of life, then Pope John Paul II must be tarred with the same brush. This courageous survivor of life under Communist rule in Poland has frequently made it clear he has plenty of reservations about the lifestyles and philosophies of both East and West. Moreover, anything the least bit radical in the bishops' statement came either directly from him or from the Bible. The calumny directed against the Roman Catholic Church, though, is still a fairly minor matter compared with what has been written and said about the WCC.

It is not surprising that right-wing institutions, such as the US-based Institute for Religion and Democracy or the South African government, are out to malign the WCC's activities. Nor can one expect anything different from Revd Jerry Falwell, who devoted most of the March 1983 issue of his magazine *Fundamentalist Journal* to an all-out onslaught on both the National Council of Churches in the United States (NCC) and the WCC—repeating the slander that money given to either group can end up buying guns to kill white missionaries and others in Africa. But even otherwise reputable sources, such as *Reader's Digest* and CBS-TV's 60 Minutes, have been duped into recycling total distortions. In its January 1983 issue, *Reader's Digest* (US edition) ran an article entitled 'Do You Know Where Your Church Offerings Go?—You'd Better Find Out Because They May Be Supporting Revolution Instead of Religion'. This followed the line of the August 1982 piece 'Karl Marx or Jesus Christ?'[1] Then on 23 January 1983, 60 Minutes flew to the attack with a program called 'The Gospel According to Whom?' Even the not-particularly-religious New York weekly the *Village Voice* called the show a 'calculated distortion' and 'one of the most delirious spasms of open red-baiting since the McCarthy era.' The NCC has denounced the program as 'distorted, sensational, and biased' and denied various allegations, including the lie that the WCC and NCC support armed revolution around the world.[2]

Having seen the program twice, I must describe it as one of the worst and most misleading pieces of alleged investigative journalism I have ever come across in twelve years of covering religion in the news. By deceitful use of pictures of guerrillas, church offerings, and dead missionaries in Zimbabwe, the false impression was given that any money put on the collection plate goes to buy guns for terrorists who then slaughter clergy and their families overseas. In truth, the only money that goes to black or other liberation groups is for humanitarian purposes (medical needs, food, education, housing) and is an infinitesimally small fraction of all the WCC money (sixty-six million dollars in 1982) that goes to traditional relief and rescue work. Despite all lies to the contrary, it has never been shown by anyone that a single cent of WCC donations has gone for a single bullet anywhere. The white missionaries killed in Rhodesia-Zimbabwe during the fight for independence were murdered not by Mugabe's forces, as criticisms such as 60 Minutes' infer (without offering a shred of proof), but—and this according to former members of the government forces—by Selous Scouts, a special army group designated to discredit the rebels. (It should be pointed out here that the WCC's Program to Combat Racism, from which grants to liberation movements come, is a special fund. Only the money that member churches specifically designate for the PCR can end up in it. Significantly, the amount being given continues to increase in spite of five years of attacks against the fund.) Most contemptible of all in the 60 Minutes slur was its suggestion that the dissident clergy and others who were shown criticizing the NCC, and by association the WCC, were typical representatives of their denominations. For example, the program showed Revd Michael Le Saux, a pastor in Logansport, Ind., urging his congregation to support a resolution calling for his United Methodist Church to withdraw from the WCC; what it failed to point out was that this resolution was later defeated by a margin of ten to one at the UMC's annual conference in June 1982.

Two of the most vocal critics interviewed, Ed Robb and Richard Neuhaus, are leading figures in an organization funded by very conservative private foundations whose only function to date has been to manufacture, according to the NCC, 'an arsenal of vague and damaging allegations against church leaders'. Their partisan, highly political affiliations and purpose were never made clear to the viewers. The truth is that all attempts to document a connection between Marxist-Leninists, or leftists, or Communists and either the WCC or various groups of Roman Catholic bishops have failed miserably. The clerical use of Marxist analysis or 'rhetoric', where it occurs, no more makes the user a Marxist than the use of Freudian terms makes the user a Freudian. As the New Testament shows, the devil can quote Scripture without being a Christian. Clearly there has been a major shift on the part of main-line denominations towards involvement with the nitty-gritty issues of day-to-day existence. But if to become involved in this way is to be leftist or worse, then Jesus was a leftist too.

NOTES

[1]Detailed rebuttals of both articles are available (from the WCC's Communications Department, P.O. Box 66, 150, route de Ferney, 1221 Geneva 20, Switzerland). But few will read them.
[2]The NCC too has printed a detailed and indignant rebuttal, which can be obtained from most national offices of Canadian churches that are members of the WCC.

The price of activism

There is a huge problem for the major churches, Roman Catholic and Protestant, as they become increasingly active in the search for social and political justice in Canada and overseas. It has nothing whatever to do with the bogus charges of leftism or Marxism already examined. Rather, it has to do with the very source of the new emphasis on human rights and social justice itself: i.e. the Bible.

The Bible points out that it is necessary to take the 'plank' out of your own eye before you can see well enough to take the 'speck' out of the other person's eye. In addition to telling us that judgement must begin at the house of the Lord, it warns us to heed the admonition, 'Physician, heal thyself'. To put it plainly, you can't press credibly for human rights elsewhere if they are trampled on in your own institution. You can't argue and theologize honestly about a 'preferential option for the poor'—a major concern of the Roman Catholic Church today—if the church you represent is embarrassingly rich and its leaders and/or members are doing the best balancing act they can between serving God and serving Mammon. Who can believe you when you say you are wholly on the side of the marginalized and underprivileged if at the same time you are always seeking to maintain your own very privileged position?

The churches complain, rightly, about the way opposition or dissent is handled by various totalitarian regimes of both the right and the left. But today, from the Jehovah's Witnesses and the Mormons through the Anglicans and the Roman Catholics, the religious hierarchies themselves can be ruthless enough with those they label heretics. (In the past, when religious leaders had the same absolute power that rulers in the USSR or El Salvador now do, popes, bishops, and clergy of all stripes were not at all squeamish about using torture or the dungeon.) It is good to

protest the great evils of institutional racism in South Africa, as
the moderator of the United Church and some of his clergy and
church members did in April 1983, outside the South African
Consulate in Toronto. It is encouraging to hear Pope John Paul
II speaking of human rights wherever his travels take him. But
in neither of these two churches do women really have the full
equality that even the Bible seems to demand. In fact, where the
rights of women are concerned, religion of nearly every kind
still stands as a real obstacle to progress.

Where the churches' position is the weakest for criticizing the
socio-economic order is in the area of special privilege. How can
these institutions call for more taxes on the wealthy to give more
to those Canadians without privilege, when they themselves pay
no taxes (other than local improvements) on their own very
extensive buildings? I well remember a case in 1976 when secular planners in the Kitchener-Waterloo area were scandalized by
the United and Lutheran Churches' selling property for tax-free
profits ranging from six hundred and twenty-five to one thousand and twenty-five per cent. The sites in question were purchased in the early 1960s for token amounts. True, the churches
had not intended to speculate on the land—a process that drives
up prices and makes housing for low-income citizens an impossible luxury—but they did not hand over any of the profits
either. This kind of thing goes on all the time, to the benefit of
all denominations. Several recent deals affecting large churches
in the Toronto core have, through the sale of 'air rights' over the
churches or of pieces of their actual properties, brought in many
millions of dollars, all of it tax-free. The truth is that if religious
institutions here and all over the world (one prime example is
the city of Rome) were to pay taxes at the going rate, there
would be more than enough funds to house most of earth's
homeless immediately.

The churches' relations with the state have been more or less
cosy ever since the Emperor Constantine converted to Christianity, more than fifteen hundred years ago. Today that arrangement seems neither moral nor just. Constantine at least had the
excuse that (at his command) all the citizens were then officially
Christians. In our much-vaunted Canadian mosaic, however,
agnostics and just plain 'religious nothings' constitute, according
to some pollsters, up to one-third of the population. Why should
the churches get a free ride partly at their expense? Many

churches, of course, minister to the whole community in dozens of ways, providing everything from day-care facilities to drop-in centres for young people or seniors. But thousands of other church buildings never open their doors except to members of the congregation. I once asked the pastor of a large, extremely conservative downtown congregation what his church did for the poor of the area. He replied with a perfectly serious face that his elders 'dispense the odd teabag' to those asking for handouts. His church is bolted shut ninety per cent of the time. The answer to those who object that taxing the churches would close hundreds of them tomorrow is, 'not necessarily.' In any case, closing some of them might actually prove a blessing.

It is hard to do much for the kingdom of God if you are struggling so hard as a church that all your time must be taken up with money-raising schemes. Better to join with others a few blocks away. If a system were to be organized whereby each church, temple, or synagogue were given a tax credit for every totally public use of its buildings that it offered, costs could be lightened and the entire community around would benefit. At the same time, the religious community would be free to play the role of honest prophet and critic. It is impossible to do that now when the churches are so closely knit into the very structures that they find fault with. You can't radically affect the status quo if you owe your very existence to it. This is as true here as it is in Latin America.

One final thought: The Anglican Church of Canada and the United Church were engaged in a fund-raising drive in 1983— for very worthy causes—in which each church aimed at a target of forty million dollars. The Sharelife Campaign of the Roman Catholic Archdiocese of Toronto the same year was for nearly six million dollars—again for very worthy projects. Churches as they are now constituted always need money. The catch is that to raise the millions involved in the three cases cited, each church had to go not just to its ordinary members but also to some of the very same huge corporations whose activities here and in other countries have so often been the target of church wrath. There is an obvious ambiguity and ambivalence in this, and it must be more than a little embarrassing for the church leaders who go hat-in-hand to make these corporate calls. I am not saying they should stop criticizing the big corporations—or asking them for money. But they must do a much better job of communication than they have in the past, with outsiders and church-members alike—after all, the ranks of business include many people who sometimes go to church. Big business needs to understand more completely why the churches are speaking and acting as they are. More dialogue and less confrontation could help to clear the path towards justice and peace.

After the
Virgin Mary

Women and religion

I was standing one Sunday morning at the door of the downtown Toronto church where I had preached for a number of years, accepting the greetings of the parishioners as they filed out. I was dressed, as usual, in a white surplice over an ankle-length black cassock. As I smiled politely and shook hands I felt a tug at my robe and looked to see a small inner-city urchin grinning grubbily up at me and saying: 'What you got that skirt on for mister?' Not a bad question! The point of the story is that the Anglican, Roman Catholic, and Orthodox Churches all dress their clergy in robes that, while they are supposed to play down sexual differences, today look actually feminine. Yet all of these churches have had great difficulty with the concept of women priests.

There is no question but that women's struggle to attain their basic human rights and become equal partners with men in religion, as well as the market-place, has been one of the top-ranking stories of the past decade. My own files show that I have written more about this single issue than almost any other since 1971. Both the story and the struggle are far from being over.

The plain truth is that religion today is still an immensely powerful force holding women back from full emancipation. While the problem is especially severe in the fundamentalist segments of Islam and Judaism, in Mormonism, in the Jehovah's Witnesses, and in fundamentalist Christianity, it is equally evident in the Roman Catholic Church, with full papal blessing. It also persists in the Anglican, Presbyterian, and United Churches—even though they have ordained women clergy for some years. The churches call for justice in South Africa, El Salvador, Poland, the Soviet Union; but they have yet to answer the demands of justice where women—who make up more than half their member-ship—are concerned. Foot-dragging male hierarchies cite all kinds of arguments, traditional and theological, against women taking their full place in organized religion, but their real reasons for stalling are sociological and cultural.

Judaism, Christianity, and Islam were all born in a sociological matrix that discriminated against women. Jesus didn't pick twelve male Apostles because maleness was essential to Apostleship or what later became the priesthood. He did so because, given the prejudices and conventions of his day, no other arrangement would have worked. Sex and sex roles have no more to do with ordained ministry than being a male had to do with Jesus' own unique mission. God is certainly neither male nor female; and if Jesus' task was to reveal God, then his sexual nature was irrelevant. Had the world been different 'in the days of Caesar Augustus', a female agent of God would have done equally well. Therefore I agree with what Most Revd Robert Runcie, Archbishop of Canterbury, told an interviewer in 1981: 'The best argument for women's ordination, in my view, is this: if priesthood is to represent God to humankind and humankind to God in these days when exclusive male leadership is no longer the case in most walks of life, it's hard to justify the fact that men alone can represent God to mankind and mankind to God.'[1]

Unfortunately mere ordination, while a major step forward, does not in itself solve the equality issue. The United Church of Canada has been ordaining women since 1936; the Presbyterian Church since 1966; and the Anglican Church of Canada since 1976. Yet women clergy in all three denominations still have real problems finding congregations. Some male clergy in the Presbyterian Church are so opposed to female ordination that there is real danger of a split. Convention Baptists too have ordained a handful of female clergy, but have no pulpits prepared to take them. As one top official told me recently: 'We haven't even begun to come to grips with this issue yet.' Regrettably, though not surprisingly, Pope John Paul II is intransigent in his insistence that there will be no women priests in his church. His arguments are based on a questionable tradition and the old chestnut (repudiated even by many Roman Catholic scholars) about the importance of Jesus and the Twelve having been male.

It seems the pontiff has chosen to ignore Sister Theresa Kane.

But many, including eyewitnesses like myself, will not soon forget her courageous words when she rose to welcome him in the presence of seven thousand nuns at the Shrine of the Immaculate Conception in Washington on 5 October 1979. Shocking John Paul visibly—since hers was the only voice to tell him something he didn't want to hear in his whole Irish-American tour—Sister Theresa stated that thousands of North American Catholic women were suffering 'intense suffering and pain' because of their exclusion from the priesthood and other ministries. She said women must be given a chance at inclusion 'in all ministries of our church.' The new Code of Canon Law, promulgated in 1983 by the Pope, essentially repudiates all her arguments. True, women are admitted to a range of new duties in church administration, but they are still barred from the priesthood. Indeed, they may not even act as acolytes at the altar: little girls are not permitted to be servers. Maintaining not only the priest's role of consecrating bread and wine but also the very minor role of assisting at the altar as the exclusive privilege of males is clear evidence of a sexual bias and discrimination for which no justification can be found either in the Bible or in contemporary insights. It is wrong, and more and more Catholic women are prepared to say so. Over eighty-five per cent of North American Catholic women approve of the feminist movement in general, and about one-third are opposed to the ban on women priests, according to the most recent polls I have read.

Significantly, the Archdiocese of Toronto recently mounted a rather sensational campaign to recruit priests in the face of a critical shortage. Large billboards depicted Jesus pinned to the cross, with a city in the background, above a stark caption: 'Dare to be a priest like me!' Imaginative as the advertising was, I doubt it will achieve much in concrete results as long as the rule on a celibate all-male clergy is maintained. What is genuinely tragic is that so many people must continue to suffer the lack of priestly ministrations, when the Roman Catholic Church has an enormous reservoir of highly trained, theologically and pastorally capable persons ready in the wings, i.e. its thousands and thousands of nuns. Nor are they the only ones: at present, about one-third of the more than two hundred Catholic students enrolled at the Toronto School of Theology are women. Together with the women of other denominations training for ministry in the churches, they represent a resource that must be used—and not simply to fill a gap.

For it would be a real mistake to imagine that most women who are or aspire to be priests or ministers want nothing more than to mimic their male counterparts. They want a radically different kind of ministry for themselves: one that truly reflects women's particular insights and strengths. Furthermore, as women gradually 'take back the church' (to use a slogan of the more militant Christian feminists), traditional theology will have to change. The present male-dominated stereotype of God will be drastically altered once there is true equality for women at all levels of church life and full acceptance of the female principle. For centuries, a god made in the image of a harsh, aggressive, macho male has been used to give divine blessing to both unlimited wars and exploitative social systems. But once it becomes natural to think—as Pope John Paul I, 'Papa Luciani', once said during his brief reign—of God as mother as well as father, the very concept of God (himself or herself) is revolutionized. For instance, the christening of a Trident nuclear submarine 'Corpus Christi' (the body of Christ) becomes an even more grotesque blasphemy when God is seen as a God of tenderness and mercy, of motherly nurturing and care for all the Trident's intended victims. Never again can we be quite so ready to see men take the implements of butchery and go against their fellows with full church blessing and the cry, 'God is on our side'.

NOTE

[1]Nevertheless, as late as August 1983, Runcie was telling reporters at the World Council of Churches assembly that the time is still not right for the Anglican Church in England to ordain women.

Feminism and the Virgin Mary

Many millions of Christians in the Eastern Orthodox and Roman Catholic Churches hold a faith in which a woman, Mary, plays a central role. Paradoxically, however, devotion to Mary has not created a climate for feminism—in fact, quite the opposite.

News that devotion to the Virgin Mary is on the upswing may bring comfort to Catholic traditionalists dismayed at the decline in saying of the rosary and other Marian devotions since the Second Vatican Council. But it is hardly cheering information for Protestants concerned about closer ties with Rome; nor does it sit well with progressive Catholics who have always been somewhat embarrassed by the 'Marian excesses' typical of many Latin countries. Just now there is a greater demand for rosaries and books on the Virgin than there has been for several years; the Legion of Mary is said to be growing (members give out 'Miraculous Medals' in their door-to-door visits); some Ontario churches have revived the Holy Hour, which includes the rosary; and others have held outdoor rosary services. Yet Vatican II had led to the abandonment of many such traditional church practices.

Most Revd G. Emmett Carter confirms that devotion to Mary is on the upswing in Toronto and says he sees it as a positive thing: 'There was a difference between what the Vatican II fathers actually said and what people perceived. They were trying to regulate the manner in which devotion to Mary was being manifested in some quarters; you could say it was putting Mary back into her proper place.' Asked whether he saw any dangers in the current revival, he answered: 'No, there never has been any excess in this country. The Council had in mind the kind of abuses where Mary sometimes took precedence over everything else.'

Undoubtedly the single greatest impulse towards a renewed veneration of the mother of Jesus has come from Pope John Paul II, who includes some reference or prayer to Mary in every address or homily. Indeed, his invocation of the Virgin at the moment of his first appearance on the balcony at St Peter's after his election caused traditionalist groups in Rome to dub him immediately 'the Pope of the Madonna'. In his talks the Pope has often returned to this theme, appealing to the faithful to pray to the Virgin for an increase in the number of young men offering themselves for the priesthood. He has frequently noted also the importance for him of the 'Black Madonna' of Czestochowa—a dark-toned picture of the Madonna which has hung in the monastery of Jasna Gora in Poland for nearly six hundred years as a symbol of divine protection and freedom from tyranny. John Paul's devotion to Mary, emphasized time and time again, not only reflects his Polish background, but may well also be connected to the fact that he lost his own mother at the age of nine.

There is little information about the mother of Jesus in the New Testament and the very earliest Fathers of the Church. However, by the end of the sixth century the doctrines that she remained perpetually a virgin and that at her death she was taken bodily up into heaven had become firmly established. (The teaching that she was totally free from original sin—the doctrine of the Immaculate Conception—was hotly debated in the Middle Ages, but was not officially defined until 1854.) During the Protestant Reformation, a series of reformers attacked the then-current beliefs about her on the grounds that they were unscriptural and tended to obscure the role of Christ as 'the one mediator between God and man'. Martin Luther (1483-1546) stressed Mary's humility, and was one of the foremost critics of excessive devotion to her as a 'false glorification'. The Church of England expressly forbade the invocation in prayer of any saints, including the Virgin Mary, but later trends in the church have restored her to a position of deep respect and even, in High Anglican circles, a degree of veneration approaching that of the Catholic Church.

Recently in the United States, ecumenical talks and studies between Lutherans and Roman Catholics have resulted in a startlingly frank statement. Two top Roman Catholics, Revd Raymond Brown, a noted New Testament scholar, and Revd Joseph Fitzmyer of the Catholic University of America, worked with two equally capable Lutheran scholars, Karl Donfried and John Reumann, to edit the results of an exhaustive study, by a combined Catholic and Protestant team, of the New Testament evidence on Mary. Now in book form, *Mary in the New Testament* (1978) notes that the two sides found they shared a common regard for the 'mother of Jesus' as John's Gospel consistently calls her. However, the team concluded that Mary probably misunderstood her son and was outside his circle of friends and believers until after the Resurrection (Acts 1:14). The negative image of Mary comes from Mark's Gospel, the earliest: the episode in which Jesus' family comes to take him home, alleging that he is 'beside himself' (3:21), and the passage in which Jesus says that a prophet has honour everywhere except in his own country and among his own relatives (6:4). The other two Synoptic Gospels, Matthew and Luke, omit the first story and soften the second. Even in John's Gospel Jesus treats his mother with more than a little firmness when she tries to interfere in his ministry (2:4). At the cross, however, John describes how Jesus entrusts his mother to the 'beloved disciple' (19:26), and so Mary becomes, in the tradition, a model of belief and discipleship for the church. The team was divided over whether the evidence points to Mary's having had other children after Jesus or not. The New Testament speaks of his 'brothers', but the word in the Greek can also mean cousins or kinsmen. Protestants take these as blood brothers, whereas the Roman Catholic and Eastern Orthodox Churches have opted for the kinsmen concept. But a 1976 commentary by the German Catholic scholar Rudolph Pesch comes out with the blunt opinion, which I share, that these relatives were indeed natural brothers. As for the later doctrines—that Mary herself was immaculately conceived, without sin, and later ascended bodily into heaven—the scholars have little to say, since there is absolutely nothing in the New Testament concerning either.

Charles Davis, a former leading British Catholic theologian who left the priesthood during the 1960s exodus and has held various teaching posts in Canada, is even tougher on Mariology. Once asked whether he agreed with the contention of some Protestants today that devotion to Mary is an antidote to male chau-

vinism in religion, Davis answered that he felt the very opposite
was true. He said: 'Mariology as a concrete, historical form of
religious outlook and piety is the counterpart of the growth of
the dominance type of authority structure in the church and the
product of unhealthy sexuality.' It is true that devotion to Mary
has produced music, art, and authentic spiritual experience in
the history of the church. But I agree with those who say it has
often distorted the church's attitude to women, sexuality, and
authority in general. Davis believes that a reformed Marian
devotion is desirable but wellnigh impossible: 'It seems to me we
know next to nothing historical about the mother of Jesus.
There is simply no adequate historical basis for a Mariology.' As
a former New Testament professor, I can confirm that his statement is correct.

For a fascinating, and at the same time devastating, assessment of the cult of the Virgin in its most extreme forms, one
should read Marina Warner's book, *Alone of All Her Sex: The Myth
and Cult of the Virgin Mary* (1976). Miss Warner was raised in a
convent and joined the Sodality of Our Lady as a 'Child of Mary'
when she was sixteen. Later, disillusioned by the threats of hell-
fire and the guilt inspired by the teaching that every sexual
impulse was 'lust' and a betrayal of the Virgin's demands of chas-
tity, she embarked on a quest. After months of research, she set
out to visit the principal Marian shrines in Europe: 'I wanted to
examine the paradox that a religion which accords the highest
honour and love to a woman keeps women in a subordinate role,
that the countries where the Virgin is most powerful are also
those where women have the least mobility and influence in the
public sphere, that in the celebration of the Ideal Woman somehow humanity and women are both subtly denigrated.' Her
book is obviously not the whole story, but it does raise serious
questions, which remain problematic both for the Pope and for
those who share his Marian enthusiasm today. Meanwhile,
Marian doctrine will continue to be a topic in ecumenical discus-
sions between various churches and the Church of Rome.

Women, Jesus, and the Bible

Jesus was a radical feminist and it follows that anyone professing to belong to him should be one too. So more and more Christian women are saying these days. They are right, and those who would like to feel that this is just one more attempt to harness the name of Jesus to a currently popular movement have a lot to contend with. Christian feminists are basing their case squarely on the Bible. Not just on one or two passages—as those who have suggested that Jesus was the first ban-the-bomber or the first hippie tried to do—but on a broadly argued examination of the Gospels.

The evidence these women have produced is extraordinarily compelling. Before looking at it, however, one has first to set aside certain contemporary stereotypes conjured up by the word 'feminist'. By calling Jesus a radical feminist, they mean that he treated women with equality and approached them primarily as human persons, and in so doing broke radically with the customs of his day: the description has nothing whatever to do with strident female supremacy or anti-male go-it-aloneness. Certainly, in terms of the negative argument, there is nothing in the Gospels to suggest that Jesus ever gave any sign that he thought of women as inferior or advocated treating them as subordinate to men—quite the contrary.

But to get the full impact of his positive attitude towards women, one must first know something of their status in the society of first-century Palestine. Women were not allowed to study the Torah or books of the Law. In the Talmud, Rabbi Eliezer declares: 'Rather should the words of the Torah be burned than entrusted to a woman. . . . Whoever teaches his daughter the Torah is like one who teaches her lasciviousness.'

Women—like small children and slaves—were not obliged to recite the Shema, the morning prayer, or the prayer at meals. In fact, the Talmud says: 'Let a curse come upon the man who has his wife or children say grace for him.' Male Jews prayed daily, thanking God for making them neither gentiles, nor women, nor ignorant men. Women—again like children and slaves—did not qualify to make up the number (ten) required for a worshipping congregation. In the great temple of Jerusalem they were restricted to an outer court five steps below the men's. A rabbi was advised not to speak even to his wife or daughter in the street, let alone any other woman. Philo, a contemporary of Jesus, argued that women ought never to leave their own households except to go to the synagogue and that at a time when most other people would be at home. Women, then, were thought of almost entirely in terms of home-making, childbearing, and nurturing. Wives were not permitted to divorce their husbands, and the normal lot of all women was to be under the tutelage of men—fathers, brothers, husbands.

It is only against this background that the radical nature of Jesus' attitude can be fully seen. Clearly, there were women who not only learned religious truth from him, but followed him about as disciples (Luke 8:1-3; compare Mark 15:40-1). The three women who visited the tomb were told (Mark 16:7) to be the first witnesses to Jesus' Resurrection, even though Jewish Law at the time prohibited them from bearing legal witness; significantly, the eleven Apostles refused to believe their report. On a number of occasions, Jesus openly refused to accept women as sex objects although in the situations narrated he was clearly expected to do so. For example, when a woman (Mary Magdalene?) who was known to have been a harlot washed his feet with her tears and anointed them, the Pharisee host is depicted as regarding her only as a sinner (Luke 7:36-50). Jesus, however, saw her as a person capable of great spiritual insight and action and spoke directly to her of love, faith, and forgiveness. Similarly, in the case of the woman caught in adultery (John 8:1-11), Jesus treats her as a human being, dismissing the petty legalisms with which her accusers hoped to entrap both her and him. 'Neither do I condemn you,' he said. 'Go, and sin no more.'

All of the first three Gospels relate Jesus' radical break with the 'blood taboo'. When a woman who has had an 'issue of blood' for twelve years (widely interpreted as meaning she was ritually unclean) comes from behind and touches the hem of his robe, not only is she healed, but Jesus makes a point of drawing the crowd's attention to what has happened (Luke 8:43-8). Centuries later this lesson was still being ignored in churches, and even today the idea lives on in some circles that women should not enter the sanctuary for fear of the 'uncleanness' of the monthly cycle.

In the fourth chapter of John's Gospel, Jesus startles a Samaritan woman by initiating a conversation with her about spiritual things, and eventually she becomes the agent of a revival in her home town. In other words, she is entrusted with both the 'word' itself and the dignity of telling it to others.

Another Gospel story shows Jesus directly repudiating the stereotype of woman as housekeeper and nothing more. This is the incident (Luke 10:38-42) in which the sisters Martha and Mary become involved in a sharp exchange because instead of helping to prepare the meal, Mary takes the supposedly 'male' role of sitting at Jesus' feet and listening to his teaching. Jesus affirms Mary's right to an intellectual life and even states that she has chosen the 'better' or spiritual part. In other words, women are called to a spiritual life just as men are.

Perhaps the most powerful evidence of Jesus affirming the dignity and equality of women, however, is the parable in which he depicts God as a woman. The story of the woman who searched for the lost coin (Luke 15:8-10) is one of a trio of parables in which the leading character is a symbol of the Divine: in the case of the prodigal son, it is obvious that the father is meant to portray God, while the shepherd who searches for the lost sheep stands for the Lord who yearns for and goes out to find the straying sinner.

Thus Jesus did not shrink from the notion of God as feminine. In fact, it would appear that he included this female image of God quite deliberately, for the scribes and Pharisees to whom the parables were addressed were among those who discriminated most against women. The conclusion deduced by Christian feminists from such passages (and there are many more) is not simply that women belong in the ministry or priesthood of the various churches, but that they must be taken into full and equal partnership at every level of church life and of society. Obviously, they feel they have a long way still to go; and anyone with even a passing acquaintance with the inner workings of most denominations knows they are right. But, they rightly argue, until the churches pay radical attention to Jesus' message regarding women, the churches will continue to be less than fully Christian, and men themselves will continue to be less than fully free.

A postscript: On Easter Sunday 1980, the front page of the *Star* featured a colour picture of a first-century fresco from a Roman catacomb showing seven women celebrating Holy Communion together as priests. In the accompanying article, I told of a Catholic theologian and archaeologist, Professor Dorothy Irvin of St Paul, Minn., who has found dozens of inscriptions, mosaics, and frescoes from the first few centuries AD which indicate beyond any doubt that there were women priests and even bishops in the early church. Some of the works she has studied even show signs of having been tampered with over the centuries, to change the sex to male! Professor Irvin affirmed that her findings utterly refute the tradition that the church was without women clergy for nearly two thousand years.

Sexism in 'God-talk'

Jesus may or may not have had a sense of humour—the point is still debated in some circles—but his followers definitely need one, especially if they are women. Consider a recent Sunday morning service at a well-known Anglican church. The congregation, about two-thirds female, fell silent as the 11 a.m. bell tolled and the robed clergy and choir took their places. The minister-in-charge then turned and announced the opening hymn: 'Rise up, O men of God!' Having sung this straight-faced, the largely female grouping was then addressed in the time-hallowed words: 'Dearly beloved brethren, the Scripture moveth us in sundry places. . . .' The clergy at the front were all male; the hymns, the lessons, and particularly the sermon were all full of male references; the stained-glass windows celebrated male saints: clearly the unseen deity being worshipped was maleness apotheosized, i.e. made God.

Small wonder that Christian feminists, who have seen beyond the funny side to the ultimate, one may even say transcendent, put-down of women implied in all of this, are up in arms. They rightly point out that language is not just a matter of words, but the conveyor of meanings, the shaper of our deepest instincts and understandings. If racism cannot be fought, let alone eliminated, without careful examination of the words we use, they argue, the same is true of sexism. Once you accept their thesis and look at religious symbols, language, and customs from this point of view, you can't help being struck by the enormity of what has happened. You no longer want to smile when you hear the old joke about the Women's Auxiliary beginning their mid-week session with the hymn, 'Lord send us men . . .' You want to be part of the transformation you know must come before women attain full religious equality.

In fact, a very basic prejudice against the female still permeates most of our church life, even in 1983, and Canadian churches (most notably Canada's largest Protestant denomination, the United Church) are in a ferment over the issue. Significantly, the United Church is currently undertaking a grassroots study of a small booklet called *Guidelines for Inclusive Language*. It has been approved by the executive of the church's top legislative body and will continue to be a hot topic of debate in local congregations for years ahead.

The guidelines, drawn up by an impressive-sounding committee, are not likely to result in changes to the basic Christian prayer. Congregations will not find themselves being asked to pray, 'Our Supreme Parent who are in heaven, hallowed be . . .' Jesus himself will not be treated as though he were female, or androgynous (male-female). But noting, correctly, that theological language is nearly always based on analogy, symbol, and metaphor—since it is attempting to speak about the unspeakable— the task force recommends the use of language that includes both sexes wherever possible. Thus church people, especially educators and clergy, are urged to avoid such terms as 'man', 'men', or 'mankind' when what they really mean is 'people', 'persons', 'humanity', 'everyone', or simply 'men and women'. The phrase 'sons of God' should be replaced by 'people of God', 'daughters and sons of God', 'children of God', or 'God's offspring'. Since the Bible was written in primitive patriarchal times, it naturally shows a preference for masculine terminology with regard to God. In other cases, however, the translators have used male pronouns even when the original Hebrew or Greek words were not gender-specific.

In truth, many Bible passages that speak of God in feminine terms have been consciously played down by theologians over the years. Remember Isaiah 46:3-4, where God says: 'Harken to me . . . [you] who have been borne by me from your birth, carried from the womb, I have made and I will bear, I will carry and I will save.' Deuteronomy 32:18 speaks of the 'God who gave you birth', while Jesus himself expresses his wish to gather the people of Jerusalem to himself protectively 'as a hen gathers her chicks'. In passing, it is worth noting that many contemporary theologians now refer to God as 'she' or 'her' from time to time, not because they believe God is female—the God concept includes and transcends sexuality—but in an attempt to redress the centuries of imbalanced thinking. Some even go so far as to suggest that the Third Person of the Trinity, the Holy Spirit, should now be regularly looked upon as the female aspect of the deity. It is significant that, traditionally, evil has often been associated with a woman in the Christian tradition. Many indeed still blame women for the fall of man in the Garden, feeling in some twisted way that the 'original sin' was sexual, with woman as 'the devil's gateway' to hell. The 'devil' himself is always thought of as male. The booklet therefore urges that all personifying of evil or the demonic as either masculine or feminine be avoided.

If the guidelines become church law, there will be a thorough-going search to eliminate sexist stereotypes from all worship and educational or theological materials in the United Church. Preachers are warned: 'In descriptions of women, a patronizing or girl-watching tone should be avoided, as should sexual innu-endoes, jokes and puns.' Women should not be treated as sex objects or portrayed as being typically weak, helpless, hysterical, or housebound. Terms such as 'the little woman' or 'the ball and chain' are taboo. Admittedly, the authors get a little carried away at times, especially in their advice to preachers quoting from lit-erature. The pains they take to eliminate sexism from the famous passage in John Donne about no man being an island (given as an example) are little short of hilarious. Here is their purified form of it: 'John Donne commented on the reality that no one among us is an island entire of itself. Rather each of us is a piece of the continent.'

On a more serious note, however, they have put their finger on a vital matter when they urge Christians to examine their lan-guage not just for sexism, but for put-downs of ethnic or reli-gious minorities as well. In fact, I have long been convinced that Christian hymns present some of the worst possible theology, sexism, and religious intolerance to be found anywhere, and that careful revision is needed. Now that we have all the great religions of the East thriving in our midst, it is surely time to give up singing lustily of the 'heathen' overseas in language like that in 'From Greenland's icy mountains' (Bishop Heber, 1819). In this hymn, the people of India, Africa, and the Pacific are alleged to:

> Call us to deliver their land from error's chains.
> Can we whose souls are lighted with wisdom from on high,
> Can we to men benighted the lamp of life deny?

Along the same lines, and still very much in use, is a famous children's hymn written in 1888:

> *Little lips that Thou has made,*
> *Neath the far-off temple's shade,*
> *Give the gods of wood and stone*
> *Praise that should be all Thine own.*

> *Little hands whose wondrous skill*
> *Thou has given to do Thy will,*
> *Offr'ings bring, and serve with fear*
> *Gods that cannot see or hear.*

The United Church is on the right track. This kind of material is long overdue for extinction.

The electronic pew

Religion and the media

In my role as a religion journalist, I have naturally had a keen interest over the years in the interaction of various faiths and denominations with the mass media. God is in the communications business, but most of those who call themselves his people are still a very long way from having got the message.

Despite the Christian religion's emphasis on communication—after all, it was Jesus' command to make known 'the good news'—the churches, with a few notable exceptions, continue to regard the news media with disdain. This 'rejection of media', as some critics have called it, is especially disturbing in the light of certain statistics. A series of polls taken over the past ten or twelve years (including the most recent findings of Professor Reginald Bibby in late 1982) have shown that the overwhelming majority of Canadians still believe in God: in spite of current religious upset and uncertainty, the figure stands at roughly eighty-nine per cent. However, these same samplings show that about sixty-nine per cent of the people believe that the influence of religion is declining. Church attendance too continues to slide. In other words, Canada is fast becoming a post-Christian country. Between these contradictory pieces of evidence there looms an enormous gulf in communications. As I noted in the introduction to this book, people want to find meaning and long for spiritual life, but somehow the churches are not communicating their message. Back in the 1960s, Pierre Berton in his church-rocking book, *The Comfortable Pew*, wrote: '. . . in the twentieth century, the churches' attitude to the new electronic media is one of distrust. There seems to be a feeling that all twentieth-century media are somehow indecent.' While there have been a few improvements, much of Berton's indictment still remains painfully justified, especially in some of the larger main-line denominations.

Take, for example, relations with the press. Basically, churches don't want the press to know anything about their inner workings, finances, controversies, or whatever—except what they choose to tell. They want reporters to take their press releases and run them, but consider it somehow 'dirty pool' when the normal investigative approach taken to politics, business, or any other facet of society is applied to religion; the churches seem to feel they are privileged, above 'that sort of thing'. For a full account of the difficulty reporters have in trying to get behind the scenes in religion, I suggest Richard Ostling's book *Secrecy in the Church* (1974). I well remember a reporter covering religion for another major Canadian paper in the early 1970s who spent two hours with a leading Anglican bishop trying to shed some light on the turmoil then shaking the institutional church. None of his questions were answered. The headline on the eventual non-story was an actual quote from the prelate himself: 'I know what's wrong with the church, but I'm not telling!'

Conferences of bishops here, whether Anglican or Roman Catholic, keep up a façade of being open to the media, but quickly go into secret sessions whenever any topic of wide importance—the controversial kind—presents itself. Most major media have given up attending. There are just too many handouts, and the open sessions usually have to do entirely with churchy, in-house affairs. Although in North America you can get to most top-ranking church leaders of all denominations as individuals, Toronto's Cardinal G. Emmett Carter is an exception: he insists on having all questions in writing ahead of time, and then often fails to reply. Groups such as the Scientologists, as well as a few suspect evangelists, have been known to threaten legal action as soon as they know a journalist is on the trail—even before a line of the story appears. Some churches or sects will refuse to speak to a reporter who has written a 'both-sides' story about them. (I feel rather gratified that Revd Ian Paisley of Ulster includes my name on the list of those to whom he will not give interviews, and that the South African government has refused to grant me a visa.)

Covering stories at the Vatican is at once the most frustrating and most challenging job of all for a religion-beat reporter. On the one hand, there is an excellent press office near St Peter's

Square, with helpful staff, lots of international phone hook-ups, typewriters, and instant translation at press conferences. Yet reporters who cover the World Synods of Bishops (held every three years), as I have done four times now, are never allowed into any of the sessions. Journalists from around the world have to be satisfied with much-abbreviated, and at times watered-down, reports from *relatores* who tell them what is going on. The only way to check the story is to try and locate individual bishops and get a translated version of their actual speeches. Some are helpful; others stonewall.

When budget cuts are announced because of inflation or other causes, church communications departments are almost always the first to suffer. Not long ago the Anglican Church of Canada more than decimated its communications department. (At the moment of writing, spring 1983, the Anglican Diocese of Toronto is without a press officer—but then it has been without one for about eight of the last eleven years.) The Anglican view seems to be that reporters, like tradesmen, should use the rear door—if they must come around at all! I well remember when the Most Revd Donald Coggan, then Archbishop of Canterbury, came to Toronto a few years back to speak to a joint session of the Empire and Canadian Clubs. He dismissed the news photographers and TV cameramen with a lordly wave of his hand and said: 'Now if you're quite through, I'd like to get on with my speech.' There was the usual applause for a put-down of the media—the scapegoat syndrome—and the reporters retreated, either cowed or else very angry. Their efforts to put the man and his message across the nation seemed unwanted, even impudent. I once asked an Anglican archbishop, at a conference in Winnipeg, why it is that so many Anglicans seem to regard the media with lofty disdain. He answered: 'Unfortunately, too many of them still remember the so-called good old days when we knew the people in the boardrooms and offices where the real decisions were made. The church didn't need the press then and this attitude still hangs on.' In some churches, the press officer is at the same time editor of the denomination's national newspaper—a situation hard to square with the need for independence and objectivity in such a journal. Theological colleges are beginning to include courses on communications for young ministers-in-training, but investigation shows that these are generally optional and seldom taught by anyone with 'hard-news' experience. The chief emphasis is still on preaching.

To be fair, the churches' suspicion of the press and other media is not totally ungrounded. Many newspapers in Canada neglect religion almost entirely except for the odd wire report or item about a church bazaar or meeting. Often a paper that would never dream of using a novice to cover a sports or political story will send a cub reporter to write on or interview some prominent religious figure. The result is frustration on both sides. But for the churches to use this as a reason for rejecting twentieth-century media would be ridiculous. The quickest way to get media to take religion more seriously is for those who are religious to make news in such a way that they cannot be ignored. As the theologian Karl Barth, once said, putting the case for media to the churches: 'Why don't you force us to pay more attention?'

Significantly, the fastest growing sector of the church at the moment in North America is the conservative evangelical wing. It is no accident that these (often fundamentalist) churches do take the media seriously; indeed, many focus all their efforts on getting their message across. The Peoples Church in Toronto, Canada's largest evangelical congregation, is a prime example. Where the local Anglican Diocese, with nearly three hundred churches, has no press officer, this one church has two public-relations people. The church's Sunday morning telecast service is currently outdrawing Rex Humbard, the popular American evangelist, by almost three to one. In addition, the congregation, which has the largest Sunday school in Canada and regularly draws a couple of thousand people to services even on Sunday evenings, buys regular radio time and makes ample use of the printed word. The Salvation Army, again an evangelical movement, has always concentrated on the media, and its ability to use the press could put many secular organizations to shame. All of these groups seem to have understood much more clearly than their main-line counterparts have that the church must communicate or perish. They see press, radio, and TV as neither good nor bad in themselves but simply there—part of the world that it is their calling to evangelize. Like Jesus, Paul, or the early church, they want to use the best media possible to broadcast the message. Better than anyone else they seem to have entered into the spirit of a remark attributed to the late Pope John: 'If St Paul came back today, I think he would be a journalist.'

Star Wars

Star Wars (1977) is one of the most religious films ever to be
shown in a secular movie theatre. In fact, George Lucas's space
fantasy is filled with more specifically Christian motifs than
many sermons are. This description may well come as a surprise
to most of the hundreds of thousands who have seen the film to
date—perhaps even to Lucas himself, writer and director of
what *Time* called 'the best movie of the year'. Obviously, as he has
pointed out, his aim was simply to make an imaginative enter-
tainment that would sweep audiences out of the theatre into the
high adventure and romance of a struggle in an unknown
galaxy many thousands of light years from earth. He wanted to
combine his love for Flash Gordon and other such heroes, past
and present, with all the wizardry of space-age technology, to
create a new epic, a myth for the future.

Nearly all the elements of the classic fairy tale are present in
the film: good against evil; the heroic few who triumph over
seemingly all-powerful hordes; the lovely princess to be rescued;
the magic sword; the aged, all-knowing counsellor and friend.
But *Star Wars* is more than a rehash of the themes of childhood
fantasy decked out with some of the most breath-taking, and at
times hilarious, technical effects and creations ever screened.

Like painters and poets, film-makers too may create works
whose meaning or impact is different from what they had conceived, and perhaps deeper. Looking at *Star Wars* from the religious angle—a perspective largely neglected by critics so far—
throws fresh light on the secret of its deep appeal and its
enthusiastic acceptance by young and old alike. Consciously or
unconsciously, Lucas has touched a nerve at the centre of our
being. Wittingly or unwittingly, he raises the key religious ques-

tions of our time in his space fable. While at one level it is possible just to sit back, suspend thought, and 'watch the good guys win', at another there is a basic message. Although the message focuses on issues central to all religion and mysticism, often the reference point seems specifically Christian. This is not to say that *Star Wars* is a 'Christian movie'—whatever that might be. But much of the symbolism clearly does derive from Christian sources.

The story itself can be summed up as follows. In another galaxy, in another time, a republic flourished, ruled by wise senators and protected by the Jedi Knights. But it fell prey to inner rot, and power-hungry men soon forged the sinister, totalitarian Galactic Empire. The Jedi Knights were exterminated and a reign of terror began that penetrated to even the remotest systems in the galaxy. Here and there, nevertheless, existed pockets of resistance, rebels pledged to overthrow the emperor and restore freedom. Luke Skywalker, a young man who is bored with farming life on an obscure planet and longs to see wider worlds beyond, is suddenly thrown into the vortex of this climactic strife. Together with a mysterious old man named Ben Kenobi (the last surviving Jedi), two comical robots, a cynical starship pilot, and his huge anthropoid companion, Luke embarks on an intergalactic mission. The purpose is to wipe out the key to the empire's power, the terrible planet-destroying Death Star, and to rescue the princess Leia who alone has discovered the one small chink in the enemy's armour.

This unlikely group battles the Grand Moff Tarkin, evil governor of the Imperial Outland Region, and Lord Darth Vader, his malevolent henchman who was once himself a Jedi Knight but has betrayed his former master, the Force. Aided by the Force, which the aged Kenobi describes as a kind of 'field of energy all around us and within us', Luke's star-fighter at last destroys the Death Star, and peace and justice are once again assured.

Kenobi's role is highly significant. His constant phrase, 'May the Force be with you', resounds like a benediction. He teaches Luke to rely on the Force rather than on his own wisdom or space technology for ultimate victory. It is by obeying this instruction at the height of the horrific final battle that Luke is able to prevail. Kenobi's obvious power—almost sorcery—over others, his extrasensory awareness of cosmic events, his assurance of ultimate victory, suggest a more-than-human source.

Finally, when he is slain in combat with the traitor Vader, his body vanishes into thin air, leaving only his robe and the echoing assurance: 'The Force will be with you always.'

Kenobi is clearly a kind of Christ figure or symbol. He assures the others he will be more powerful in death than in life. For example, he continues to guide Luke through the final battle. As in the story of the empty tomb in the Gospels, only his robe remains after death. Vader, Kenobi's arch-enemy, is described as once having been a disciple of the Force and of Kenobi. Now the symbol of all that is sinister and evil, he was once a 'prince of light', like Lucifer who fell from being the brightest of the angelic host to become Satan, the prince of evil. We are reminded also of Judas, the disciple who held a privileged place at the Last Supper, close to Christ.

To the basic religious questions—Is man alone in the universe? Is he but the plaything of fate? Will the crushing weight of evil necessarily triumph? Is death the end?—*Star Wars* answers with an unequivocal *no*. Again and again the movie sounds the note of freedom of choice, the challenge to become involved against the forces of evil, the call to be the 'salt of the world', the creative, saving minority. The spontaneous applause so often heard at the film's conclusion suggests more than simple relief that the baddies have been defeated or delight in the exquisite cinematic hardware. There is a sense of the rightness of these deeper affirmations.

As all recent surveys in Canada and elsewhere have shown, modern man is profoundly religious in his searching, however turned-off he may be to organized religion. Most traditional or professional theologians will probably scoff at the notion that Christ can be seen in a rather weird figure in a science fiction plot; some Christians may even take offence. But as Bishop John (*Honest to God*) Robinson has said in a recent book, for many people today traditional language about God and Christ has broken down. He argues that some of the most profound religious statement are likely to be found hidden 'in fiction or art, in psychology or drama'. *Star Wars* does not fall into the 'most profound' category. But it does talk about religious ideas in terms the average person can identify with. Religious leaders would do well to see it, discuss it with their congregations, and use it as a starting point in seeking to bridge the obvious communication gap between the pulpit and the pew.

The star-spangled pew

Jesus wrapped in the Stars and Stripes—you won't find it in the New Testament, but it is the substratum of nearly all the TV evangelism beamed across the Canadian border. In fact, this invasion of American political and social values under the guise of the 'old-fashioned gospel' is one aspect of Canadian independence (or rather the lack of it) that has so far escaped notice. Pierre Berton should write a sequel to his book *The Comfortable Pew*, and call it *The Star-Spangled Pew*.

By far the most formidable—and outrageous—of the electronic prophets who see the Great American Dream and the kingdom of God as one and the same thing is Revd Jerry Falwell, pastor of Thomas Road Baptist Church in Lynchburg, Virginia, and star of the leading syndicated religious program in the United States and Canada, The Old-Time Gospel Hour. Listed generally under the title Jerry Falwell, the show is carried by three hundred and eighty-one stations in North America, including fifty in Canada (two in the Toronto area). More than three hundred radio stations carry it as well. Equally important, Falwell is founder and head of Moral Majority Inc., a Washington-based coalition that purports to be politically neutral in its crusade to 'turn America around and back to God'. But Falwell makes no secret of the fact that he considers 'political liberalism' the chief enemy of all that is sacred. Moral Majority's aim is to mobilize at least two million Americans to work for 'pro-God, pro-family policies in government'.

Falwell's church seats four thousand and has an average Sunday attendance of about ten thousand. Its vast complex includes a liberal arts college, Liberty Baptist College, with three thousand students who in order to enrol must promise never to hold hands, smoke, drink, dance, or listen to rock music. Falwell describes himself as a separatist, independent Baptist, which is really another way of saying that he is his own denomination. Nevertheless, and despite the sniping of some fundamentalists who (hard to believe!) are even more right-wing than he is, he says he is willing to co-operate with anyone who shares his religio-political stance on specific issues such as abortion. For instance, in 1980 he told the Mormons he welcomed their co-operation in fighting the proposed Equal Rights Amendment (ERA) in the United States, but that he would keep on trying to convert them to his view of Christianity in the process.

Articulate, dynamic, and persuasive, Falwell is also basically very honest. He has done everyone a favour by candidly stating where he is and what he stands for in his book *Listen America!* (1981). He concedes at the outset that more than half of all adult Americans, according to the most recent polls, say they have had a 'born-again' religious experience. Roughly one hundred and seventy million Americans, he says, want their children to grow up in a 'moral society'. More than eight of every ten—eighty-four per cent—believe that the Ten Commandments are valid for today. Still, he is unhappy. Even though the two contenders for the 1980 presidential election were born-again Christians, even though many American churches are bulging at the seams and you can scarcely turn on either radio or television there without a religious bombardment of the hot-gospelling type, Falwell wants a religious revival. Instead of asking what is wrong with the brand of religion being preached—why it has so little real impact on people's private and public lives—he says the passivity of the silent majority is to blame for decay. But the kind of religious revival he has in mind is a heretical blending of the politics of Ronald Reagan and the (carefully selected) ethics of Jesus.

For Falwell, the United States is the uniquely appointed agent of God in the world: 'We have the blessing of God upon us . . . I believe God promoted America to a greatness no other nation has ever enjoyed.' The capitalist system has God's own hand upon it, he claims, arguing that free enterprise is outlined in the Book of Proverbs. Moreoever, he says, Jesus made it clear the work ethic was part of his plan for man. Ownership of property is biblical. Competition is biblical. (Unfortunately for him, the same book can be used to support other views; Proverbs 23:4, for example, says quite bluntly: 'Do not toil to acquire wealth; be wise enough to desist.')

164 | The electronic pew

Falwell is opposed to the feminist movement, homosexuals, foreign aid, abortion, pornography, Communism, the ERA, big government, extended day-care for working mothers, and most public-welfare schemes. He favours unswerving patriotism, more defence spending, capital punishment, unquestioning support for Israel (he even told Prime Minister Menachem Begin that the Israelis have the right to settle anywhere in the West Bank region they want to) and, of course, *laissez-faire* capitalism. To be sure, all these are viable options for Christians in any country. But to equate this package with the 'true gospel' or true Christianity is as close to blasphemy as it is possible to come. The gospel belongs to no political creed of either left or right. Falwell is obviously intelligent, but that is no guarantee he may not be dangerous. He argues for freedom and liberty but then makes a palpably nonsensical statement: 'If a person is not a Christian, he is inherently a failure because he has rejected the holy Spirit.'

What about devout Jews, Muslims, Buddhists, and the like? Small wonder that Falwell also has little to say about the real outsiders in society. According to his view, the poor (whom Jesus singled out for particular concern) have simply failed to make it, to get their slice of the social pie by trusting God and working hard. 'Many women have never accepted their God-given roles,' he tells us—a familiar theme of most of the TV-evangelist tribe. Sex on television is for him much worse than violence: 'I am concerned about excessive violence, but I am far more concerned about the invasion of illicit sex into prime time.' Being against abortion, he claims to be pro-life. Obviously his pro-life stance is selective, however, since he also argues strongly for taking the lives of some criminals. He is against child abuse, but very much in favour of spanking children. As a fan of the Book of Proverbs, he clearly suffers no pangs of conscience over a passage such as this: 'Do not withhold discipline from a child; if you beat him with a rod, he will not die. If you beat him with the rod you will save his life from Sheol [hell].' (Prov. 23:13.)

The truth is that behind his espousal of the cause of Christ lies an extremely violent philosophy—a sanctification of war, and a sanctification of structures of injustice, which he somehow regards as the basis for a golden age. Viewers are of course free to disagree with the Falwells of the world. The pity is that alternatives to this mishmash of religion and American politics are virtually non-existent on television. A visitor from Mars, viewing religious programs on Canadian TV sets for the first time, could well be forgiven for wondering what Christianity was all about. If the major religious bodies in the country care about this situation, it is surely time they did something.

A postcript: Now that the CRTC has granted permission for a religious satellite channel (June 1983), the ball is firmly in their court.

100 Huntley Street

The host of the Global Television Network's 100 Huntley Street, Revd David Mainse, created no small stir in 1982 with his request to the CRTC for a licence to broadcast religious programming twenty-four hours a day, with his own hook-up to satellite. (As of August 1983, it is a moot point whether he or a consortium of the main-line churches will eventually get the licence.) The show is less hyped-up than its American counterparts, and less hard-sell in its appeal for cash, but it suffers from the same tendency to use Jesus as an instant solution for every conceivable ill. I wrote the following article in 1977, not long after the program's inception.

All the razzle-dazzle of big-time daily religious television programming has arrived in Toronto. Called 100 Huntley Street, after the studio's address, just a stone's throw from the corner of Jarvis and Bloor Streets, the show is slickly professional and charged to the hilt with Charismatic emotion and style. Its mix of upbeat gospel music, visiting celebrities, and interviews with local religious leaders is patterned closely on the American-based 700 Club and its host of imitators. The star of 100 Huntley Street, however, is a Canadian, and the whole production is Canadian-owned and -operated.

Five minutes to air-time in the huge, glittering TV studio, the makeup girl pats the nose of a blond singer to remove an offending shine. The marimbist and a trombonist simulate a duet as they warm up silently in a corner. Suddenly, rising religious TV superstar Revd David Mainse grabs a microphone and moves up into the audience for some pre-show patter. 'You're from Manitoba? God bless you!' The floorman erupts with: 'Two minutes to air-time, praise the Lord!'

Volunteers (about twenty-five women and five men) waiting to counsel people who want jobs, healing, or knowledge of 'how to come to Christ', sit poised at their telephones as Mainse prays for the 'Holy Spirit, the communicator' to bless the program.

The final cue given, the cameras zoom in on Mainse as he introduces 100 Huntley Street—'ninety minutes of live broadcasting
from the heart of downtown Toronto.' The floorman and two
cameramen lead the applause, and the telephones begin ringing
wildly as the New Creation quartet sings the joys of 'one-
hundred-per-cent-living for the Lord'. Then, while the telephone counsellors raise one hand in silent prayer, there is more
applause and Mainse introduces singer-songwriter Gene
MacLellan.

MacLellan, who wrote such popular hits as 'Snow Bird' and
'Put Your Hand in the Hand of the Man Who Stilled the Water',
sits in the spotlight, guitar balanced on one knee, and tells how
he has finally decided to take his own advice. 'I've decided to put
my own hand in the Lord's hand now,' he says. 'I'm a yes-man
for the Lord.' (Cries of 'Amen' from the audience.) 'I was seeking a long time and even went to a psychiatrist four years ago,
but I got no help there. Then I went back to the Word of God
and found the answers. The Lord can trust me a little better now
and he's just dropping new songs in my head.' He sings his latest
song: 'Jesus is calling, midnight is falling; the signs are everywhere . . .'

Every now and then Revd Al Reimers, an Anglican priest who
is part of the Mainse team, reads a report on the incoming calls.
Marriages are being healed, he says. There are two reports of
people 'finding salvation'; one of the men is a Metro police
officer. A man in hospital with lung cancer has called to say his
prayer has been answered and the doctors have decided they
don't have to operate now. A young Jew has 'come to Christ'.
(Jewish people are given very special treatment. One man who
called in this week asking what spiritual advice they had for him
in his search for a deeper faith was told: 'Praise the Lord! This is
a very special call. God loves you very much as part of his chosen
people; Jesus, you know, was a Jew. You've read Isaiah? Well,
the Messiah spoken of there is Jesus.' The woman continued:
'Look, God is doing just beautiful things for Jews. They're
accepting Jesus as Messiah and becoming what we call completed Jews.' The caller said: 'You mean they're becoming Christians?' The reply was affirmative. She then asked him to hold
until someone more experienced could talk to him, but he hung
up. Personally, I believe he did the right thing: the day of trying
to convert Jews to Jesus surely should be long past.)

The building where 100 Huntley Street and its various spin-offs originate has been leased for twenty years to Crossroads Christian Communications Inc. (for what a Crossroads spokesman calls 'ridiculously low rates') with an option for an additional five-year lease when the twenty years are up. One of the finest TV production set-ups anywhere in Canada, it includes a cafeteria and dozens of offices. Crossroads, which also operates Circle Square ranches for children in a growing number of locations across the country, has a total paid staff of eighty. The 1976 budget was one million, two hundred thousand dollars; 1977's is almost double that, at two million, one hundred thousand. Mainse's staff say the money comes entirely from free-will donations by viewers and Christians who are excited about 'winning the nation for Christ'.

There is no hard-sell approach to raising the cash, they insist. But this past week the program has been making a special appeal—what it calls a 'stewardship emphasis'—to meet the new budget. And from time to time I have heard complaints that when the broadcast is over, people who have attended the show, even the elderly, are pressured to give money. According to several callers, the sales pitch is guilt-producing and coercive: 'the unsaved will go to hell if we can't reach them', they are told. Often, as with the American 'hucksters', the theme is that God will grant success, financial and otherwise, to those who support 'his work'. Thus Mainse wrote in the August 1977 edition of his publication *Crossroads Direction*: 'It is a fact that God blesses those who support this ministry. For example, one man who has been supporting us financially . . . is a salesman. He reported he has been with his company for five years but this past month has had double the sales of any other month in his career.' Of course, Jesus did say it is blessed to give—but he gave no such promises about getting in return.

Mainse, in his forties, seems on a perpetual high (Charismatics say they are 'high on Jesus'), and never stops smiling as he moves from one 'beautiful' person or theme to another. Often he stops in the midst of an interview or phone report to join hands with the people on camera—inviting the audience to do the same—as he is moved to pray for some specific need or person. Viewers at home are invited to kneel by their television sets: 'You can come to Calvary in your own home!' A Pentecostal himself, Mainse has assembled an impressive ecumenical team for his daring attempt at a twentieth-century approach to the large masses of the unchurched. In addition to the Anglican Al Reimers, the team includes a Jesuit priest, Revd Robert L. MacDougall, a criminologist and former addict who once spent time at Southdown, a centre just outside Toronto for alcohol- and drug-addicted Catholic priests. Since 'being filled with the Spirit'—as the Charismatics describe their experience of the Holy Spirit—MacDougall talks like a Pentecostal enthusiast. There are four or five other ministers on staff as well.

Without a doubt, 100 Huntley Street is an imaginative attempt to use modern media and take the message of religion to where the people are. Some of MacDougall's descriptions of calls received during his once-a-week early-hours show—children left alone, people coming down off drugs—are very moving. The scope and professionalism of the productions are also a challenge to the major churches, which have been fumbling in mass communications here for some time. But the program raises important questions. Is this, as critics say, a shallow emotional approach to the faith, presenting a kind of instant bandaid Jesus who gives simple answers to complex issues? Does the emphasis on Charismatic gifts—speaking in tongues, healing, and prophecy—tend to obscure or even eliminate the social impact of Jesus' message, making Christianity out to be a matter simply of personal success and adaptation to the status quo? I think so.

Evangelicals in Canada report mixed feelings over the whole phenomenon. They are delighted that the gospel has found such an attractive, effective outlet. At the same time they worry that, as one leading evangelical put it, the programming seems to be nothing but 'hidebound Pentecostalism'. Canada's top evangelical preacher, Revd Paul Smith of the Peoples Church in Toronto, said in an interview: 'We're delighted that the faith is getting now the kind of TV exposure here it has long had in the United States. But we cannot agree with the Charismatic emphasis. I wish they had taken a broader approach. We'll pray for them—at a distance.'

1. In Calcutta. Christmas, 1979.

2. A small boy hears himself on tape for the first time. Calcutta, 1979.

3. The 'parking lot' outside the Anglican cathedral. Frobisher Bay, 1977.

4. Building an igloo. Frobisher Bay, 1977.

5. With Mother Teresa in her orphanage. Calcutta, 1979.

6. With Jean Vanier at his centre for the handicapped. Trosly-Breuil, 1978.

7. At the manger in the Church of the Nativity. Bethlehem, 1976.

8. On top of Mount Sinai. Christmas, 1980.

People

Mother Teresa

'Love came down to us at the first Christmas that we might love one another. Every human being needs that personal touch of love; that's all any of us was created to do—to love and to be loved.' So Mother Teresa replied when I asked her what she would like to say to the people of Canada at Christmas, 1979. The words are simple, ordinary. In a world where talk so often takes the place of action, they seem frail.

In fact, no person could look more frail and ordinary than the seventy-three-year-old Roman Catholic nun who was awarded the 1979 Nobel Peace Prize. In repose, her face is etched with lines so deep you think she must be a hundred, and know she has seen the gamut of human suffering. Yet when she smiles and speaks to you, she appears to be illumined from within, vibrant with warmth and caring, ageless. You forget that she is barely five feet tall, for her presence fills the room. You feel something of the force flowing through her: the reason she has been able to challenge and to do the impossible. She lives a reality that radiates hope and inspires millions around the globe. When the Marxist government of West Bengal held a state reception for her in recognition of the Nobel award, she was hailed as 'a pure symbol of peace' and told: 'Though we are politically divided, in Mother Teresa we are one.'

The order of the Missionaries of Charity, which she founded and heads, is the only religious order in the Catholic Church with a waiting list. Its more than twelve hundred sisters in their simple blue-bordered cotton saris work among the poor and outcast everywhere from Calcutta to the slums of London, from the Bronx to the Gaza Strip. There is also a men's order of nearly three hundred Missionary Brothers of Charity, which she helped to form. In addition, Co-Workers of Mother Teresa are now established in almost every land. Numbering many thousands, these are people of all religions, young and old, who share a common commitment to see and love God in their fellow men and give their service freely to the very poor.

Photographer Bob Olsen and I travelled half-way around the world to see Mother Teresa and the work she does in her adopted city of Calcutta. After recovering from the thirty-hour trip, which took us by way of London, Rome, and Muscat, on the Persian Gulf, we set out to explore the streets where she labours. The experience was mind-boggling. To spend a week here, as we did, is to undergo a constant bombardment of the mind and senses. We felt as if we had taken a dive into a deep well of humanity, one by turns exotic and nauseating, fascinating and frightening. Yonge Street at its busiest would seem deserted and antiseptic compared with the teeming streets of this city where the population is estimated at between ten and twelve million. To get the feeling of it, you would have to imagine the midway at the Canadian National Exhibition at its peak, then add wandering cows and buffalo, a stream of worn-out cars and buses steadily honking their horns and belching black exhaust, a host of hand-pushed or -pulled vehicles—from rickshaws to massive wagons—and, finally, every scent from spicy food to animal and human waste. And that would be only a mild approximation.

To it you would have to add the smell of real poverty. Much the same the world over, it is at its worst in Calcutta. Beggars, many with sick children or self-inflicted wounds to arouse pity or guilt, are numerous and persistent. Hungry people rake over heaps of rubbish by the road in search of something to eat, sell, or burn for cooking fuel. The army of the homeless, roughly a hundred and fifty thousand abandoned children and fifty thousand adults, spend the whole of life—eating, bathing, sleeping, excreting—in the streets. At night, heads and faces wrapped in cloths, their huddled forms look like large cocoons lined up in rows. Trucks regularly pick up the bodies of the dead. We ourselves saw several corpses.

One is amazed that any person would dare to think he or she could even begin to make a difference here. But, in answer to her 'call within a call', this tiny woman from Albania did just that. In 1946, during a train journey, Mother Teresa felt led by God to devote herself to those for whom no one else cared, the poorest of the poor. She left the Sisters of Loretto, the order she had served since 1928, and the Calcutta school where she had

been teaching the daughters of the rich. Permission to establish
her new movement came from Rome two years later. Today in
dozens of homes and other centres in Calcutta, her sisters and
brothers heal the sick, care for the dying, immunize the young,
and offer rehabilitation to the handicapped. No one, however
needy or cut off from society, is beyond her reach.

The first time we tried to interview Mother Teresa—before 6
a.m.—we found her too busy to attend either to us or to the
crowd of people already waiting in the cool courtyard below.
Barefoot, sitting cross-legged at the rear of the simple second-
storey room that constitutes the chapel in the mother house on
Circular Road, she was praying with about two hundred of her
nuns and novices—seeking the strength to tackle a day that
would see her presiding over a twelve-hour meeting with the
heads of her various missions throughout the world. Later,
when we did manage to spend a day with her, she explained how
she keeps going, and how she gets the energy to accomplish her
gargantuan task: 'You saw us at the holy mass. Love is the fruit
of prayer and prayer is the fruit of faith. Without these none of
us can do anything. Love is the gift of God who gave us his Son
at that first Christmas two thousand years ago.'

Together with Dr Ronald Smith (a retired English physician
who has had two coronaries but says he has never felt better in
his life than since he came to help Mother Teresa as a volunteer)
and Daphne Rae (an English nurse who works as a magistrate in
London) we went to visit Nirmal Hriday, Mother Teresa's hostel
for the destitute and dying. One of her earliest projects, the one-
storey edifice is part of the great temple of Kalighat, dedicated
to Kali, the Hindu goddess of destruction. Outside, in a street
bustling with shops, beggars, and mad traffic, we saw an old
woman dip her tin cup in the filthy water of the gutter and take
a drink. Inside, out of the heat of what passes for winter in Calcutta, all was still, bathed in a soft light from windows near the
ceiling. We were able to make out two tiers of simple cots on
each side of the long room that was the men's ward (a similar
ward for women ran at right angles off the cooking area in the
middle). Although a few patients were sitting up and looked as
though they would recover, most of beds were occupied by people who had been found dying on the pavement. Half of them
might be dead by the next day, yet there were no laments, no
pleas for help. The brothers, assisted by a wonderful corps of

volunteers who pay their own board and offer their service freely for the privilege of bathing, feeding, and helping these outcasts in any way they can, moved with skilled and caring hands along the ward. As the doctor and nurse administered medicines, two brothers were washing maggots out of a huge wound in the hip of a man who had fallen from a train.

I was shocked and, frankly, dismayed when Mrs Rae suddenly handed me a tin plate with a chunk of bread and a mug of broth on it and said: 'Feed that man.' She was pointing to a grizzled Hindu lying paralyzed from some unknown fever on a pallet near the door. With all the fears of a sheltered North American, I shrank from contact with the unlovely, to say nothing of the risk of disease. Yet as I knelt to break the bread, put it in his mouth, and pour the broth when his eyes showed that he wanted to drink, a remarkable change took place in me. It was in no way anything to boast of—after all, the nurse really gave me no choice—but I found myself overcoming my revulsion and fear. I caught a glimpse of what Mother Teresa calls 'the Christ in every man or woman' and was deeply moved.

In the women's ward, one of the volunteers was a twenty-three-year-old woman from Waterloo, Ont., who asked that her name not be given: 'I'm no heroine, nor am I religious,' she said. 'I'm just attracted by what Mother Teresa is doing for humanity.' Mother Teresa and her helpers make no attempt to convert these captive souls to Christ. If they want Ganges water, they get it. If they just want a cigarette before they die, they get that too. She wants them to be able to die in dignity and to know, at least once in their devastated lives, the touch of genuine human love. She told me: 'Christian, that's just a name in a way. What we try to do, if they want it and are looking for forgiveness, is to assure them God will accept them and grant them his blessing.' Hindus and Muslims alike call her Mata Ji, 'highly respected mother', because they recognize her spiritual power and her unwillingness to force her faith in Jesus on them. 'No one, not even God himself, can force another person to become a Christian,' she says. 'He too respects our freedom.'

When we arrived at the mother house early the next morning (Mother Teresa's day begins at 4.30 a.m.), we were worried because there was already a long line of people—rich and poor, Indian and European—waiting to see her. The pastel-coloured building, very plain and functional, rang with the chanting voices of the sisters at mass in the crowded chapel. In a nearby courtyard, barefoot novices in all-white saris (the traditional garb of the humble and poor) drew water in a pail from a deep well in one corner and chatted as they stooped over the laundry. A Norwegian TV crew had just left. There was a very wealthy tea planter who wanted her to write a letter so that his son could be moved from one private school to another; a young woman in a sari who was writing a thesis on key moral leaders of our time; and a Hindu mining engineer, Henry Godell, who said his mother was desperately ill, and that he was sure Mother Teresa could 'work a miracle' if only she would come and see her. He had kept a taxi waiting at the door for over an hour. And there were dozens more.

Incredibly, Mother Teresa makes a point of being available to all who come, and keeps an agenda that would kill many younger and stronger people. Finally she asked us into the extraordinarily spartan room reserved as her office and place for meeting visitors. The prayer of St Francis—'Lord, make me an instrument of thy peace . . .'—hangs on the wall, together with a signed portrait of John Paul II and cables from great and small around the world in tribute for the Nobel award. A sticker on a glass door reads: 'Jesus Christ lives today, saves the sinners, heals the sick, liberates and gives peace.' We found her one of those rare people who give you such full attention and emanate so much warmth that you feel you are the only one who matters to them at that moment. This attitude is basic to her whole philosophy and success. When I asked if she was not overwhelmed by the seekers outside the door, let alone all the needy of Calcutta and the world, her smile lit the dingy chamber, and she answered: 'I just tackle things one bit at a time; it's just like seeing you two men from the crowd waiting out there. Otherwise everyone would be lost in the numbers.'

On Christmas Day, Mother Teresa said, she and the sisters and brothers would be busy visiting all the Calcutta homes and missions: 'There will be special feasts for all our poor, and holy mass. We ourselves will celebrate Christmas on the twenty-sixth here at the mother house.' She graciously received a porcelain bell with Eskimo children on it, which Olsen had brought as a gift from Canada, and said it would be used at chapel and in the refectory. Then she told us she was going to see the Hindu engineer's mother. We wanted to follow in a cab to see and photograph her in action, but at the last moment she asked us not to come. Our disappointment turned to elation when she added that she would take us on a tour of her orphanage for abandoned babies, just down the road, as soon as she got back. It became the most exciting and moving experience on the trip.

When we arrived at the rambling two-storey house, hundreds of starving people were lined up in the hot, humid street waiting to carry away a pot each of the lentil-based gruel in vast sixty- or seventy-gallon drums in a courtyard at the entrance. The sisters and volunteers spend the whole night preparing for this ritual, which feeds about seven thousand people a day. Pandemonium broke out when the older children of the orphanage spotted Mother Teresa and rushed squealing to clutch her skirts and get a greeting. Of the more than one hundred and fifty children there, forty-seven were under three months old. We saw two tiny mites who had just been rescued from an abortion clinic, and another premature baby found on the railway tracks was brought in while we were there. Mother Teresa pinched one fat baby cheek and told me: 'We are fighting abortion by adoption. Thousands have gone through our hands. We even have a waiting list of parents in Europe and elsewhere who want to have a child.'

Olsen said later he had never, in his whole career, worked so hard to capture someone on film. She darts about with such bird-like speed and energy that we were both sweating when the visit was over. Yet 'the saint of the gutters' seemed unruffled, ready for whoever was next in line to meet her. Although neither of us is overly mystical or easily impressed, both Olsen and I came away convinced that we had seen and touched a living saint. She radiates the reality so much talked about in Christian circles but so rarely seen: a reality with its roots in another dimension, yet totally locked into life. As she says: 'We see the Babe of Bethelehem, but we also see Jesus on the streets—under the distressing disguise of the poorest of the poor.'

Jean Vanier

The ravages of two world wars are visible all around Trosly-Breuil, a tiny village in the valley of the River Oise, about forty miles north-east of Paris. Yet for millions around the globe, Trosly-Breuil is a unique symbol and source of hope. Here, since 1964, one of Canada's most distinguished sons has championed the cause of the mentally handicapped, and in the process has distilled his insights into a wisdom with powerful things to say to the so-called normal world.

Jean Vanier, whose father Georges was ambassador in London and Paris before serving as Governor-General of Canada from 1959 to 1967, has had more opportunities for personal advancement than most. But he renounced them all, and has devoted his life to living with and caring for the weak of the earth. In so doing he has become convinced of what he believes is a crucial truth for the sad, the depressed, the frustrated, and the insecure (a group that includes all of us, at times, when the masks of our defences are removed): that the seeds of human hope lie not in the values so eagerly espoused by our society—money, power, success, sex, good looks—but in learning how to accept weakness, our own and others'. 'The birth of the child at Christmas, God's appearance to us in weakness, means you are allowed to be weak, to be yourself as a person capable of growing,' he says. 'Once you really grasp that in your innermost being, it's good news indeed.'

Born in 1928, Vanier is tall and rangy, with a long, angular face and a gift for both high good humour and potent seriousness. Clearly he is a mystic—many would say a saint. Yet his outlook and intellect are anything but other-worldly. He thinks, talks, and writes as a man who feels deeply the divisions of our strife-torn planet. His work with the weak has never let him forget those who are, to all appearances, the strong.

In 1978 I spent two days at L'Arche, as his scattered community at Trosly-Breuil is called, and came away feeling I had been given a privileged glimpse into what is means to be truly human. L'Arche (the ark, a place of refuge) takes its name from the biblical story of Noah and the flood. The movement Vanier started has so expanded that there are now over one hundred such 'arks' in almost every corner of the earth, including India, Africa, Haiti, and Honduras; Canada alone has twenty-five. Basic to his philosophy is the certainty that any do-gooder approach to those less fortunate than ourselves is wrong. Volunteers—about one hundred and sixty of them, from a wide range of countries, including close to a hundred from Canada—who come here with the idea of 'doing good' for the retarded are soon sent packing. 'L'Arche is a place of meeting,' Vanier says. 'It's a place where we all must learn from one another. The volunteer assistants have to lose their sense of the kick of doing good to others and see the handicapped as people who have much to teach us too.'

This is not just pious jargon. Vanier points to what passes for normality in the world and says he is terrified by our acceptance of what it too often means: acquiescence in aggressive competitiveness, domination of others, striving for needless possessions, fear of what others think, greed, lust, massive insecurity, and even violence. 'Normal people are often blind, so caught up in their own desires or frenzy of pointless activism that they can't even see others around them,' he says. 'The handicapped person wears his weakness for all to see; he can't hide it. The rest of us are actually less honest. We hide our handicap behind a façade of success. Outwardly we may smile, but inwardly there is a flight from anguish.' Ultimately, he argues, it is this putting up of barriers, this pretence that we are strong, that is the source of all conflicts—and of the absolute conflict, war itself.

Trosly-Breuil, a picturesque hamlet of about eight hundred inhabitants, is almost buried in the vast forest of Compiègne. In winter a damp, bone-chilling mist seeps up from the river, obscuring the outlines of trees and buildings and fringing the whole village with white lace when the evening frost sets in. The straggling houses and outbuildings are almost medieval-looking, made of yellowish-grey local stone and heavily beamed with rough-hewn timbers; in a lovely open square there is a quaint outdoor wash-house where village women once did the communal laundry. The smell of burning leaves and apple boughs hangs hauntingly in the air. L'Arche has a number of focal buildings—a gorgeous chapel made from what was once a stone storehouse or barn, a meeting hall (another converted barn), and some offices. But in keeping with Vanier's conviction that the key to healing is real community, the one hundred and sixty handicapped live in separate houses, each group teamed with an equal number of volunteers. The average 'family' numbers about sixteen persons.

Vanier himself lives in a house with eight handicapped and eight volunteers who share meals and household chores in a mutuality shot through with all the joy, heartache, and plain hard work that mark the life of any healthy family. But, as I ate with them at dinner and helped with the washing-up afterwards, it was the deep sense of caring and the spontaneous laughter that struck me the most. Some of the *foyers*, or homes, are in nearby villages, and in a couple of cases, where the handicapped are being prepared to move out on their own, a volunteer lives in an apartment with two others of the same sex, helping them adjust to being self-sufficient. Everyone has a job to do, according to his or her ability. Some of the handicapped work in L'Arche's workshops, sub-contracting minor but essential tasks such as fitting together hinges for refrigerator doors or assembling insulation tubes. Others, more able, make mosaics, pottery, or ikons for sale. Still others work on the land; acres of garden have been created out of what was once a swamp. A sense of useful business pervades the scene.

In fact, all through our interview, under the sharply slanting beams of his garret-like office, the sound of wood-cutting could be heard coming in the window. Vanier smiled as he recalled how he gave up two careers, one as an officer in the Canadian navy, and the other as a popular professor at St Michael's College in Toronto, to work with the handicapped. 'I came here to visit a friend of mine who was chaplain to about thirty handicapped men,' he said. 'I bought a house and moved in with two of these retarded people. Somehow I felt very quickly bound to them; I felt I could never leave them or allow either of them ever to be put back in an asylum again. When the chaplain had to leave, I took over care of all thirty of them with only five assistants.' It was then, he told me, that he discovered both the extraordinary tenderness of people who are mentally handicapped and the terrible anguish they endure of feeling unwanted and deceived: 'They have an immensity of suffering and at the same time the sense that society is either looking at them with false pity or totally rejecting them. People look at them and say: "How terrible that they are retarded." They don't see that they have suffered, that they can be a friend, that they too are persons. We tend to accept people only as long as they live as we live or as we want them to live.'

At L'Arche, Vanier said, the handicapped must learn to let go of their sadness and accept their disability. The volunteers must learn to drop their cockiness, their trust in whatever it is they can do well, their technique, their 'normality'. There was real passion in his voice when he explained: 'The handicapped who have accepted it can help us accept our handicap—our fear of what others think, our lust to be richer than we are, better looking than we are, more influential, or what have you. We're more influenced by current fads than by the truth. People need to stop blaming the economy or politicians or their fate and get in touch with their own brokenness. Only then can they be free to become what they are with what they have.' In his view, our whole civilization is built on despising weakness and struggling for personal or corporate power, when in the long run all that counts is being yourself and developing deep personal relationships with others. 'Society can only be built on relationships, otherwise we have only a flight from anguish—hence all the misery we see around us,' he pointed out. 'We're not in touch with ourselves, with the child within each one of us. Jesus said we should become not childish, but childlike. There are no barriers between young children, no matter what their background. Significantly, there are no barriers between the handicapped of various countries and cultures either.'

Noting that the two pivotal images of the Christian message are the manger and the cross, Vanier stressed that both moments, birth and death, are times of weakness. 'But we don't want to look at death, and today there is even a flight from the child because we hate to be reminded of our own weakness,' he said. 'Perhaps what Christmas is all about is to help us rediscover the child in all of us, the fact that we have hearts and are capable of loving.' Thus, Vanier argues, while our culture tells us to seek out the strong, and treats anyone who doesn't as a nut, the gospel says to seek out the weak and be close to them. 'We're not here to do good to the weak, but to discover the value of the weak for us all,' he exclaimed. 'We can't opt out of our culture, but we can be conscious of what it does to us and make our own choices about what is really important. The alternative is to be caught up in forces over which we have no control and which end up by destroying us.'

No one can visit L'Arche without being impressed by the calibre of the young people working as assistants. Loretta Bucher, a twenty-six-year-old university graduate from Moore Park in Toronto, has spent nearly four years here. She currently spends most of her time caring for Nicole, an aging woman with Down's Syndrome. Miss Bucher said: 'The handicapped have taught me how to love and to see myself as Christ sees me. They demand a total transparency so there's nothing to hide behind. You can't pretend to be a great this or that or get away with any power trips. It's a kind of constant calling of yourself back to yourself, your true self.'

I met dozens of volunteers with similar experiences. There was Mary Louise Evans, professor of psychiatric nursing at the University of British Columbia, who is spending a sabbatical year at L'Arche teaching dance therapy and co-ordinating three of the *foyers*. Her specialty is integrating the handicapped into regular society. Tricia Reynard, from Halifax, teaches sewing. She came in 1971 simply to have free room and board while learning French. But L'Arche won her, and she says she has learned in a remarkable way how to share life with others and to accept people as they are. Her husband, Michael, runs one of the workshops. John Martin, a young man in his late twenties from Charlottetown, told us he is here working with Vanier because he wants to help set up an 'ark' community in Cape Breton Island when he returns to Canada.

The most impressive 'volunteer' of all, however, is Madame Pauline Vanier, Jean's mother. Far from being coquettish about her age, she told me she was 'quite happy to say that I'm eighty.' She could be enjoying the salons of Paris, London, or Ottawa, but about seven years ago she decided to take up permanent residence in a simple stone cottage in Trosly-Breuil. It was not in order to be near her son. 'People think I'm here sitting in front of the fire having tea with Jean,' she chuckled. 'Why, I'm lucky if I see him for half an hour once a month.' The real reason, she said, was to 'stay young'. Oddly enough, she once told Jean she would never come because, like so many, she was afraid of the handicapped. Now all that has changed. While low-key, her role at L'Arche is crucial. Often those handicapped dealing with crises come by to talk, or just to sit near her for a while. Madame Vanier also keeps a watchful eye on the young assistants. At the first sign that things are getting them down—the language problem, the frustrations of living in the community—she invites them round for tea or a meal and a fresh infusion of morale. She spoke with pride of the way in which Canadians started the work not just at L'Arche in France, but in Africa and India as well.

Vanier himself told me he was concerned that his duties—the travels around the globe to visit his far-flung communities, the frequent retreats and seminars, all the counselling and administration at L'Arche—sometimes prevent him from being as close to the handicapped as he would like. That's why, he said, he was planning to take twenty or thirty of them on a Christmas holiday to some warmer beach area or resort where they would go for walks together or play simple games. 'In a sense, every day for me is a day off,' he said, laughing. 'But we need some time just to relax and have fun together.'

Dr Helen Huston

In December 1979 I stood on the very edge of the roof of the world, the Himalaya Mountains, and talked with a unique Canadian. Dr Helen Huston, the United Church of Canada's 'physician in the clouds', has served in the mountainous interior of Nepal for nearly twenty years. For the past fifteen she has worked to relieve pain and suffering at Amp Pipal, a tiny jungle village perched on a peak about forty-seven hundred feet above sea-level with the snow-capped Himalayas as a backdrop. 'When I reflect on how God has spoken to us in the glory of creation,' she said, pointing to where the awesome peaks of the Annapurna Range gleamed pale gold, then pink in the sunlight, 'I marvel that he was content to come and speak to us, "a tiny baby thing, that made a woman cry".'

As we spoke, I had the illusion I could almost reach out and touch the mountains opposite (the so-called Third Pole of the earth) as they suddenly turned so white they made my eyes ache. Gigantic and saw-toothed, like the maw of a great shark about to consume the azure ocean of the sky, they are triple the height of the mountains around Banff. Yet all about us was lush tropical growth: huge poinsettias twelve to eighteen feet high, with crimson blooms as large as oversized dinner plates, orange trees, banana groves. At our feet the ground slipped away nearly two thousand feet to the fertile valley below with rice paddies in graceful, looping contours, and tiny clusters of thatched, earth-coloured homes. Everywhere brilliant birds were singing, and naked children played in the baked-mud compound above the shed-like corrugated steel roof of the hospital. As we watched the clouds drift below us, Dr Huston explained that this is not quite the paradise it seems at first sight. For here—nine or ten hours' gruelling hike over rivers and foothills from the nearest road and over seventy miles from fabled Kathmandu, the closest major hospital centre—infections and diseases of every kind abound.

Nepal has made enormous progress since it emerged from feudalism and isolation in 1951, she said, but there is no doctor from Amp Pipal to the Tibetan border. Most of the country's population of roughly twelve million have never seen one. Malnutrition is rife, partly because there are just too many people (about one hundred per square mile), and partly because of bad eating habits. The people polish their rice smooth with primeval tools and feed the vitamin-rich bran to their goats, pigs, or buffalo. We saw a child of eleven who had the look and build of a four- or five-year-old as a result of undernourishment. Though there are mountain streams, most water supplies are contaminated, and in some regions as many as fifty per cent of the infants born die within their first year. Tuberculosis, polio, typhoid, and leprosy run rampant, along with hordes of parasites such as hookworm, which can cause chronic anaemia. And since all travel is on foot (distances are still measured in the number of days required to trek them), with every step a climb either up or down, often over precipitous and slippery trails, serious accidents are common.

We had an escape from death ourselves while backpacking the eighteen-mile trek into the hospital from Dumre, about eighty miles northwest of Kathmandu. Having forded rivers, crossed torrents on shaky swinging bridges, and toiled in the hot sun over terrain that makes the Bruce Trail seem easy, we were within sight of Amp Pipal. Suddenly, after stepping on what looked like solid ground, I was falling headlong into space. I landed on my back and, if my pack hadn't caught on some brush, would have continued sliding into a gorge hundreds of feet below. When photographer Bob Olsen heard my cry, he also took one step too many. The next thing he knew, he was hanging upside-down with nothing but a vine tangled in his legs to keep him from falling. Our Nepalese porter—sixty years old, thin as a rail, and strong as an ox—saved our lives by helping us to climb out.

From snake-bites to mauling by a Himalayan bear, Dr Huston has seen and treated it all. 'Infections of various kinds are a major problem, especially in little children,' she said. 'Sores or cuts are left unattended or treated in some primitive way, out of ignorance, and by the time they get in to see us it's almost too late.' She has little patience with the West's current admiration for 'folk medicine' in the light of what she has seen over the years. 'Some of it may be good but most is not. A man came in the other day with his hand terribly infected. He said he had rubbed rat dung on the wound. Another who had cut the cornea of his eye on a blade of corn as he walked through the fields— the corn here grows over ten feet—said he had taken a raw lemon and squeezed it into it. He eventually lost his sight on that side.'

A tall, gracious figure, with strong, sure hands and a profound capacity for caring, born of her sense of God's love for her, Helen Huston would shudder at the thought of being called a saint. In fact, she was so keen not to take any limelight, and to make sure that the story would be about the work of all the hospital staff, that it was very difficult to get her to talk about herself at all. She was born in western Canada and graduated in medicine from the University of Alberta in 1951. In 1953 she began serving as a medical missionary in India, and in 1955 made her first visit to Kathmandu. At that time there was no road from India to Nepal, and the twenty-four cars in Kathmandu had all been carried by Nepalese porters—forty-six to each car—over the many miles of mountainous trail between. She became very shy when asked about her dedication to sharing herself with the sick and needy in Nepal when she could be making a large salary in practice in Canada, but one source of inspiration soon became obvious. Dr Huston's eighty-six-year-old father, a retired United Church minister in Alberta, had just written to tell her that he was moving out of his house to a senior citizens' home in order to make room for a newly arrived Vietnamese family. His spirit has clearly borne fruit in her life.

Our conversation was cut short by the arrival of a patient in the hospital 'ambulance': an eight-foot-long wooden pole about five inches in diameter, from which was suspended a hammock. Two Sherpas, small but enormously strong, were carrying him, and two others followed, to serve as relief when they became exhausted. They had been travelling over mountain and valley for two days. Then another patient arrived, a woman carried in a basket on her husband's back. She had been bleeding for a month after a miscarriage, and her husband had walked for a day and a half—an arduous, hazardous trip of about twenty-five miles—to bring her in. The concern and caring in Helen Huston's eyes as she received them and arranged for their comfort spoke more than words can describe.

The hospital is run by the United Mission to Nepal, an ecumenical organization with workers from over a dozen countries and about thirty different mission boards from Anglican to Mennonite and Pentecostal. It is a simple, one-storey structure set on the lip of the mountain. While adequate, the equipment is simple, even primitive, and consists mostly of discards from other hospitals in the United States, Britain, and elsewhere. The water for the laundry is heated by methane gas processed from cow manure. To keep costs down, all cooking for the patients is done by one of the people who brought them in (there is a special cookhouse nearby) and, because there is no hotel or other accommodation, a bench is provided beside each of the thirty beds, on which the friend or family member can spread a straw pallet and sleep. The beds in the children's ward are extra large so that the mother can sleep with her child. Together with a visting surgeon from England, Dr John Parry-Jones, and a young general practitioner from Liverpool, Dr Ken Snider, Dr Huston sees about three thousand out-patients a month. She is supported by five or six nurses from around the world, including Ruth McCaslin, a Mennonite from Vancouver Island. Her husband Walter McCaslin, a thirty-seven-year-old agricultural expert from Saskatchewan, is currently looking after hospital maintenance. Another doctor, an Australian, Dr Eleanor Ross, runs a community health centre in the nearby jungle village of Amp Pipal itself. She too has served in Nepal for twenty years. 'We do everything from immunization to family planning in the out-patient clinic,' sayd Dr Huston. 'But without our trained Nepalese assistants I don't know where we'd be. They're expert at vasectomies, mid-wifery, and such procedures as the treating of abscesses.'

We saw proof of her words while touring the wards. A baby with a badly burned hand had just been brought in, and Ram Sharam, a young Nepalese paramedic, let us watch as he deftly peeled off the dead skin, dressed it, and applied clean bandages. Although no anaesthetic was used, the infant was soon contentedly nursing at its mother's breast. In an outbuilding not far from the TB wing—a little row of mud and stone cabins each with a fireplace for cooking outside—a young, bright-faced Nepalese girl was making 'superflour'. A combination of several grains and lentils, it is far more nutritious than rice or any other single grain. In fact, part of the hospital's policy is not just to provide the food but to teach others how to make it.

When we finished our tour of the mission it was 5 p.m., and the Himalayan peaks were aflame in the dying sun. Deep purple shadows draped the awesome crevasses while the sheer rock faces where no snow can cling gleamed like molten copper. Then, almost as if by command, the colour vanished and the mountains seemed wrapped in a cold, silent mystery—almost malevolently brooding. Indoors, over a meal of buffalo curry and rice, Dr Huston recalled a woman who once came to her with a sick child and said: 'I've had five children and this one, the only one left, is dying.' The child was healed. As she remembered, it was easy to see from the look on Helen Huston's face that all the solitude and hardship she has known as a medical missionary have been more than worth while.

An interview with Robertson Davies

I have interviewed Robertson Davies several times over the years. The following conversation took place in 1974.

DAVIES   To give you my religious background, I'm an Anglican by what I suppose you would call persuasion. I was brought up in a Presbyterian family and I found Presbyterianism, even as a child, a strikingly cold and unsympathetic faith. I couldn't say that I was very conscious of what it was, but at an early age, church chilled me; it seemed to be a combination of concert and lecture. As I grew older I became much more interested in the sacramental approach of the Catholic Church and the Anglican. As I was very ill-suited by temperament to be a Roman Catholic, it was pretty obvious that I would be better off in the Church of England. I was confirmed in Christ Church Cathedral, Oxford, while there as a student and away from home, so it avoided disturbing my parents.

HARPUR   Are you still a practising Anglican?

DAVIES   I would hesitate to say that, though I attend church fairly often. You see, here at Massey College we have a chapel and it's ecumenical. We've had many different chaplains; the present one is Anglican, but his predecessor was a Presbyterian. We use our own form of service and it stays the same throughout.

HARPUR   You consider yourself a believer, then?

DAVIES   Yes, indeed. But you know, if I were asked to nail down and defend what it was I believed and why, I would be in a pickle, like a lot of people. I think this is the thing which is not perhaps very widely or sympathetically understood. Religious belief is not susceptible to the kind of discussion and proof which appeals to sceptical minds that generally want to work on scientific principles. They're so imbued with the scientific method that intuition and a sort of native awareness don't count for anything.

HARPUR   I wonder if you could enlarge on that a little.

DAVIES   Well, I mean, you're not asked, if you say you've fallen in love, to give an absolutely watertight and world-convincing explanation of what you're doing. In a very different way, it's the same with religion. I don't see why it should be demanded that you justify, explain and excuse it to people of another opinion.

HARPUR   Do you think there has been too much emphasis on theology, then, in the churches?

DAVIES   I don't think I'd want to say that. In too many modern churches there is no emphasis on theology at all. There is a kind of justification by works or by keeping up with modern trends—anything that will drag in a few more people. I think that if the church were more, not uncompromisingly, but firmly, theological, it might attract a lot more intellectuals.

HARPUR   In your novels, especially *Fifth Business* and *The Manticore*, you write in some depth about evil. What is the human problem here as you see it?

DAVIES   This is something with which I am very much concerned and think a very great deal about. You see, I cannot. consider myself a totally orthodox Christian because I can't accept the Christian urging towards perfection. I don't think that perfection is possible or even, in psychological terms, desirable for human beings. I think it is absolutely necessary for a man to recognize and accept the evil in himself. If he does that he is in a position to make the evil work in a different way; the charges of psychological energy involved can be redirected in, not necessarily good paths, but at least in understood paths. When you behave badly, at least then you're sufficiently far ahead to know what you're doing and to count the cost. It is Dr Carl Jung who is always quoting a saying of Jesus from the Gospel of Thomas to the effect that if you know fully what you're doing, you are blessed; if you don't know, you are damned. This is a very great saying and I wish we had it in the orthodox Gospels. You've got to know yourself and take personal responsibility. Just to go ahead living blindly, assured you're on the right path, is almost certain damnation. I don't mean the theatrical damnation of red flames and torture, but just to be an ineffective nuisance.

HARPUR   What of the devil—is he just a mythical symbol?

DAVIES   The devil seems to me to be not the commonplace symbol of evil but the symbol of unconsciousness, of unknowing, of acting without knowledge of what you're intending to do. It's from that that I think the great evils spring. The devil is the unexamined side of life; it's unexamined but it's certainly not powerless.

HARPUR   What about the rightness or wrongness of any particular action? Are there, for example, standards for human sexuality?

DAVIES   I think every act must be weighed individually; there can be only general principles. Sexual contacts which are primarily just for their own sake, for thrills, can be very deceptive, and ultimately disappointing. I'm very depressed by a lot of stuff you read nowadays—articles about sex as though it were a kind of open gate to happiness and fulfilment. This is not a matter of being puritanical. Sex that is not an evidence of a strong human tie is just like blowing your nose; it's not a celebration of a splendid relationship.

HARPUR   How do you yourself arrive at the general principles you use in deciding what is right and wrong?

DAVIES   It's an endless process and you just have to do the best you can. It's almost like belonging to Alcoholics Anonymous— you just live one day at a time and hope you won't make too much of a mess. Attempting to set up gorgeous principles and then stick to them is an awful way of disappointing yourself. It's like the way we used to make New Year's resolutions when I was young. If they lasted a week you were practically a hero.

HARPUR   There are risks, then, in setting a code for yourself?

DAVIES   You have to have one which works without too much pressing. If you're perpetually nagging yourself, there's something wrong. It's time for some serious self-examination. You have to be on reasonable terms with yourself; you've got to forgive yourself for being an awful lot of things which you just are.

HARPUR   You spoke earlier of the churches as attempting to keep up with modern trends. Is this what you feel is happening in the push to ordain women as priests?

DAVIES   No, I don't. I think that the bringing of the feminine principles, feminine values and insights, into greater prominence in Christianity will be the greatest revolution in the faith in the last thousand years. But it's got to be the real thing, and not just women's lib. The trouble with Christianity is that it's too Hebraically based, with its single Father God and its masculine Saviour. We've got to get rid of that fearful masculine insistence if we're going to have a religion which is a workable, comforting, and dear one to humanity at large. We've got to stop pounding away at the *logos* idea [word, reason] and do some serious thinking about the *eros* principle, i.e. the principle of love and relationship as women know it, instead of a frosty, disembodied love of God which seems so often to exercise itself in such horrifying ways.

HARPUR   Do you believe that religion has fostered discrimination against women?

DAVIES   The Jewish and Christian religions have been hard on women. When you read how Orthodox Judaism looked at women you realize what a gigantic revolution was ushered in by Jesus. Now the church needs another one. People talk about the coming Messiah; how do they know the Messiah isn't going to be a woman? It's a fair deal!

HARPUR   I take it you don't accept the Christian claim that Jesus is the unique Messiah for mankind?

DAVIES   No, and I don't think he would have either. It seems to me that Jesus as an ethical teacher and Jesus as the symbol of the best in man are different creatures. When they're mixed up together you get some bad results.

HARPUR   You think there was a myth that grew up around Jesus after his lifetime?

DAVIES   Yes, and I think that the myth is of infinite value; but the teaching also must be realized as that of a man of an astonishing degree of insight. In my view, the symbolic Jesus and the historical Jesus are just not the same creature. This, of course, would get me into the most awful wrangles with theologians, but that can't be helped.

HARPUR   You don't like the ideal of struggling for perfection. What would your definition of a truly good life be?

DAVIES   I think—and here I run counter to virtually all theologians and a lot of others, too—it's the fully realized human life, the fulfilling of one's potential. The person who lives that way can't help but be enormously valuable to an awful lot of people. And he's not going to do harm, because he knows himself. But when I talk about goodness, it's with inverted commas. What goodness so frequently means is giving to the community chest or campaigning against cancer, etc., while at the same time leading an utterly unexamined life which may be a source of despair or less effective life for others. The place to start living a better life is at home instead of using it as a launching pad from which to sally forth to impose virtue on other people.

HARPUR What do you think of the current widespread interest in meditation, mysticism, and other religious experiences? What is this trend saying?

DAVIES Well, it depends so much on the individual involved. I think that the attempt to incorporate Eastern religious practices into the Western world is enormously suspect, because I don't think we're temperamentally and psychologically well-suited for it. Meditation is a good Hebrew and Christian practice, so why do you have to sit around with your legs tied up in knots, saying, 'Oh manee tam mey room', which nobody understands, in order to promote spirituality? If you want to meditate no one's stopping you, but do it in a manner which is historically yours instead of kidding yourself you're an Indian. I think the romance of it, eating sesame seeds and funny foods, appeals to some; but it's a mechanical way to perfection. You know, the idea that if I stop eating meat I'll be more spiritual. Baloney! Some of the greatest saints ate meat every time they got their hands on it.

HARPUR What do you think of the role of the clergy today and of trends towards priests who earn their living in a secular job?

DAVIES A committed person who works at something else while authorized to lead worship, etc., seems to me to be in the truest Christian tradition. There's great value in having men who are committed to carrying their beliefs into some kind of daily work and who don't walk around as professional victims for every beggar and hustler or for every neurotic woman or whining man. Often a minister is just a kind of poorly paid, ill-equipped psychiatrist. I don't mean this cruelly. You can't expect these fellows to be Jesus Christ, Sigmund Freud, and John Paul Getty all rolled into one! A minister is expected to be able to scale the pinnacles of finance as a fund-raiser while he's usually getting a rotten stipend himself.

Travels in the Holy Land

Jerusalem

This holy city is sacred to three of the world's great faiths—Jewish, Christian, and Muslim. Seers and prophets have enshrined it in fiery visions. Empires have struggled to possess it. Poets and hymn-writers have sung its glories. Today countless millions the world over still look to it as a symbol of their highest aspirations. For Orthodox Jews, Jerusalem is not only synonymous with the soul of a people long-persecuted and exiled, it is the place where the Messiah will one day appear. For Christians, it is the spot hallowed by the death and Resurrection of Jesus and forever a symbol of the heavenly city, the New Jerusalem that God will establish one day, 'when tears and crying are no more'. For Muslims, who share with Jews and Christians so much reverence and feeling for the places and personages of the Old Testament, Jerusalem is ranked third in importance only to Mecca and Medina. (Two strikingly beautiful mosques, the Dome of the Rock and Al-Aqusa, remain major centres for Muslim pilgrimages. The Dome of the Rock, begun in AD 685 and completed six years later, stands on the rock where the Jewish temples of Solomon and then of Herod once stood—the same rock, Mount Moriah, on which tradition says Abraham offered to sacrifice his son Isaac in obedience to God's command; according to Muslim tradition, it was from this rock that the prophet Muhammad departed on his famous Night Journey to heaven.)

Quite apart from its religious significance, Jerusalem today, as in antiquity, is extremely beautiful. The impression is all the more striking when you approach the city on foot from the east along the Jericho road, as *Star* photographer Dick Loek and I did near the end of our hectic five-day trek from Nazareth to Bethelehem at Christmas, 1977. The road from Jericho, the oldest as well as the lowest-lying city in the world (about twelve hundred feet below sea-level), winds precipitously up for more than twenty miles through one of the most barren-looking, fascinating pieces of terrain in the whole world: the wilderness of Judaea. Suddenly, as you breast a hill not far from the ancient ruin of the Crusader-built Inn of the Good Samaritan, you see shining on the top of a distant peak the domes and minarets of a city that seems to have no right to be there. All around is barren and desolate, and yet there it is, hugging the mountaintop and shining golden in the light of the setting sun. For all the myriad of events that have intervened, from such a distance Jerusalem appears much as it must surely have looked to Jewish pilgrims as they wound their way up for the Passover two thousand years ago; much as it must have looked to Jesus and his disciples as they set out for the final clash with the authorities that culminated in his death and Resurrection.

Once in the city itself, the first-time visitor can only stand amazed at the strange mingling of old and new, of biblical times and the age of the jet and the high-rise. An Arab with a donkey has his water jugs filled by an attendant at a modern service station not far from the fashionable King David Hotel. A Mercedes vies with another donkey and its driver for space in the narrow confines of a street where Roman Legions once marched. Inside the ancient walled city, now surrounded by the seemingly endless complex of shops, houses, and gardens that is modern Jerusalem, you feel as though you have stepped back into history itself. The sights, sounds, and smells of the Oriental market, with its hundreds of tiny shops opening out onto streets that are little more than crowded alleys, go back to time immemorial. The place is a festival for the senses.

We climbed along the Via Dolorosa, believed by many to have been the route taken by Jesus as he carried the cross to Calvary, and stood in silence in the Church of the Holy Sepulchre where, according to tradition, he was laid in the tomb and rose again on the third day. At the Western, or Wailing, Wall—part of the vast enclosure wall constructed by Herod the Great when he rebuilt the temple—scores of Jewish people, young and old, were praying, reading Scripture, or scribbling prayer requests on tiny scraps of paper which were then screwed up tightly and pressed into crevices in the stones. A squad of lean, weary-looking soldiers, with automatic rifles slung at casual angles, poured off an army bus and headed for the same spot. Above, on several rooftops, Israeli sharpshooters kept a constant vigil in case of trouble in the square. Nevertheless, the overall impression is one not of trouble, but of harmony and peace.

It was in November 1947 that the United Nations voted to partition Palestine and internationalize Jerusalem. But the Arabs rejected the resolution, and fighting broke out. In 1949 a ceasefire came into effect, which left the city divided into Jewish and Jordanian sectors for nearly twenty years. One of the most significant results of the Six-Day War of 1967 was the reunification of the city under the Israelis. The Jews regained access to the Temple Mount, the Wailing Wall, and the Jewish quarter of the old city; Muslims and Christians regained the right to visit their shrines. Walls and fences dividing the city were taken down and municipal services improved. Since then the city has expanded rapidly. Ten years ago there were one hundred and ninety-six thousand inhabitants in the Israeli sector and sixty-six thousand in the Jordanian sector. Now there are two hundred and fifty-six thousand Jews and ninety-six thousand Muslims and Christians, making the municipality the largest in Israel. A city alive with churches, synagogues, and mosques, it seems to be a place where Jews, Christians, and Muslims can live and worship in freedom and accord. Perhaps Jerusalem is an omen for the future of the whole of the strife-torn Middle East.

Masada

Towering more than thirteen hundred feet above the western shore of the Dead Sea, about one hundred miles from Jerusalem, stands the ancient rock fortress called Masada. Though the events that made it famous took place nearly two thousand years ago, it has come to have a unique religious and cultural significance for Jews not only in Israel, but around the world.

As you approach, driving south from Jericho, awesome sheer cliffs and an almost flat, table-like top clearly distinguished Masada from the mountain chain to which it belongs; behind, stretching off to the west, lies the arid waste of the Judaean wilderness or desert. From earliest times, the obvious military value of the location commended this rock bastion to a succession of tribes. But it was Herod the Great (appointed King of the Jews in 40 BC) who really succeeded in turning Masada into a massive and formidable fort. This Herod, who ruled with skill and utter ruthlessness until 4 BC, was the same Herod under whom Jesus was born and who is said to have ordered the slaughter of the innocents when the wise men failed to tell him where the infant could be found. According to the Jewish historian Josephus Flavius, Herod fortified Masada between 36 and 30 BC as a refuge against the Jews—who hated him for his cruelty and his links with Rome—and against Cleopatra of Egypt, who had designs on his throne. He built a wall around the entire top of the rock, defence towers, luxurious palaces, storehouses, and cisterns capable of holding enough water to last for eight years.

It was some seventy years later that Masada became forever seared into the consciousness of the Jewish people. In AD 66 a long-simmering Jewish revolt against Roman rule burst into a full-scale war that lasted for four years. Finally, in AD 70 the Roman legions led by Titus stormed into Jerusalem, demolished the temple, burned the city, and transported most of the population off to be slaves. Some of the Zealots (Jewish rebels) escaped, fled to Masada, overpowered the small Roman garrison, and took possession of this lonely outpost. Using the fortress as their headquarters, they carried on guerrilla harassment of the Roman conquerors for two years. Unable to endure this flagrant insult to imperial power, Flavius Silva, the Roman governor, moved his troops into position around the base of the rock in AD 72 and prepared for a long seige.

Josephus tells how he advanced through the desert with his Tenth Legion, its auxiliary troops, and many thousands of prisoners of war who carried water, food, and military hardware. Silva built a wall completely around the foot of Masada, to prevent anyone from escaping, and erected eight fortified camps at strategic points on its circumference. Direct assault, by climbing the tortuous Snake Path that winds up the eastern face of the cliff, proved impossible, for the Jews easily daunted all comers by rolling huge boulders down on top of them. Drawing upon all his Roman strategic and engineering skill, Silva then decided to embark on the incredible feat of building an earth ramp on the west side of Masada so that he could bring his seige weapons (towers and catapults) right to the very top. Finally a breach was made, and the defensive wall destroyed. As the noted Israeli archaeologist Yigael Yadin wrote in his book *Masada* (1966), this was the beginning of the end for the rebels. Forced to choose between surrender and death, their commander, Eleazar Ben Yair, 'resolved that a death of glory was preferable to life in infamy'. Thus the nine hundred and sixty men, women, and children at the top of Masada took their own lives, and no one remained for the Romans to conquer.

Josephus writes: 'And so met the Romans with the multitude of the slain, but could take no pleasure in the fact, though it were done to their enemies. Nor could they do other than wonder at the courage of their resolution, and at the immovable contempt of death which so great a number of them had shown. . . .' Before their mass suicide, the Jews destroyed anything that might be of military use to the Romans, yet deliberately left their stores of food and water intact to show that it was not lack of provisions that had led them to it, but the determination never again to be slaves.

Between October 1963 and April 1965, Yadin and an international team of experts and student volunteers endured the heat and the rigours of life on Masada's top to excavate the Herodian and Jewish sites. Today the astounding genius of Herod's building and the grim realities of the Zealots' last stand have been laid bare for all to see and marvel at. Ignoring the modern cable car that runs to the top, I took the rugged Snake Path on foot. The climb takes about forty-five minutes, allowing for a few moments' rest here and there to enjoy the breath-taking panoramic view of the Dead Sea below and the misty mountains of Moab in the distance to the east. Once at the top, you can see something of the magnificence of Herod's pleasure palace, clinging to the sheer side of the northern face where he would have the most shade and always be assured of a cooling breeze fanning down the valley. Here, too, are the remains of his luxurious bathhouse with its sauna rooms and pools. Perched precariously on the edge of the rock are the remains of the ancient synagogue where the ill-fated Zealots worshipped until the very last. I sat on the top seat and gazed out over the unending desert scene beneath, the surface of the valley corrugated by winter floods and centuries of time.

Today, many pious Jews from Canada and every country in the world come here to pray or to mark special religious occasions—even Bar Mitzvahs and weddings. And it is in the large open space near the synagogue that all members of the Israeli army, after they have finished their initial training, are brought to take their solemn oath of allegiance to the state and its defence. Masada stands forever as a mute witness to one of the fundamental values of all true religion: moral and physical freedom. As such, it belongs to the saga of all mankind.

A tale of two mountains

I. Mount Sinai, Egypt

The runway at Eilat, Israel's gateway to the Red Sea, shimmered
in the glare of the early morning sun. Suddenly the twin engines
of the Piper Chieftain aircraft roared to life and, as we sped
towards a fringe of distant palm trees, I was off on what was to
prove one of the most moving adventures of my journalistic career. *Star* photographer Dick Loek and I planned to climb
Mount Sinai—the place, in the heart of the Sinai wilderness,
where God is believed to have spoken to Moses from the burning bush and where, after escaping from Egypt, the Children of
Israel received the Ten Commandments.

We sat directly behind the tall Israeli pilot, who had flown a
Phantom jet in the 1973 Yom Kippur War, and as we became
airborne we could see the whole panorama: surf-caressed
beaches, resort hotels, and the vast sweep of bare hills and endless sandy desert beyond. The plane banked sharply to avoid
crossing into Jordanian air space, giving us a magnificent view of
the Jordanian port of Aqaba and the eighty or more ships of all
sizes at anchor out in the gulf. Rumour had it they were jammed
with arms and supplies for the Iraqui-Iranian conflict. Soon, at
an altitude of about ten thousand feet, we soared over the blue
Gulf of Aqaba south towards its meeting with the Red Sea. On
our left the mountains of Saudi Arabia rolled on to what seemed
like infinity, while on our right the 'great and terrible wilderness'
of the Sinai loomed, brooding and desolate, yet with a wild gran-
deur and allure unrivalled by anything either of us had ever
seen before. As a fifteenth-century monk and explorer once
wrote: 'In the Sinai, every day—indeed every hour—you come
into new country of a different nature, with different conditions
of atmosphere and soil, with hills of a different build and colour

so that you are amazed at what you see and long for what you will see next.'

Crossing the coast and heading inland at the Israeli kibbutz of Neviot—a tiny cluster of buildings and a smudge of green fields mocked by the surrounding solitude and arid wastes—we had the feeling we were in a spacecraft orbiting a new and forbidden planet. Some scholars believe the name Sinai was derived from the ancient Akkadian or Chaldean moon-god, Sin. If so, the choice was a happy one, for the land's contours are certainly more lunar than terrestrial. Immense rivers of sand pour between jagged ridges of rock, while lakes of sand gleam in the valleys between the gaunt peaks of gorge-filled mountains that look as if they had been tortured and twisted by some giant hand. The annual rainfall here is only a few inches, but it comes in the form of sudden downpours that turn the wadis (dried-up river-courses) into raging floods and sweep huge boulders down the gullies. Most of the water is lost, either racing to the sea or evaporating in the baking sun, but enough remains to sustain a few springs and wells. Even from the air you can spy the sporadic miracles of the desert, a few palm or cypress trees surrounded by bone-dry wilderness.

The intercom crackled and the pilot announced that we were now entering Egyptian territory (the peace treaty signed by President Anwar Sadat and Prime Minister Menachem Begin in March 1979 had set a three-year timetable for withdrawal of all Israeli forces and settlers from the Sinai.) The terrain below became more rugged, the mountains appearing to jostle one another and towering ever higher in the thin haze ahead. The hills and mountains of the southern third of the Sinai Peninsula—at the very centre of which lay our destination—are the oldest and highest of the entire region. Formed chiefly of Pre-Cambrian crystalline rock into which great shafts of igneous rock were welded in some fantastic ancient upheaval of the earth's crust, they glowed a coppery red as they caught the morning sun. Churning sullenly at the precipitous southern edge of these fiery hills was the water to which they gave the name, the Red Sea.

As we approached the tiny airport of St Catherine's (named after the monastery at the foot of Mount Sinai) and began to lose altitude, we asked the pilot to circle the jagged peak, about eighteen miles away. But he shook his head as Egyptian ground control ordered him to fly straight in. A brusque major, very conscious of the pips on his shoulders, examined our documents and was puzzled to find that we were not scheduled to fly out with the other tourist passengers later the same day. When we explained our plan to camp overnight on the top of Mount Sinai, he told us this was 'strictly forbidden'. In spite of our arguments and explanations, he insisted: 'Stay either at the small hotel here or at the hotel run by the monks of St Catherine's.'

But as we bumped along in the bus through the desert en route to the monastery, the Israeli guide accompanying the others told us to pay our courtesies to the Greek Orthodox fathers there and then 'do what you like'. Encouraged, we were at the same time overwhelmed by the moonscape terrain, void of any vegetation except for a patch here and there of tough, withered broom on which the hardy sheep and goats of the Bedouin eke out an existence. Yet miraculously, the guide informed us, there is water for those who know where to seek it. Pointing out a band of black rock that ran diagonally down the cliffs of a nearby mountain, he explained: 'That's called an igneous dike. Somehow it acts as a conduit, or rather a dam, when it rains, and you can nearly always find water at its base. The Bedouin know that and so did Moses, when he fed his father-in-law's sheep here thousands of years ago.' He ordered the driver to stop at the mountain's base, and there, astonishingly, almost hidden from view in a wadi, was a cluster of four or five palm trees and a small Bedouin encampment around a well.

The monastery of St Catherine's—whose history goes back to at least AD 330 when the Emperor Constantine's mother, St Helena, built a small church and tower at the base of Mount Sinai near the traditional site of the burning bush—is built around a similar though much larger oasis. We took a sudden left turn into a box-like canyon, with towering granite walls, and saw, like a mirage, the pointing green fingers of cypress trees surrounded by the yellow stone of fortress-like forty-foot walls. We had to leave the bus about a mile from the entrance, and as we shouldered our packs and hiked closer, we could soon make out extensive walled gardens with olive trees, date palms, grape vines, and a small orange grove. We began to see why Moses first came here after he fled from Egypt, and how the Children of Israel could camp here during Moses' long sojourn on the mountaintop, to receive the Ten Commandments: there is water here, and as the Israelis say, 'Water is life!' In the cool shade at the entrance, by the well of Moses, a Bedouin sold soft drinks to a busload of tourists who had taken the hazardous twelve-hour bus trip from Cairo. The price was one dollar (US) but he could have charged five dollars and sold just as many to the parched visitors.

Inside, in the other-worldly silence of the Greek Orthodox monastery, we sought out Father Gregory, secretary to the fifteen members of the community, and explained our mission. He tugged for a while at his flowing beard and then, with a wave of his hand, said not only that we could camp on the top of Mount Sinai, but that he would assist with any provisions we needed. He disappeared with a shuffling of sandals and returned with a round loaf of bread (it had a crust as hard as the Sinai rocks), some olives in a twist of paper, goat's cheese, and six mandarin oranges. Just before 1 p.m., with the blazing sun at its zenith, we headed up the valley beyond the monastery—an easy climb at first, even though our packs, loaded with camera gear, sleeping-bags, a tent, clothing, and plenty of water, plus the food, weighed about eighty pounds each.

There are two routes to the summit, one—the easier—a winding switchback trail made up of sharp rocks almost the size of footballs. The other consists of a steep, twisting 'stairway' of massive stones built, it is said, by pious monks over the centuries as a penance for various sins. The 'steps' number close to four thousand in all. This is the shorter route to the seventy-five-hundred-foot summit; but while it can be climbed by anyone who is reasonably fit in under three hours, it is no place to haul up a heavy pack. We took the trail instead. Once you have hiked along the other trail for about half an hour, the monastery is swallowed up by the canyon, and you are alone in a world of sheer rock cliffs, dizzying chasms, and sawtoothed peaks overarched by a sky of cloudless blue. Shortly after 4 p.m. we mounted the narrow crest, and save for Mount Catherine, whose twin peaks rose another eleven hundred feet higher into the sky to the southwest, we had the strange world of the southern Sinai at our feet.

Since our shirts were soaked with sweat and the temperature was dropping swiftly with the waning sun, we donned woollen sweaters, hung the shirts on a rock, and set up the tent on a gravelly ledge. In a silence so intense it penetrated our very marrow, we sat on the edge of a more-than-one-thousand-foot cliff-face in the deepening cold and ate the monks' bread. By 5.15 velvet night had fallen completely, and the mountains took on a ghostly shimmer as stars filled the sky and the dying moon cast its pale rays just above the far horizon. We got into our Arctic sleeping-bags at about 6 p.m. and fell almost instantly asleep as a now-bitter wind keened eerily through the crevices and caves below. Not far from where we slept was the cave where tradition holds that God put Moses: 'while my glory passes by, I will put thee in a cleft of the rock, and will cover thee with my hand while I pass by.' (Exod. 33:22.)

At 4 a.m. we were awakened by the sound of voices on the path, and rose to see two Egyptian soldiers, Muslims, on their way to offer prayers in the tiny stone cell that serves as a mosque on the summit. Their chanting accompanied the dawn as the sun gradually won its way above the peaks of Saudi Arabia in the east and began the most fantastic 'light-show' we had ever seen: the peaks and rocks seemed molten in a sheen of pinks and golds and crimsons. Small wonder President Sadat, who wanted to be buried on top of Mount Sinai, proposed that a church, a mosque, and a synagogue be built upon this peak as an international shrine, where pilgrims of all faiths could come and pray for peace. The earth has many 'holy places'. But surely none is holier than this place where, according to tradition, the belief was born that God is One, with its great, liberating corollary that all mankind is one brotherhood. Nothing could be closer to the spirit of true religion than that.

II. Mount Sinai

'And the Lord came down upon Mount Sinai, on the top of the mount: and the Lord called Moses up to the top of the mount: and Moses went up.' (Exod. 19:20.)

To stand on the top of Mount Sinai and watch the sun come up, ravishing this lunar-like mountain wilderness with a kaleidoscope of colours, is to witness one of the wonders of the world. But it is so much more than that. It is to stand at one of the crossroads of human history—at the centre of the crucible where civilization sprang to life. We take it for granted now, perhaps never give it a thought.

But the discovery that there is only one God over all and beneath all and through all; that the universe is one process designed by one Maker; that therefore all people everywhere are one family under him; and that he has built the demand for justice and love of neighbour into the very fabric of our existence—this was an epoch-making event, the greatest discovery ever made. Chaim Potok, in his book *Wanderings* (1978), says the idea that there were no other gods marked 'a fundamental transformation in thought and belief, and an abrupt turn by our species towards a new horizon.' He adds that the notion of a God over and above man and nature who yet loves mankind, being concerned even with the welfare of slaves and strangers, had no link of logic with previous ideas: it was 'an epiphany [manifestation of God], an inductive leap of extraordinary seminality, or a vaulting of the imagination—call it what you wish.'

About 1300 BC, the rabble of slaves who had escaped from the tyranny of Pharoah Ramses II of Egypt were led by Moses back to this very mountain where as a shepherd, the tradition says, he had encountered God at the burning bush. (The Monastery of St Catherine's, at the base of the mountain, has the main altar of its church built over the roots of a large bush that flourishes just outside. The monks claim it is the original bush that burned and was not consumed. To sceptics this may seem unlikely, but, remarkably, the bush is said to be of a species found nowhere else in the twenty-three thousand, five hundred miles of the Sinai Peninsula.) The world the Hebrew slaves knew as they waited impatiently for their leader to come down from the mountain was very different from the one they would soon be challenged to see.

Everyone at that time knew the universe to be a chaotic, fearful thing; a jungle of so many warring gods, demons, and hostile spirits that, as Joy Davidman points out in her book *Smoke on the Mountain* (1970), 'a moral law was impossible, for what pleased one deity would offend another.' But the single God who spoke on Mount Sinai would not be flattered or bribed: all he demanded was justice. Standing on the windswept peak, bible in hand, I read again of the supernatural physical phenomena that accompanied the giving of the law. The account of the events in Exodus (beginning in chapter 17) tells of thunderings and lightnings and dense clouds of smoke covering Mount Sinai. Perhaps it was volcanic activity, perhaps imaginative exaggeration. Perhaps the witnesses really were in the presence of the uncanny, what scholars would call the numinous—that which evokes a sense of the wholly other. Be that as it may, it is a fact of history that the Hebrew slaves entered this awesome landscape an unruly, divided pagan rabble and left it for the promised land, some forty years later, a wholly monotheistic people devoted to the rule of law. The tradition tracing this transformation to Moses and Mount Sinai is too strong to be denied, however much scholars may quibble about the details. And what was thundered out in the Ten Commandments and the covenant between God and humankind on this ancient peak has echoed down the ages. It sounds from the minarets of Muslim mosques in the muezzin's haunting cry that Allah is God; it resounds in the synagogues where the cantor chants in unchanging Hebrew that the Lord our God is one Lord; it reverberates from all the churches and chapels of Christendom. The message is the same, the voice is the same, the meaning is one.

Mention the Ten Commandments today to many people and they immediately think of 'Thou shalt not kill, thou shalt not commit adultery, thou shalt not steal.' The 'thou-shalt-nots' are indeed the cement that holds civilization together. But there is a great deal more to the law God laid down at Mount Sinai than these negative-sounding rules might suggest. (It helps to recall the story of the 'shalt-not'-inclined missionary trying to convert an aged African chief. After listening long and patiently the chief said: 'You tell me I must not take my neighbour's wife?' The missionary replied in the affirmative. 'Or his ivory or his oxen?' said the chief. 'Yes, that's right,' said the cleric. 'And I must not dance a war dance and then ambush him on the trail and kill him?' the chief continued. 'Absolutely right!' Then the chief said regretfully: 'I'm too old to do any of these things anyway! To be old and to be a Christian must be the same thing. I am a Christian already.')

While the prohibitions have their place, the deeper, spiritual meaning of the law is emphatically positive: thou shalt acknowledge and love the one God (be it by whatever name) and thou shalt love and show justice to thy neighbour. God knows—and most of us do, too—what a completely different world this would be if the countless millions of Jews, Christians, and Muslims who look to Mount Sinai as a holy mount precisely because of the Ten Commandments were to truly devote themselves to these two simple precepts. There would be a radical revolution such as the world has never known, a revolution without bloodshed, a revolution of harmony and peace. It is urgently needed.

I was pondering this as I threaded my way down from the top of Mount Sinai. There is a frantic amount of 'God-talk' around these days. But in the stark and vast solitude of Sinai it struck me with new force that religion has a great deal more to do with actual living than with pious verbalizing; with deeds than with words and rituals. The commandments are about attitudes and actions, not creeds and beliefs. After Moses, Jesus himself was to hear the voice of God in the wilderness, and from another mountaintop proclaim a new vision of human relations and human society: he would speak of being and doing what God wills. It's a long, long way from that radical vision to the undemanding, stained-glass religiosity we so often settle for.

III. Mount of the Beatitudes, Israel

We felt ourselves to be two of the luckiest people alive. We had just spent three days back-packing 'in the steps of the Master' around and beyond the Sea of Galilee—from the bustling streets of the hill town of Nazareth, where Mary received the Annunciation of the birth of Christ and Jesus lived as a boy, to the sources of the Jordan at the foot of snow-capped Mount Hermon in the north. Now we were about to fulfil the long-held dream of camping out on the Mount of the Beatitudes where, according to Matthew (chapters 5 to 7), the essence of the Christian ethic, the Sermon on the Mount, was preached. I knew that the voice that echoed here two thousand years ago was the voice of a man, for whatever else the Gospels say about Jesus, they insist he was fully human, not some extra-planetary Superman. Yet I knew as well that for countless millions through the ages— indeed, for all who share in Western civilization, Christian or not—the words spoken here have seemed to come from the heart of the inner reality of the universe itself. They ring with the most profound truth.

Like its twin Mount Sinai, the Mount of the Beatitudes represents a pillar of our moral values, symbolizing a searing perception into what it means to live in the global society that is the fullness of humanity as it was meant to be. A Roman Catholic church of exquisite beauty stands on the brow of the hill traditionally believed to have been the place where Jesus spoke to the

eager crowd so long ago. By coincidence, there is a mass in progress when we arrive, dusty and weary after a journey of several
hours. The service is being held outdoors, in the afternoon sunlight of a gorgeous garden that lies between the chapel and a
guest-house run by Italian Franciscan nuns. Propping our packs
against a low stone wall beneath a date palm and groping for our
water canteens, we are acutely aware of our dishevelled appearance, in contrast to the Sunday-best of the tourists who have
come by bus. But the magic of the moment soon makes us forget
all that. The circle of believers chanting their responses, the
voices of the white-robed priests around the altar, the cool green
of the garden, and the calm surface of the Sea of Galilee, surrounded by ancient volcanic mountains in the distance and lush
orchards along the shores, cast an uncanny spell. Then, as the
central priest begins to preach, in French, we hear again the
immortal lines with which the Sermon on the Mount begins:

> *Blessed are the poor in spirit, for theirs is the kingdom of Heaven.*
> *Blessed are the meek, for they shall possess the earth.*
> *Blessed are they who mourn, for they shall be comforted.*
> *Blessed are they who hunger and thirst for justice, for they shall*
>   *be satisfied.*
> *Blessed are the merciful, for they shall obtain mercy.*
> *Blessed are the pure in heart, for they shall see God.*
> *Blessed are the peacemakers, for they shall be called the children*
>   *of God.*
> *Blessed are they who suffer persecution for justice's sake, for theirs*
>   *is the kingdom of Heaven.*

We strap on our gear reluctantly as the priest begins expounding the meaning of the text. But we have to leave. With Eli Spec-
tor, our Israeli guide and interpreter—who accompanied us on
our hike from Nazareth to Bethlehem for the *Star* four years
ago—we still have to find or negotiate a place to camp, and it will
be dark in another couple of hours.

Apart from the actual site of the chapel, the garden, and the
Franciscan guest-house, the entire sugar-loaf-shaped mound
called the Mount of the Beatitudes is farmland, orchards of
grapefruit mixed with rocky pasture for large flocks of sheep
and goats. Finding a flat spot to pitch our tent means stumbling
down a steep, boulder-strewn slope and climbing several wire
fences to get to a ledge-like corner of an impossibly tilted field.

As we unpack and put up the special mountain tent we used on Mount Sinai and then eat a simple but delicious meal of fresh dates, pita bread, and assorted nuts, Eli tells us again 'the old, old story' of this region and the biblical events that tradition says took place here. A veteran of four Arab-Israeli conflicts and a professional guide for over thirty years, he has more knowledge of both the Old and the New Testaments than most clergy do.

Below us, almost on the shore of the lake (though called a sea, Galilee is only about twelve miles long and eight miles across at its widest point), are two small shrines said to be the sites of the miracle of the loaves and fishes that fed five thousand people, and the Resurrection appearance of Christ to Peter (John 21:1-19). Almost the whole of Jesus' three-year ministry took place within a day's walking distance of this very spot, Eli reminds us, from the calling of the first disciples who were fishermen to the wedding feast at Cana (modern Kana) of Galilee, where John says Jesus turned water into wine. As the sudden darkness of the Eastern night begins to fall, Eli takes his leave, promising to return early next day. He tells us he will stop at the farmhouse of the Arab who tills the soil where we have become transient squatters, 'to let him know what you crazy Canadians are doing here.'

The depth of peace and tranquility in the air of the mountains and hills around the Sea of Galilee has been a source of wonder for all who have come here down the ages. Tonight it surpasses telling. Crickets are chirruping as on a Muskoka summer evening, while the lights of Tiberias twinkle off to our right and to the left, here and there, those of the villages along the top of the Golan Heights. An occasional flicker of light out on the lake below reveals the presence of fishermen toiling late at their nets. The Sea of Galilee itself is six hundred feet below sea-level and the Dead Sea, the lowest spot on the earth's surface, is more than seven hundred feet lower still. The whole region is part of a great fault in the earth's crust that runs from the Taurus Mountains in Turkey, down through the Red Sea, to the Great Rift Valley of East Africa. Perhaps, then, the secret of this place is partly a matter of geography—the clean lines of the treeless mountains against the starlit sky, the amazing sense of space, the rich supply of oxygen at this low altitude, the fertility of the valleys, and the harsh contrast of the ever-menacing desert areas beyond. Perhaps it is also partly because so much of human history has been forged in this region, and because, in the opinion of many, the fate of world peace always hangs in the balance here. But for the spiritually aware, it must be chiefly the knowledge that, down the ages, this has been the place where God has spoken most plainly to humankind. It was in this land of the East that the three great religions of Judaism, Christianity, and Islam sprang forth and changed the world.

Later, as we fall asleep, we can hear the waves lapping the shore below. The thought occurs that Jesus and his disciples must often have slept out on just such a night, perhaps somewhere on this very slope, with only the sky for a roof. As he once said: 'The foxes have dens, the birds have their nests, but the Son of Man has no home in which to sleep.' The crowing of roosters from the nearby farm and a dawn chorus of songbirds in the orchards between us and the lake wake us a good half-hour before the first hints of morning sun 'put the stars to flight'. By 5.15 a.m. the sky behind the Golan and the Mountains of Gilead to the east is aflame. We breakfast on some fresh-picked tangerines and grapefruit brought unexpectedly by one of the farmer's teenaged sons, who is on his way down to his favourite fishing spot. Then, while Dick works with his cameras and captures angle after angle of the Galilean scenery, I drag out my pack and, using it as a seat, open my bible. For the first time in my life it is my chance to read not only the Beatitudes, but the entire Sermon on the Mount near the place where it was originally spoken. It is a moment I will never forget.

IV. *Mount of the Beatitudes*

Scenically, there can be few greater contrasts than to stand one day on the top of Mount Sinai, in the middle of a desert, and a few days later on the Mount of the Beatitudes, overlooking the Sea of Galilee. Yet the two places are bound together, embedded in the history and consciousness of humanity. Both have an overwhelming relevance for the present. Both speak of human brotherhood and peace, not in terms of the mushy sentimentality that vanishes with the annual Christmas tree, but in a radical, even costly way that we neglect to our peril.

The view from Sinai's craggy peak is of an arid mountain wilderness. Yet there on the great land-bridge between battling empires, where the beginnings of our alphabet took shape, God spoke. The scene from the Mount of the Beatitudes, where we are now encamped, is one of mind-dazzling serenity, of soul-piercing peace. And here again God spoke. This time it was in the words of Jesus—words we all pay tribute to, but which, if they were ever to be put fully into practice, even by those who call themselves believers, would turn the world upside-down. Scholars, scoffers, and sceptics can quibble over specific details, and there are verses of the Sermon on the Mount I do not profess to wholly understand. But the main points of Jesus' revolutionary call for a new relation between people and societies leap out at us bold and clear. In particular, they cry out for a global response at this hour of nuclear peril.

Sitting there on the slope, with the Sea of Galilee at my feet and the silence-wrapped hills beyond, I was reminded of what the German scholar Adolf Deissmann once said of the Beatitudes: 'They are not quiet stars, but flashes of lightning, followed by a thunder of surprise and amazement.' The worldly wisdom that has prevailed throughout the whole sad history of wars and savage oppressions, and that has been largely responsible for the 'balance of terror' on which peace now rests, says : 'Happy are those who make it to the top of the heap, who know how to bear a grudge and get even, who never shed a tear for either their own mistakes or another's distress.' Jesus flatly contradicts that wisdom. He calls those truly happy who, no matter how unsuccessful, weak, or insignificant they may seem, have a passion for justice; who are quick to show mercy and forgiveness; who are motivated by compassion for others; and whose lives are committed to striving for peace.

There is no sloppy, utopian emotionalism here—rather, a stern command to seek first the kind of social order that God wills, based on global justice for all. The stabbing relevance of that command strikes home in a thousand ways. As the Roman Catholic Bishops of Canada pointed out in 1982: 'Some five hundred million people are suffering from starvation and more than eight million die each year due to lack of drinkable water. Yet the nations of the world spent one million dollars a minute, more than four hundred and fifty billion dollars a year, on military expenditures!' As they and other Canadian church leaders have repeatedly stated, especially in regard to native rights and unemployment, there are plenty of injustices in our own society as well.

Rereading the Sermon on the Mount, we realize, too, how deeply it touches not just the life of society at large, but the inner fabric of our own lives. The greatest personal enemies any one of us faces are fear, worry, and anxiety, as any doctor or psychiatrist will confirm. This is precisely the diagnosis Jesus himself gives in the Gospels. In his view, the most deadly blight of humankind is not 'sin', but that fear which corrodes the spirit, saps the body, and enervates the heart. That is why his most characteristic words to people in the Gospels are 'Be of good cheer' and 'Have courage'. The faith to which he calls us is not faith in some set of dogmas and creeds, but a fundamental confidence in life and the universe itself. For him, it was based not on wishful thinking or whistling in the dark, but on the most profound conviction that God is like a parent to all his children. In other words, at the core of the universe and of life there is a caring, 'personal' reality who can be wholly trusted. In the end Jesus himself was prepared to stake his life on it. Thus in the middle of the Sermon he tackles needless anxiety directly, and says the secret of living is to be found in this kind of trustful acceptance of the task of the moment: 'Tomorrow shall worry about its own anxieties.' (Matt. 6:34.)

In a world where thousands of people can be wiped out by an earthquake, even congregations in the midst of worship (as happened a few years ago in Italy), where people die daily in crazy accidents, savage killings, or the grip of some inexplicable disease, how can such a childlike trust in a caring God be possible? Only a fool has a glib and ready answer to the problem of pain and evil. Jesus was as aware of the problem as anyone. Life in the first century in Palestine under the Romans was often brutish and short; plague, war, famine, and accidents were all part of life as he knew it.

But if one accepts the very minimum assessment of who he was (one that even the toughest agnostic would concede)—i.e. a religious genius as unique in the realm of the spirit as Bach, say, was in music—his statement that the ground of all reality can be trusted, even in the face of tragedy, has to be taken seriously. The statement, 'Blessed are they that mourn, for they shall be comforted', was made by one who knew that his radical call for trust in God and new relations among men would ultimately bring rejection and a cross; the crowd would clamour for Barabbas, who believed in the power of the sword, instead.

Today, some two thousand years after he walked and spoke among these Galilean hills, it would be easy to suppose that his vision and his truth have failed. The fact is that they have never yet been fully tried.

On death and dying

The ultimate reality

The old man leaned against the wheel of his tractor and cried. Tears flowed down his lined and weather-beaten face as if they would never end, falling to mingle with the freshly ploughed earth at his feet. I put an arm about his shoulders as his strong frame shook with grief beyond control. With stammering tongue he poured out the anguish, the guilt, the sense of utter, dark despair he had held back for weeks—ever since the morning when he had backed his truck out of its shed and accidentally killed the joy of his life, his only grandchild. In a state of numbed shock, he had tried to be strong for his wife, their only daughter, and her husband through all the days that had followed. All the time the angelic-looking three-year-old had lain amidst mounds of flowers in his son-in-law's farmhouse, he had been unable to show his heartache. It had nearly killed him. Now, in the silent expanse of his beloved fields, he found release—and healing. His world could never be the same again, but once the inner dam had thus been broken, he was free to find the courage to live once more.

That was over twenty years ago, when I was a student minister on my first summer charge, just north of Toronto. Today it is more acceptable for people in general, and men in particular, to express grief and tears. Our ethnic populations, especially the Italians and the Greeks, have helped in some degree to modify our thinking: death still comes as a horrific emotional trauma, but it leaves fewer scars for those who can vent their grief. Yet clergy, social workers, and psychiatrists report that postponed, repressed grief continues to be one of North America's major causes of mental and emotional problems. The truth is that although there has been a literal explosion of books and articles on death and dying, although courses on death and bereavement (thanatology) have almost become a new academic craze, and although the care of the dying and their families has finally become a serious medical concern, death itself is increasingly invisible in our society.

About fifteen thousand people died in Metropolitan Toronto in 1980. Of these, nearly eleven thousand died in hospitals or nursing homes. The overall figures for North America show that approximately seventy-five per cent of all deaths occur in such settings. The hospital, not the home, has now become the standard place of death. In part, of course, this trend is a tribute to the success of modern medicine. It is natural and right to place those whose life is at risk where they can obtain the best' treatment available. In many cases, where all family members are working and/or the facilities at home—in a one-bedroom apartment, for instance—are too restricted, it is the only way that the dying can receive proper care. But interviews with clergy, sociologists, and a range of other experts reveal a more sinister factor at work as well: we want to hide from all the unpleasantness and ugliness that go with death.

It is partly our denial of death that makes us try to sweep away out of sight the terminally ill, the chronically infirm, and the aged. Once a community affair, with all the supporting rituals this provided, death is now witnessed by a decreasing number of people. Few adults, never mind children, actually know what it is to be near someone who is dying. Killings and deaths on television, whether in news clips or in fictional stories, only serve to make dying seem even more remote and unreal. Jordan Pearlson, a senior Toronto rabbi, comments: 'We've gone from a period such as the Middle Ages, when death was on everyone's mind and the focus of life was dying well, to a hedonistic society which pretends death is not there. In pursuit of the myth of eternal youth, we have plastic surgery, hair implants, jog ourselves silly—anything to pretend we are immortal.' Dr Margaret Scott, clinical director of the Palliative Care Unit at Grace Hospital, agrees: 'Death has become more invisible and the results are far from healthy. Death has a new mysteriousness about it, so the fear of death has escalated—the fear of the unknown and unnamed.'

Philippe Ariès, author of *The Hour of Our Death* (1981), a 651-page history of how humanity has faced death over the past thousand years, argues powerfully that until comparatively recent times death was 'tame'—faced with calmness, openness, and full community support. Now, he says, we have returned to 'savage' death, where the ultimate symbol is the patient dying alone in a small, sanitary hospital cell, stuck full of tubes and heavily sedated. (In a moving article, first published in the *New Physician*, the journal of the Student American Medical Association, and later reprinted in *Reader's Digest*, Dr Nancy Caroline tells of one of her patients, who, contrary to his expressed wishes, died in this manner. She records her shock when she found he had died after turning off the respirator himself. A note scrawled in his very uneven hand said simply: 'Death is not the enemy, doctor. Inhumanity is.') Thus Ariès writes: 'Although it is not always admitted, the hospital has offered families a place where they can hide the unseemly invalid whom neither the world, nor they, can endure. It also gives them a good excuse to let someone else deal with all those awkward visitors, so they can continue to lead a normal life. . . . The hospital is the only place where death is sure of escaping notice; and it is the place of solitary death.'

Visibly or not, however, as the ancient wisdom put it, 'man is born to die'; to quote the Anglican Prayer Book, 'In the midst of life, we are in death.' This is not a morbid epitaph, but plain realism. Today, around the world, some two hundred thousand people of all ages and conditions will die of causes ranging from disease and hunger to murder and war: about seventy million men, women, and children this year. In Canada, the most recent national figures available show that one hundred and seventy-one thousand, four hundred and seventy-three people died in 1980. And Ontario alone reports an average of sixty-two thousand deaths annually. Yet as Sigmund Freud wrote in 1915 (quoted in Ariès's book): 'Our own death is indeed unimaginable. . . . Hence at bottom no one believes in his own death, or to put the same thing another way, in the unconscious, every one of us is convinced of his or her own immortality.' True, the number of people in Canada who are arranging their own funerals and prepaying everything from the cemetery plot to the service is rapidly increasing; in the past decade or so it has jumped from about thirty-two thousand to double that figure. Still, the vast majority seem to feel that it will be soon enough to think about death 'when the time comes'.

Unfortunately, this attitude means enormous hardship and confusion for those are left behind, just at the moment when they are too shocked to cope adequately with anything. Ministers and funeral directors know only too well the literal horror of the bereaved when they have to decide what kind of funeral they want and walk through lonely cemeteries trying to pick out a suitable grave for their loved one—often, in their numbness, making mistakes that will only add to their anguish in the weeks to come. Some people are so afraid of even thinking about death that they persistently refuse to make a will, ignoring the havoc and financial hardship that may result.

Yet both the dying themselves and those who have won the victory over grief often have much to teach us about our own mortality, and about facing the final mystery with dignity and growing peace of mind. Coming to terms with death can help us live more fully day by day. In the summer of 1982, on a quiet, sunlit street in a quaint Ontario town, Ella Holmes, a seventy-three-year-old great-grandmother, talked very calmly with me about the verdict she had recently received: inoperable cancer of the lung. It began with a bad cough in May 1982. By mid-June, X-ray results showed a shadow on the lung. At first it seemed like pneumonia. But a biopsy in Owen Sound Hospital indicated the malignancy: 'I had an intuition there might be something very seriously wrong,' she said. 'But it was a terrible blow when the doctors told me very directly what it was.' She went to London in July for twenty radium treatments over a five-week span. But when subsequent X-rays showed more blurring on her brain scan, she decided not to go back for suggested further therapy. 'I want to die at home surrounded by my husband and family,' she told me. 'My own doctor has promised he won't let me suffer needless pain.' Drying a solitary tear, she said: 'I know we all have to go, but it is a shock knowing it will be soon. It's not the fear of dying; I can face that. It's the thought of leaving my loved ones and the hurt I know they'll feel.' Mrs Holmes said that while she was not 'wildly religious' she believed in a life hereafter, and her United Church minister had been a great help by talking to her about the new books on near-death experiences. 'Being able to talk openly about death with my doctor, my minister, and my husband has been the greatest therapy of all,' she said. 'I guess I'm lucky that way. You could step out on the highway or be in a car and be killed suddenly without any time to prepare or say goodbye to anyone.' (Eight or nine weeks after this interview, Mrs Holmes's doctor called to tell me she had died, quietly and at peace, with her family at her side.)

Less than half a mile down the same street, Beth and Ken Johnstone, both in their late twenties, had a different though equally poignant grief to bear. Early that spring, their only son, Jason, had died of the mysterious 'crib death' at the age of twelve weeks. They had taken the baby and his sisters, Christa, five, and Lisa, three, to visit Ken's mother. On their return, they left Jason in his carry-cot while they put the girls to bed. When they went to pick him up he was rigid and blue. Ken, captain of the local firefighters, immediately applied CPR (cardio-pulmonary resuscitation) while Beth called the doctor. Heartbeat and breathing were restored and the child was rushed by ambulance to the Hospital for Sick Children. But he never regained consciousness, and died five days later. Because Jason had suffered irreparable brain damage, the Johnstones knew that he could never have lived fully even if he had recovered. But they were left with the tragic enigma: 'He was a perfectly normal baby; there was no warning ahead of time, and no explanation afterwards,' Beth said. 'I have some comfort in that I know that between Ken and our doctor everything was done that could have been done. What's more, Jason's eyes were given to the eye bank and so, for me, it gives some meaning to his little life.' She admitted she used to find the whole idea of donating human organs 'gruesome', but the thought of Jason passing on the gift of sight to someone else has now become for her and Ken the key to turning devastation into hope.

In our society, the death of a child is the 'ultimate loss'; it seems the ultimate insult, the death of the future. Many, in fact the majority of couples who experience it, find that it places intolerable strains on relations between them. Grieving at a different pace and in different ways, they often find that communication breaks down completely. But though Ken and Beth have each grieved in their own way—'Ken was very quiet about it, losing himself in his work and the other children'—Beth said the tragedy has actually brought them much closer together. She became pregnant again, and life could go on. Unfortunately, unlike Mrs Holmes, the Johnstones said the church had not been much help to them in their crisis. 'At the funeral, the minister hinted that Jason's death might be God's way of trying to tell us something, of punishing us for not being church-goers,' Beth said. 'I was shaking more with anger than grief at the service. It was our own faith deep within that saw us through.' The two children responded to Jason's death at first with open grief and then with quiet, almost serene acceptance. 'Christa was very upset—partly because of our tears—until we explained that Jason had gone to heaven,' said Beth. 'Her immediate response to that was: "Let's go and get him back." But a few days later she came to me and said: "Grandpa's in heaven, isn't he? He'll look after Jason." ' Lisa, the younger of the two, had been given a puzzle by an older male friend of the family shortly after Jason's death. Two months later the man too died suddenly. Christa announced to her parents at supper that night: 'He'll give Jason a puzzle to play with in heaven.'

Sitting with the Johnstones, being privileged to share in their grief and their deepest thoughts, I knew that at one level they would never 'get over' their loss. But I also knew that—because of their openness, because of their daring to grieve, because of their faith—they were being healed, and that for them life had already begun again.

Humanizing death

I was leaving Scarborough General Hospital after seeing some patients from my church when a couple approached and asked me to visit their dying mother. The seventy-five-year-old woman was lying in a coma, an oxygen tent draped around her bed. A wave of anxiety passed through me as I looked at the frail, apparently lifeless body. As a green curate, faced with an unconscious stranger, I felt acutely helpless. With the nurse's permission, I reached through the plastic folds and held the old lady's hand as I read the twenty-third Psalm, said the Lord's Prayer, and ended with a blessing. She died peacefully the following night. When I saw the family before the funeral, their gratitude seemed out of all proportion to the falteringly little I had done: 'Mother regained consciousness just before she passed away. She said she had been fully aware of your visit, though she could neither move nor speak, and that as you read and prayed she had experienced an amazing sense of light and of peace surrounding her entire being. She died in great peace.'

During my seventeen years as an Anglican priest, I was to encounter this phenomenon often. Thousands of priests, ministers, rabbis, and elders of other churches and faiths can testify to something similar. I attended seminary at a time when special courses on caring for the dying and the bereaved were as yet undreamed of. Today, that situation has changed remarkably. Dr Elisabeth Kübler-Ross, author of such books as *Living with Death and Dying* (1981), *Questions and Answers on Death and Dying* (1974), and *Death—The Final Stage of Growth* (1975), has herself given thousands of death-and-dying courses in the United States and Canada. In 1965 this Swiss-born psychiatrist pioneered what has now become a major preoccupation of all the helping professions, from medicine to religion. Since then, courses on thanatology (death and bereavement) have mushroomed across the continent in colleges, seminaries, and schools of medicine and social work.

When Harvard offered its first course on death and dying a short time ago, about twenty-five students were expected. Nearly two hundred and fifty eventually registered. This response has been reflected in every major centre in North America, according to Robert E. Kavanaugh, author of *Facing Death* (1974). At the prestigious Toronto School of Theology (a federation of the seminaries of five major denominations, including Roman Catholic, Anglican, Presbyterian, United Church, and Baptist students) a course in Clinical Pastoral Training takes future clergy into hospitals for first-hand training with the terminally ill. Humber College, which in 1982 sponsored the seventh annual Canadian conference series on Death, Grief, and Bereavement, that fall presented one of the fullest, most ambitious series of courses in the country on Life-Threatening Illness, Dying, and Bereavement. Greg McQueen, chairman of Allied and Community Health Services at the college, said the program is the first of its type in Ontario. Designed in collaboration with the Clarke Institute of Psychiatry, it is restricted to clergy, doctors, nurses, teachers, social workers, and other members of professions related to human service.

Even more significant is the growth, in both England and North America, of the hospice or palliative care movement aimed at humanizing the dying experience and rescuing people from the agony of 'prolonged dying' in the grip of an overzealously applied medical technology. In September 1981, at the fiftieth annual meeting of the Royal College of Physicians and Surgeons of Canada, Dr Harley Smyth warned of 'a new generation of doctors who may be putting technology [the mere ability to prolong life] ahead of clinical judgement regarding dying patients.' Smyth, a neuro-surgeon at Wellesley Hospital and a member of the college's bio-ethics committee, said: 'We have to prolong life, but not prolong dying.' That's the new distinction the hospice and palliative care movement is making. The dying are helped to live their last days as completely as possible and are then supported as they die with dignity, free from all artificial paraphernalia.

Institutions offering this kind of care can be found across Canada, from St John's to Vancouver. The best-known are the Royal Victoria Hospital hospice in Montreal, the terminal-care unit of St Boniface Hospital in Winnipeg, and the Palliative Care Unit at Grace Hospital in Toronto. Four other hospitals in Metropolitan Toronto also have special wards for the terminally ill, while in several more, a special unit for the terminally ill provides palliative care services throughout the institution. 'The essence of the care is focused on quality of life; we want to be sure they really live as fully as they can before they die,' said Dr Margaret Scott, clinical director of the Palliative Care Unit at Grace Hospital. 'What matters to the patient and his or her family comes first. Do they have unfinished business or dreams? We support them in whatever they need in this, as far as it's realistic and possible.'

As we toured the twenty-bed facility, on the sixth floor—the site of the old maternity ward and nursery—Dr Scott explained that the unit, begun in 1979, was the first fully funded such hospice in the province. 'Here, it's the person, not the disease that counts,' she said. 'The emphasis is on comfort, spiritual and emotional, combined with a deep respect for the patient's own inner values. People ministering to the dying have to take great care they're not really treating their own needs. You have to avoid any inflicting of your own views or preconceived ideas about dying on others—the current emphasis on death-and-dying is spawning a lot of would-be Messiahs.' The unit has three private, four semi-private, one three-bed, and two four-bed rooms. Families, even small children, are welcome, and everything has been provided to make the atmosphere as home-like as possible—including a large, glass-covered rooftop patio area with a view of the bustling life along Bloor Street, and a pet canary. The patients, aged from twenty to seventy-five, are almost all terminally ill with advanced cancer. Pain is controlled by morphine or methadone. Heroin is used in British hospices, but is illegal here and in the United States. 'I don't think we need it,' Scott said. 'There's the odd case of extreme pain we can't handle as well as we'd like, but heroin wouldn't help there either.' Shirley Herron, head nurse at the ten-bed palliative unit at St Michael's, agreed: 'We use a mixture of morphine, alcohol, and honey. We don't need heroin and, in fact, its use is very much on the decline in British hospices today as well.'

At Grace Hospital, as at all special units for the dying, doctors, highly trained nurses, physiotherapists, clergy, and social workers combine to give maximum assistance to all concerned.

The whirlpool bath at Grace is the envy of staffs elsewhere, but other hospitals have their own special features. St Michael's has a fully stocked kitchen where families can cook their own food in emergencies. Recently, the wife of one patient spent the day baking for her husband and others on the ward, filling the place with the familiar aromas of home. Significantly, both of these hospitals are among the growing number that encourage patients to spend time at home. Some, in fact, go home to die, secure in the knowledge that they can be readmitted should severe problems arise.

Connie Heberlein, chaplain to the St Michael's unit, said she sees the whole hospice movement as 'a bit of a return' to a family orientation for the dying. 'There are no restrictions on visiting for families; we spend almost as much time counselling them as we do listening to and talking with patients. They can stay over-night on pull-out beds, and often families meeting other families in the same situation of grief and anxiety can help each other in ways we can't.' At both hospitals I asked about the criticisms now being directed (most sharply and negatively by Ron Rosenbaum, in a piece entitled 'Turn On, Tune In, Drop Dead', *Harper's Magazine*, July 1982) at Dr Kübler-Ross's five stages of dying. According to Rosenbaum and others, some dying patients are being made to feel they are failures if they do not swiftly progress through the five phases she describes: denial, anger, bargaining, depression, and acceptance. It has become a form of 'behaviour control', they charge, as if quiet passivity were some kind of superior spiritual state. Scott and her head nurse at Grace, Jean Murphy, agreed with Heberlein and Herron at St Michael's that the 'five stages' are very clear emotional states associated with dying, but that in real experience patients do not move neatly from one to another in order. 'We never mention them here,' said Scott. 'They're often indistinct as people slip back and forth.' Heberlein said: 'The stage theory doesn't really work in practice; people don't have a sign on their head indicating what stage they're at. We support them wherever they are. They're free to be themselves, and to deny they're dying right to the end if they wish to.' Scott, however, felt that some timely warnings are needed for those who risk making death too much a subject of study: 'Death is a very human, not a scientific, event.' She said there is danger of developing a group of death technologists 'using a microscope on the soft data of human emotions' and trying too hard to evaluate and analyse what is going on at a death-bed. Those who care deeply about a 'holistic' and human approach to the dying, she pointed out, have to walk a tightrope every day between an overly analytical approach on the one hand and an emotional or pious one on the other: 'It needs a clear head to do it.'

What is most on the mind of the dying patient? Naturally, the welfare of his or her family, the fear of dying alone or in pain, and questions about life after death. Scott said that almost always there is a new awareness of spiritual values; people with a religious past that they have forgotten often rediscover it in a new way, while those with an active faith find it growing deeper. 'Those who have this comfort find it an enormous source of strength. For those who don't, you can't help wishing they did have it—but we never attempt to intrude.' There are no respirators in a hospice, and extraordinary measures to prolong dying are never taken. Having received all the reassurance, comfort, and encouragement that dedicated humanity can offer, the patient slips away, usually in sleep or a coma, and his or her last experience on earth is the touch of love.

Religion and death

My father died, in my mother's arms, in 1968, on a lonely concession road leading back to his beloved parish of St Thomas Anglican Church in Millbrook, Ontario. I cried unashamedly when my brother, a doctor, called with the news. Since I was myself also a priest at the time, I read the lesson (1 Cor. 15) at the funeral. It was not easy, and most of the service remains a blur. Yet even now the kindness of a host of friends and of the clergy present is etched on my mind.

Strangely, many of the rituals that had often seemed foreign and artificial to me during the hundreds of funerals I had taken during my ministry gained a new meaning. Even the viewing of the body—a ritual I had always regarded with distaste—helped me to face the fact that he was really dead. But more: it made palpable the knowledge that this was not the real essence or 'person' of my father lying at the steps of the chancel. The shell remained, but the personality it had embodied was somewhere else. As I read the familiar words, the truth of St Paul's rhapsodic 'hymn to the Resurrection' struck home like a hammer blow: 'When this mortality shall have put on immortality, then shall come to pass the saying which is written: "Death is swallowed up in victory. O death where is thy sting? O grave, where is thy victory?" ' (1 Cor. 15:55.)

Countless others interviewed in the preparation of this series, both the religious and the technically irreligious, have testified to the same truth. At the hour of death, whether one's own or that of one's dearest and best, faith plays a sudden and surprising role, and rituals, perhaps even those once despised, throb with the beginnings of comfort. According to all the latest polls, including the 1982 Goldfarb Report, organized religion is losing its influence in Canada. Yet at the hour of death the vast majority still turn to religion for support and strength. (Echoing recent studies by sociologist Reginald Bibby of Lethbridge, Goldfarb's findings show that fifty-seven per cent of those polled saw religion as 'clearly not keeping pace with the times or the spiritual needs of Canadians.' Only sixteen per cent, compared to twenty-two per cent in 1980, saw religion's role as becoming 'more important' in the nation's life.)

The fact that people say they have a negative attitude towards institutional religion or neglect church attendance, however, does not mean they have ceased to believe in God or other spiritual values. Revd Edmund F. McKeown, forty years a priest, has attended the sick and dying at St Michael's Hospital, where he is assistant chaplain, for the past five and a half years. Wearing a white hospital coat over his priest's garb, McKeown has comforted untold hundreds of patients of all faiths as they faced major surgery or death itself: 'I have been constantly startled by how many patients put down "no religious affiliation" on their hospital admission forms; yet when you talk with them, they all say they believe in prayer and in God. They admit their neglect often—but a merciful God allows for that.' Most people, he said, feel as they near the end that there has to be something more: 'Faith, whatever their denomination or creed, makes a terrific difference to how they face death and die.'

At the Palliative Care Unit at Grace Hospital I had heard the same story from Dr Margaret Scott, the clinical director; at St Michael's Palliative Care Unit, Chaplain Connie Heberlein confirmed it as well. The kind of faith at work here, and the ways in which the various religions meet the ultimate experience of life, are as different as the individuals and denominations involved. Fundamentalist Christians and conservative evangelicals, about ten per cent of the population when you include their counterparts in the main-line churches, still adhere to a very literal doctrine of heaven and hell. Dr Paul Smith, senior pastor of Canada's largest fundamentalist congregation, the Peoples Church, said he thinks hell's torments may not be fire but 'something much more severe'. In this view, people who die as Christians go at once to heaven to be with their Lord. All the rest—including those, however pious, of other faiths—go to hell to await a final judgement, 'which, in effect, has already been made'. The only concession he sees possible for those who die as devout members of other faiths is that there may be degrees of punishment meted out. When he takes a funeral where he feels the deceased was not a born-again Christian, he said, 'I almost ignore the dead person and preach the gospel to the living. Sure, it's a captive audience; and I take full advantage of that!'

However, many top-ranking clergy, with whom I profoundly agree, have now dropped hell altogether as an archaic concept unworthy of the loving God declared by Christ. It is still part of the traditional dogma, but in practice it is ignored. The prevailing thought is that everyone will be 'saved' eventually. Even those main-liners who cling to the doctrine of hell do so with some embarrassment combined with a great deal of compassion. Canon Tom Gracie, an evangelical Anglican and rector of the Church of the Messiah in Toronto, sees hell as 'a place where you are simply left alone, forever apart from God.' But, he pointed out, no one can make a pronouncement about anybody else's eternal destination: 'It's between God and the person; did they really and finally reject God's presence or not?' At every funeral he sees his role as comforting the bereaved by holding out the hope of resurrection: 'I always assume the loved one is in God's presence, because all judgement belongs to him.' Heaven he sees as a place of adoration, praise, and singing. Boring? 'Not for me. I've never been bored with singing in my whole life.'

Revd McKeown said he believes, with his church, in hell as a place of punishment, but he added: 'It's very vague how many or who goes there. To end in hell, you've have to deny and defy God to his face. How many people really feel like that?' The priest said that when people tell him, 'There's no chance for me, father, I've been bad, stayed away from church, etc.', he reminds them of the thief pardoned on the cross: 'Our God is merciful, and healing, and kind; that's what we have to say to the dying.' Roman Catholic funerals, since the reforms of Vatican II, emphasize the joy of the resurrection as never before, he said. No more black vestments are worn, but rather white or purple. Since none of us is good enough—'except possibly the saints'—to go directly to God's presence upon death, McKeown sees the doctrine of purgatory, an intermediate stage of cleansing, as entirely reasonable. Masses are said on behalf of the dead, as well as special intercessions, so that their souls may 'be released and go directly to God's presence.' At the service for the dying, the priest recites: 'Give him (her) eternal rest, O Lord, and may your light shine on him (her) forever.'

Canada's three hundred and five thousand Jews, including one hundred and sixty thousand in Metropolitan Toronto, have much in common regarding funeral practices, but hold views of the afterlife ranging from the mystical transmigration of souls (akin to reincarnation) to the more traditional, Orthodox idea of a physical resurrection in the Messianic Age. Whenever possible, the deceased is buried within twenty-four hours. There is no lying in state or viewing of the body, and the funeral service at the graveside does not take place until the casket has been covered with earth; close relatives actually take part in filling in the grave. Orthodox rabbi Henry Hoschander, of Shaarei Shomayim Synagogue, said his branch of Judaism sees death as 'a continuous part of the eternal structure of life'. There is no hell in the old Christian sense of a place of torment. Rather, heaven is pictured as a great study hall where the blessed sit closest to the Lord and the least worthy are kept at the extreme end, furthest from what they desire the most. Rabbi Jordan Pearlson, spiritual head of Temple Sinai, a Reform Congregation, explained that he sees Jewish customs regarding death and mourning as 'the sanest pattern of post-death therapy the world has ever known.' Following the prayers and eulogy at the temple or chapel, and the interment, the bereaved family goes home and remains there for seven days 'while the world comes to them—those you like and those who drive you up the wall.' Grief is confronted again and again as the visitors talk about the deceased: 'Tears are wholly appropriate; it is not the time for the stiff-upper-lip routine. Then, at the end of the week, you are ready to go out and face life again.' In many Jewish homes of grief, all mirrors are covered for this time of mourning; men do not shave and women do not apply make-up. 'The aim is to avoid thinking about yourself and, instead, to concentrate on the death of the beloved and how you intend to lead a more purposeful life,' said Hoschander. The period of grief is also graded in intensity. The first three days of the seven are the most severe; at the end of the week, a restricted period follows for the balance of thirty days, in which frivolous and social affairs are avoided. This represents the first month of a year during which prayers are offered on holy days and especially on the anniversary of the death.

The growing number of Hindus in Canada (roughly one

hundred thousand) practise cremation, and the various crema-
toria often co-operate by permitting the age-old custom of having the fire lit by the next of kin—for example, the oldest son in
the case of a deceased parent. 'The soul never dies; so fire is the
cleanest, most scientific way of returning the body to the elements,' said Kirpa Ram Sabharwal, president of a Toronto
Hindu temple. The ashes may be sent home to India to be scattered on the sacred waters of the Ganges; otherwise they are
consigned to local waters such as Lake Ontario. Hindus believe
the soul is immediately reborn (reincarnated) in some other
form according to the person's deeds. 'If he or she was evil, a
murderer or a robber, then the rebirth could be as a dog or cat—
even a donkey,' said Sabharwal. 'The great aim is so to live as to
complete the cycle of rebirth and be absorbed into God forever.'
The funeral service itself, complete with viewing of the body in a
regular funeral home, is traditional. During a fixed thirteen-day
period of mourning, friends visit the bereaved to pour out their
grief and retell the virtues of the deceased. Hindus too believe in
praying for the dead, to assist them in their next reincarnation,
and every year during the 'month' of Sharads (4-17 September)
there is a special mourning for the dead marked by gifts of
money and flowers to the temple.

Numbering approximately seventy thousand, members of
Canada's Buddhist population also practise cremation and,
according to Revd Samu Sunim, a Zen Buddhist priest, hold a
view of the 'wheel of rebirth' that runs parallel to that of Hinduism. The ashes are either scattered over water or a mountaintop in a ceremony known as wind-burial, or buried in an urn in
the earth (a three-hundred-and-eighty-acre Buddhist Peace
Cemetery has recently been purchased near Kaladar, Ont., 'for
all people who love peace'). Buddhism holds that, alive or dead,
we are all part of the universe—individuality is an illusion—and
that the cycle of being reborn is broken only when the soul is
fully enlightened and can then achieve nirvana: perfect peace, at
one with all things. 'Buddhists believe it is healthier to grieve
than to hold it in, if one has to,' Sunim said. 'But the ideal is to
maintain a total calmness in the face of what seems like tragedy.'

Many others in our society also believe in reincarnation,
including members of ancient orders, such as the Rosicrucians,
that have been influenced by Eastern religions. At the University

of Toronto, psychiatrist Dr Joel Whitton, author of several research papers on reincarnation, explained: 'I'm a deeply religious person interested in the universal problem of why people are born so unequal—one is a cripple, another a slum orphan, another is part of a starving tribe in the Sahel, yet another is born in a wealthy home with every advantage. My belief in reincarnation helps in this.' The reason is that reincarnation means you aren't struck there; you can have another chance. Whitton said that those who criticize this doctrine the most usually understand it the least. In his view it is entirely compatible with Christianity—although church councils early ruled against it. He admitted his research has yet to produce scientifically acceptable proof of reincarnation, but added: 'The theory simply postulates that everyone is sent into the world with a purpose. If one lifetime is not enough, you'll get another chance—or as many as you need. All religions agree life has a purpose, though they differ over what it is. Reincarnationists say that whatever it is, God will let you try again. Reincarnation doesn't rule out the idea of judgement. God or someone has to say: "That wasn't good enough. Go back and try again." That's hell, if you like.'

One of the most elaborate afterlife scenarios belongs to Canada's approximately one hundred thousand Mormons. They believe that all who die will be resurrected eternally. But before they are judged they go to two separate places: the righteous Mormons to Paradise, a place of rest, and all others to a 'spirit prison' where they have the Mormon gospel preached to them. Those who persist in rejecting this gospel will, they believe, eventually spend eternity in hell—the outer darkness where Satan dwells. According to spokesman Dick Robertson, there are 'three glories' or three different 'orbs' on which the righteous will dwell, depending on their degree of saintliness. A 'celestial life' with God and Christ is reserved for the most elect. Asked whether such a heaven would then be totally Mormon, he replied: 'This makes me feel awfully uncomfortable, but, yes.'

Whatever the afterlife may be, however, it would be wrong to suggest that any one faith prepares a person better for dying than any other, or indeed that one must have a religious faith at all to 'die well'. Countless studies of dying patients have shown that whether one's faith is in a personal God or simply in the dignity of godless man makes little difference to the peace of one's death. As Robert E. Kavanaugh, a former priest, and now an expert on death-and-dying, put it in his book *Facing Death* (1974): 'It is not the substance or content of a man's creed that brings him peace. It is the firmness and quality of his act of believing . . . the believer, not the belief, brings peace.'

Is there life after death?

Dr Carl Jung, the famous psychiatrist, once suffered 'clinical death' as the result of a heart attack. He described his experience at the brink of death in his book *Memories, Dreams, Reflections* (1963): 'I was high up in space. Far below I saw the globe of the earth . . .' Turning around, he then saw a gigantic stone containing a temple: 'as I approached . . . I had the certainty that I was about to enter an illuminated room and would meet there all those people to whom I belong in reality. There I would at last understand . . . why I had come into being . . .' At that moment, he felt himself being pulled back into his body: 'I was profoundly disappointed . . . a good three weeks were still to pass before I could truly make up my mind to live again.'

In a recent and very extensive poll conducted through lengthy personal interviews, George Gallup, jun., found that about twenty-three million people in North America have had close encounters with death, or 'died briefly' by current medical definitions. Of these, roughly eight million said they had undergone some sort of mystical near-death experience (NDE). The full results of the study are contained in his book *Adventures in Mortality* (written with William Procter; 1982). This is only one in the spate of books on the subject that have appeared since Raymond Moody's *Life After Life*, already translated into some thirty languages, was first published in 1975 (Moody's own sequel, *Reflections on Life After Life*, came out two years later).

Some of the more sensationalist tabloids have even offered rewards for the month's most gripping, far-out account of a patient's brush with eternity. People brought back from cardiac arrest or other forms of unconsciousness where their life hung in a precarious balance have described in vivid detail seeing their own bodies on the battlefield or on the operating table while frantic medical crews strove to revive them and anxious buddies or relatives wept nearby. Literally thousands have recounted seeing brilliant lights, beautiful landscapes, dead relatives, and/or divine figures waiting to greet them. Many say they were aware of a hasty review of their past life, of wanting to remain 'there' instead of returning to their bodies, or of being told they must go back for the sake of others or to fulfil some task as yet incomplete.

The latest, and to date most scientific, account of the NDE phenomenon is *Recollections of Death: A Medical Investigation* (1982) by Dr Michael Sabom, an associate professor of cardiology at Emory University in Atlanta, Ga. Sabom personally investigated the NDEs of one hundred and sixteen patients, most of whom had medical records available to corroborate both their illnesses and the medical action taken to resuscitate them. He found that the experiences (which he concluded occur in about forty per cent of all patients who come close to dying) represented either one or the other of two distinct types, or a combination of the two. In the 'autoscopic' type, the patient feels himself or herself move out of the body and view the whole scene with calm detachment. In the other, labelled 'transcendental', the patient moves through a kind of dark tunnel towards a light—'like someone holding a flashlight', 'beautiful sunglow and shadows of gold'—and a meeting with religious figures such as Christ or God, and/or deceased relatives. For example, Sabom reports that a sixty-year-old man from Florida who suffered a cardiac arrest in 1975 said he saw his mother and Christ smiling and urging him to 'Come on home.' Another man, lacerated and unconscious after being struck by a car, described floating above the doctors and nurses in the operating room, then brilliant light and the presence of angels. Later, he said, he heard a voice telling him that he had to go back and complete his work on earth.

Predictably, the popular response to all this—supported by such prominent figures in the death-and-dying movement as Dr Elisabeth Kübler-Ross—has been to conclude that life after death has now been 'proved' scientifically. This is, of course, a glaring error—one that Sabom avoids making. 'Those reporting these experiences were NOT brought back from the dead but were rescued from a point very near death,' he writes. 'My belief in an afterlife comes from my Christian faith and not from my research with dying patients.' Even so, he does insist that current medical knowledge lacks an adequate explanation for what is going on in those who report an NDE: 'The various attempts to explain these phenomena as dreams, drug-induced hallucinations, etc. do not meet the data. I am being led to the conclusion that the mind or spirit can and does exist on its own—apart from the physical brain.' Sabom speculates that something 'neurochemical or otherwise' in the experience of being very near to death triggers some sort of 'mind-brain split'. Answering the criticism made by some that most of the people he interviewed for his book had had their NDEs some years previously, he told me: 'That's a legitimate observation. But since then I've interviewed dozens of patients following a cardiac arrest—even a man two days ago—and they all give stories similar to those who had them thirty years ago.' Sabom said that in six years of research he has met only one patient whose NDE was 'frightening'. Still, his work, as well as that of Moody and scores of others, is hotly contested by the medical profession.

Dr Ronald Siegel, a psychologist at the University of California in Los Angeles, said he has found that survivors of an NDE often describe their feelings as 'terrifying' and insist that what is happening in all cases is 'absolutely identical' to drug-induced hallucinations. He compared them with the hallucinations suffered by persons in deep shock: for example, those reported by people held hostage in a bank vault, or who firmly believe they have been abducted by creatures in UFOs. Dr Nathan Schnaper, a psychiatrist at the University of Maryland in Baltimore, has also done studies with patients just hours after they have been resuscitated from some life-threatening unconsciousness. 'Most people describe their experience of cardiac arrest as frightening,' said Schnaper. 'In any case, good or bad, the NDE is a state of altered consciousness. It is unfortunate that people keep trying to mix religion and science.' He reported that one patient at the Baltimore shock trauma centre described to a trauma-surgery team leader how great he had been during the rescue effort. 'I was floating at the ceiling of the room and could see you in action,' he said. 'I watched you give the orders.' There was only one problem with this, Schnaper said: 'The team leader was nine floors away at the time of the emergency surgery.' At the International Association for Near-Death Studies, at the University of Connecticut, the prevailing attitude is one of scepticism. Dr Bruce Greyson, director of research for the institute and chief of psychiatric emergency services at Michigan Hospital, said: 'There's not much hope of getting information on life after death from NDE-type happenings. The spiritual features are simply not verifiable.'

Since the Moody book appeared, I have interviewed several people claiming to have had an NDE—including one man who 'died twice' during an operation to remove bullets fired in attempted robbery—and found the features they reported were similar. But nothing I have either heard or read in this field in the past eight years constitutes anything like 'proof' of a life beyond death. However, what the NDEs do indicate, at the very minimum, is that dying may be a much less fearful thing than most of us tend to think. The majority of those who have had NDEs say that as a result they have largely lost their dread of dying. And life has taken on a deeper meaning. Sabom quotes Dr Lewis Thomas, president of the Sloan-Kettering Cancer Institute, writing in the *New England Journal of Medicine* (June 1977): 'There are some things about human dying . . . that don't fit at all with the notion of agony at the end . . . The act of dying seems to be associated with some other event, perhaps pharmacologic, that transforms it into something quite different from what most of us are brought up to anticipate. Something is going on that we don't yet know about.'

It is time, however, to be much more personal. I have never been given to mystical experiences, visions, or whatever counts in the world of psychic phenomena. My own father, an Anglican clergyman for a number of years before his death, often seems very present in my mind and thoughts—as well as my dreams. Other than that I have never had any close awareness of 'those who have gone before'. Yet I feel a deep, granite-like conviction that the hour of our death is indeed the gateway to a new adventure, a step to a fuller life beyond. This is not something I can prove empirically or scientifically. But those who contend that the only kind of knowledge is that which can be verified scientifically cannot 'prove' their dogma either. There are, in fact, a number of ways of knowing other than by the senses or by reason alone. There is the knowledge of the heart—intuition, call it what you will. As Pascal said, the heart has its own reasons, which reason itself knows nothing of. You cannot 'prove' most of the things that matter ultimately in life.

This is where faith comes in. Not a blind, unreasoning, head-in-the-sand credulity that cares not for facts; not simply a projection of what one wishes were true. Rather, a basic trust that is founded upon an inner conviction and supported by an examination of external reality. In other words, one's faith or hope in a life to come may spring from within, but it makes sense and has cogency only when it accords with what can be known by other means—what Paul called 'a reasonable hope'. For me, then, there is first of all this inner certainty. I find it impossible to believe that behind and beneath all earthly harmony and beauty there is not a glory yet to be revealed. It makes no sense to me that all human striving, excelling, loving, and hoping should end in silent nothingness. Each moment of insight— whether in the rapture of a sunset over a northern lake, the moving innocence of a sleeping baby, the soul-quickening experience of hearing one's favourite concerto or symphony, or of intimate conversation with a trusted friend—seems to point beyond itself to an eternal joy. No artist is ever able to translate fully to the musical score, canvas, poem, dance, or sculpture the complete vision of beauty he or she has known. One day I hope to hear the music Mozart only partly 'heard' before he composed it, and to see the glory Michelangelo knew by glimpses as he painted. This could be considered mere idealistic fantasy and personal eccentricity—a feeling or hunch that I, as a person with an extensive background in religion and religious studies, just happen to have—were it not for something much more compelling.

Belief in an afterlife is one of the oldest, most widely held beliefs known to mankind. My own intuition, matched by that of countless millions of my contemporaries, is as old as the earliest traces of human history. The most recent Gallup polls indicate that about two-thirds of all North Americans believe in some form of afterlife. Buried deep in the collective unconscious psyche of humanity is the conviction that the tomb is not the end; that the human self evolves through death to something so much richer that words fail to grasp its essence. The authors of the Bible did their best, describing streets of gold and gates of sapphire. But only the crudest literalist would suppose that such images were meant to be taken at face value. These writers knew that the afterlife would be a reality beyond compare, and so they used the most valuable things they knew of to give it form. They come closest when they speak not so much of harps and precious stones as of healed relationships and an end to tears. Hear what some of them had to say:

For now we see through a glass, darkly; but then [in God's presence] face to face; now I know in part; but then shall I know even as also I am known. (1 Cor. 13:12.)

The wolf also shall lie down with the lamb, and the leopard shall lie down with the kid . . . and a little child shall lead them. . . . They shall not hurt nor destroy in all my holy mountain: for the earth shall be full of the knowledge of God, as the waters cover the sea. (Isa. 11:6 ff.)

And I saw a new heaven and a new earth . . . And God shall wipe away all tears from their eyes; and there shall be no more death, neither sorrow, nor crying, neither shall there be any more pain: for the former things are passed away. . . . Behold, I make all things new. (Rev. 21: 1 ff.)

In *Choruses from 'The Rock'*, the poet T.S. Eliot writes: 'Life you may evade, but Death you shall not. You shall not deny the Stranger.' But in the 'Little Gidding' section of his *Four Quartets*, he says: '. . . to make an end is to make a beginning. The end is where we start from.' That's what I believe about death.

There is a third strand to the cord that binds my belief in a life to come—the strongest one of all. For ordinary people are not the only ones who, throughout human history, have held firm convictions regarding life after death: all the great spiritual masters have taught that there is some form of life hereafter. Laying aside Christian claims for a moment and taking the minimal view of Jesus, even agnostics would grant that he was a moral and spiritual giant, a genius. And just as I have to take seriously the position of any genius in his or her field, so I must do with those who unquestionably hold this rank in matters of ultimate truths.

Since, like the majority of those who live in North America, I have been shaped largely by the Judaeo-Christian tradition, Jesus' teaching—however much coloured by the Gospel writers—commands attention. Jesus believed unequivocally in the power of God to overcome humanity's final 'enemy' and in the reality of a life to come, not just for himself but for all of us 'made in God's image'. What's more, he believed in a bodily resurrection: not the resuscitation of corpses, as in the case of Lazarus who was raised from the dead only to die again, but a life in which people would have a 'heavenly' or perhaps 'astral' body set loose, as his own was after the first Easter, from the old bonds of space, time, and disease. (He did not provide 'proof'; nor did he, or any other great spiritual genius of any faith, give a blueprint of whatever reality the word 'heaven' stands for. There are no grounds in his teaching for the later notion of an eternal sitting-around in choir robes, playing upon stringed instruments.) If Jesus was wrong about this, he was in no position to claim authority on any other spiritual matter either. The same is true of the saints, gurus, and sages of all the other great world religions.

When I was a young curate, many years ago, the wise old archdeacon who was my boss and mentor taught me always to end a funeral service with the following brief stanzas from three ancient and beloved hymns. The words were intoned as the coffin was carried down the aisle of the church and out to the churchyard beyond:

> *And when the battle's fierce, the warfare long,*
> *Steals on the ear the distant triumph song,*
> *And hearts grow brave again, and arms grow strong.*
>
> *O sweet and blessed country, the home of God's elect,*
> *O sweet and blessed country which eager hearts expect.*
> *Jesus, in mercy bring us to the dear land of rest,*
> *Who are with God the Father, and Spirit ever blest.*
>
> *And with the morn, those angel faces smile.*
> *Which I have loved long since, and lost awhile.*

To some, these may seem sentimental thoughts. I happen to accept them. Death cannot be trivialized. It remains the ultimate enigma and tragedy. Yet through faith death has been 'swallowed up by victory', and love and life and hope have the final word.

Conclusion

'Dare to be a priest like me', the billboard advertisement says. Showing Jesus on the cross against a background of big-city towers, it is part of a bid to attract young men into the priesthood. In fact, however, there is no evidence in the New Testament or anywhere else that Jesus ever thought of himself as a priest or appointed his Apostles to be priests. A priest stands between God and humans to re-tie—the Latin word *religio* is made up of two terms meaning to bind again what has been broken—the severed connection, to intercede with God for others, and to make sacrifices on their behalf. (In Rome, the pagan high priest was known as *Pontifex Maximus*, the greatest or highest bridge-builder—a title that survives today in the name 'pontiff' for the pope.) It is true that the entire body of believers is referred to as a priesthood, and that others in the New Testament period, including the author of the Epistle to the Hebrews, called Jesus a high priest. But nowhere does he give himself that name.

This is an important point, for it illustrates again that what Jesus said and did and what later developed in his name are two very different things. To be more precise, it raises in an acute form a question that, though seldom mentioned in our pulpits, has occupied many leading New Testament scholars: Did Jesus intend to found a new religion, the Christian Church, at all? Did he have in mind anything remotely like the churches as we know them, the many denominations, the whole apparatus from soaring cathedrals to the electronic pew? The answer, it seems obvious, is no. He clearly expected the end of the world to come within a generation—a view shared by Paul and all the early Christians. In any case, it is a vast leap from the Aramaic and Hebrew words behind the Greek word *ekklesia* (translated 'church', as in 'on this rock I will build my church') to 'church' in the modern sense. What we have now is an enormous, sprawling, complicated network of organizations and institutions, often fiercely hostile to one another, that over the centuries has evolved with much bloodshed into something quite different from the church as it originally appeared following the Resurrection, in or about AD 40.

Jesus did not speak of himself as a priest because, in contrast to the religious thinkers both preceding and contemporary with him, he did not believe that God required a third party to mediate between himself and his children. Jesus' teachings about the kingdom, prayer, forgiveness, and doing the will of God all rested on his own deep awareness that the loving 'Father' was nearer to people than their own breath, closer than hands or feet. The kingdom of heaven was within; people had only to pray 'Our Father . . .' or to ask in faith, and they would know, could count on, God's presence with them. In fact, I am convinced that Dietrich Bonhoeffer was right when he said that Jesus in a very real sense came to abolish religion forever. If he intended to establish any creed at all, it should be called 'religionless Christianity'. To make clear what is meant by this statement—at first sight paradoxical, even iconoclastic—we must begin by asking what we mean by 'religion'. As Bonhoeffer noted, 'religion' usually stands for one slice or aspect of life as distinct from all the rest, like the religion section in a newspaper or magazine. This use tends to suggest that the content and thrust of religion have to do with a very narrow segment of human activity and thought, a view that is reflected in the way religious people can very often separate their faith from their work or other important aspects of their existence. 'Religion' in this sense trivializes one's relation with God and dichotomizes experience into the sacred and the not-sacred. Thus we feel we are being religious when we observe certain days, set apart certain buildings, use certain words, ceremonies, dress, and the like, when the vision Jesus had seems clearly to have been one in which everything was impregnated, shot through with spiritual significance. Knowing God as 'Father' and believing in his kingdom brought a holistic approach to living: all things became vehicles of spirit, places of epiphany, opportunities for doing his will.

Religion not only divides life (and people) into separate compartments, but denotes special privileges for its adherents—

especially the leaders. Traditionally, religion has always fought to gain special status: under the pleasant-sounding guise of theocracy (the rule of God), what it really seeks is full political power for itself, as both history and current events in such places as Iran plainly show. In our society churches and other religious buildings are subsidized by the state, while cardinals, archbishops, moderators and others like them are accorded special treatment on official occasions. Having a religious title or charitable charter for a church or cult is at least a partial protection from certain forms of police investigation (say, in the case of careless bookkeeping). In other words, the churches enjoy a privileged position that hardly reflects Jesus' teachings about humility—declining the head position at table, avoiding titles, being a servant to one's neighbour, and so on.

This is not meant to disparage most of what currently goes under the name of religion, or to advocate its immediate demise. What is necessary, as suggested elsewhere in this book, is to take a really radical look at attitudes, institutions, rites, language, and leadership in all religions, to see how true they are to the spiritual visions of their founders—not in an attempt to turn back the clock, but rather to clarify what the key principles once were, and then try to embody them in relevant ways for people today. It is not for me to say what this will mean in terms of specific faiths: for instance, Christianity. I do not know precisely what kinds of myths, ways of worship, organizational structures, or modes of leadership will provide a truly meaningful spirituality for human beings moving into the third millenium AD. Nevertheless, I predict that unless such matters are made top priority in every major faith, in every denomination, some utterly new religious revelation will soon burst forth to eclipse them all. Man is ultimately a spiritual animal—*Homo spiritualis*—and he will not take stones for bread forever. It is my fervent prayer that this book will help in some small measure to provoke the kind of thinking that is essential for this spiritual revolution to take place. I dream that one day the quantum leap will be taken in which those who profess to know and love God, whatever their 'religion', will in fact see one another as members of the same family on planet earth. And that, recognizing the whole universe as one seamless robe, knit together and bound by love, they will join minds and hands in the task of healing the nations and welcoming in the coming kingdom of God. It is the only way left.